bit of a blur

bit of a blur

Alex James

Little, Brown

LITTLE, BROWN

First published in Great Britain in 2007 by Little, Brown
Reprinted 2007

A CIP catalogue record for this book
is available from the British Library.

Hardback ISBN 978-0-316-02995-7
C format ISBN 978-0-316-02758-8

Typeset in Sabon by M Rules
Printed and bound in Great Britain by
Clays Ltd, St Ives plc

Little, Brown
An imprint of
Little, Brown Book Group
Brettenham House
Lancaster Place
London WC2E 7EN

A Member of the Hachette Livre Group of Companies

www.littlebrown.co.uk

For Claire

Thanks to Simon Kelner, Tom Hodgkinson, Cat Ledger, Antonia Hodgson, Sarah Rustin, Tamsin Kitson and Linda Silverman.

And the cast. Darlings, you were marvellous.

contents

	prologue	1
1	dreams come true	3
2	goldsmiths college	17
3	food ltd	42
4	the beginnings of success	67
5	the genesis of britpop	89
6	triumph	112
7	regroup	134
8	rocket science	157
9	how I made them sing	180
10	flying!	202
11	rounded and grounded	226
12	beginnings and endings	252

prologue

It's bang in the middle of the bay, the Showbar, at the end of Bournemouth Pier above the very mouth of the Bourne Stream, which gives the town its name.

Despite the supreme location, sandwiched between the perfect geometry of sea and sky, the Showbar has never been popular. But I always liked it and I often sat there, dreaming. The proprietor booked my first band. He did us a favour. We were crap. Seven years later I'm returning the favour. Blur are playing here tonight on a tour to celebrate 'Country House' getting to number one, a number one with more commotion than any, since records began.

Blur are the biggest band in the land, at once renowned and reviled, sleazy and glamorous, larger than life and louder than allowed. Wherever we stop the tour bus, within moments it's swamped with people. Pretty soon they're shouting. More arrive, forgetting their concerns and flocking to the bus. Then they're screaming, literally screaming, banging and pulling strange faces. Traffic comes to a standstill, but nobody seems to mind.

Tonight is more unusual than most because Oasis, the other band involved in the record rumpus, are also playing, about a hundred yards away in the Bournemouth International Centre.

We're under police escort but people are still throwing themselves at us, trying to get a piece of hair or trousers. Legions of grinning ticket holders are massing through the thronged constabulary at Pier Approach. It's mayhem. I've turned the town upside down. Somehow, I'd actually done what I'd dreamed of doing on empty, confused teenage afternoons, as I gazed out at that immaculate horizon.

1

dreams come true

Ross Killed on Doorstep

Bournemouth is nice. It doesn't overwhelm, like St Tropez, or even Blackpool, but it's good and it's growing. The poet Shelley, who lived in Boscombe, where I was born, might have said the view from the clifftops was sublime: a sublime seascape. But however you say it, it's nice.

The beaches start way back from the cliffs in the wooded chines – steep valleys full of pine trees and rhododendron bushes. Cool in the summer and calm, a world away from the crowded seashore. The rhododendrons grew dense, as tall as houses. We'd climb to the top of the highest bush and fling ourselves off to be caught somewhere on the way down by a mass of giving boughs.

We jumped off more or less everything. We jumped off the piers and the cliffs without a care. There was always something there to catch us. At Fisherman's Walk in Southbourne the soft, sandy overhangs are high and sheer and we'd just run and jump right off. Arms flailing we'd fly over the edge after school. If you can jump off a cliff, you can do anything.

We lived, to start with, in suburbia. I went to Peter Robinson's house after school on Tuesdays. His dad had the stamp shop in Pokesdown; it's still there, Philately. There were more stairs than usual in that house, as it was above a shop. We had some good stair games. The best one was called 'Ross killed on doorstep'. Ross McWhirter was on our favourite programme, *Record Breakers*, with his twin brother Norris. The McWhirters seemed to know everything: all the important things, like who was the tallest man ever, which was the fastest car ever, what the rarest stamp ever was called – Peter knew that, already. Limits were important to us, as our imaginations raced around. Ross McWhirter knew far too much and was assassinated coming home one night. The event and the newspaper headline stayed with us, and we'd take it in turns to play Ross, who lived under the stairs.

It was in that house that I first started to watch *Top of the Pops*. Peter had some good records. The ones we played the most were 'Those Magnificent Men in their Flying Machines', by the singing piglets Pinky and Perky and 'The Entertainer', the piano rag from *The Sting*. Our favourite song was a television theme, 'Eye Level', from a detective series called *Van Der Valk*. Neither of us had a copy of that one, but I remember it well. I was playing it on the guitar yesterday. There aren't many things you can take from childhood into adult life, but I still love that melody, thirty years later.

There was a carol concert, every year, at the Winter Gardens. All the junior schools combined their choirs and all the mums went along and cried their eyes out. Our teacher said that the first eight people who learned the words to the carols could represent the school. I loved singing carols; I still do. I learned all the words. I was the only boy in the class who did. I couldn't sing in tune but my teacher had to admit that I knew the words. By the time the concert came around, I was singing harmonies. I loved Clodie, who sang harmonies, too, but I couldn't tell her.

My dad gave her a lift on the last night of the concert and took us for chips afterwards. Music had brought me closer to this girl. We stood next to each other onstage and sang the high notes. On the last day of junior school I kissed her, but then she disappeared forever. I glimpsed her one more time. She was walking her dog with her mum. I didn't know what to do and ran away.

Glen View

I was eleven and we were all on our way to London to see *Annie*, the musical. It was my mum's birthday. Mum and Deborah, my younger sister, were very excited about it. Dad was going with the flow, which is quite a rare quality he really excels at. He can sense a flow and empathise with it. It's the best thing there is, having your flow enhanced and encouraged by someone you love. He knew he was in charge, but he always steered from the back, like in a small boat. An ability to join in is the most important thing you can have if you want to play bass and I guess that comes from my dad.

While we were in London, Sparky, the dog, was to spend the night with Papa, my granddad on my dad's side, but when we got to Papa's he was dead.

Our lives changed then. We moved into Glen View House, Papa's place. It was a mansion near the beach and the centre of town, built in Bournemouth's first heyday in the 1890s. Debs and I didn't want to live there and we cried all the way from Strouden Park. Papa had been a chef, first in the army and then in Bournemouth's best hotel, The Royal Bath. We were all proud that he had been the chef there and we told everybody about it. He ran Glen View as a hotel, but it was our home. There were rooms that we didn't go in very often. It had thirteen bedrooms and the dining room seated thirty. There were lounges in all directions; a smoky television room; a commercial kitchen with a huge larder full of catering tins of ratatouille that had been there so long they were becoming spherical. There was a ghost in room four and steps from the back garden led to pleasure gardens with tennis courts and bowling greens, dog turds, tramps and prostitutes. My sister and I lived in the cellar to start with. It had been full of creepy furniture and there was slime growing on the walls. There was a light well, though, and once it was damp-proofed and painted magnolia it was a cosy little burrow.

I started secondary school around the time we moved. Because I'd dropped out of recorder and violin lessons at junior school, I was always a bit behind with music at Bournemouth School. The kids who were having lessons on trombone, saxophone, flute and other ill-advised apparatus were always a few steps ahead in music lessons. Mum had begged me to have violin lessons when I was younger, but I didn't get very far. It is very hard to play a tune on a violin. They smelled quite nice, those violins, of old things, but even symphony orchestras need about twenty of them to make a half-decent sound. A solo fiddle played by an eight-year-old boy is one of civilisation's most objectionable sounds.

I've still got the recorder that I had at junior school. It's not a nice noise that comes out of one of those either, but the worst thing about recorders is what they smell like. We spent more time daring one another to smell each other's than actually blowing down them. I got really stuck on 'Loch Lomond', and gave up. From then on I was relegated to the rhythm section of the primary school orchestra, with all the naughty kids. It was really good fun messing around at the back, pulling funny faces and banging triangles. I was thirteen when the piano arrived. It was a surprise. Dad bought it for a hundred quid. That's still how much a piano like that costs. Every home should have a hundred-pound piano.

Dad opened the lid and raised his eyebrows. There was a slight but deliberate dramatic pause. Then he slammed into the keys and rattled out some rock and roll. It was amazing. I'd never heard him play. I had no idea that he could. I hugged him, pushed my sister out of the way and demanded to be shown how to make a noise like that. It was much easier to listen and repeat than to read the blobs on the page. He taught me 'Blue Moon' first. His party piece was called 'Nutrocker' by B. Bumble and the Stingers. It has a skiffle beat and lots of heavy loud accents and he'd wooed my mother with it.

I liked school. I took a 17 bus every morning, a yellow double-decker. It zigzagged all around the houses, picking up those who lived off-piste and got us to school fifteen minutes before everybody else. It ran against the flow, away from town in the morning rush and practically no one got on or off. Peter Arnold also got on at my stop. He was in my class, a bad dribbler but a good talker. We talked all the way. He had an older brother with records, and we talked about those, mainly. His brother got the bus, too, but he sat at the back hugging his bag.

Danny Collier and his brother Duncan also got on the empty bus, at Beechy Road. They were the coolest boys in school. After he'd completed his education, Duncan, the older one, was in a band called Mulberry Phut. They were famous for having seventeen guitar players. Danny, the younger one, was the bass player in Readers' Wives. They were famous for all kinds of reasons. For a start, their drummer had ten A grade 'O' levels. They were brilliant. I sat next to the guitar player's brother in chemistry.

I liked chemistry. I'd had a few chemistry sets. I was drawn by the neat test tubes, the flames from the burner, the little vials of chemicals with unstable and toxic qualities. Jimmy Stubbs was my best friend, then. We put our chemistry sets together and tried to make them explode, and we joined the Sea Scouts.

The scoutmaster lived with his mum. One Saturday, he invited me over to his house. I said, 'What for?' He said, 'Monsters.' When I arrived for monsters, there were a couple of other boys there. He was wrestling with one of them. It was Brian, from Otters Patrol. They were making monster noises. I must have arrived too late for monsters, as the next thing that happened was that we all dressed up: me, Brian and Tim from Badgers, as girls; with frocks and wigs and lipstick, and the scoutmaster was filming us singing along to his old record player.

It was him who gave me my first break in showbusiness. Possibly as a result of my performance in drag on camera, although that film never came to light again, I won the role of 'Big Brownie' in *The Gang Show*.

I'm in a Band

I joined my first band in Jay Burt-Smale's bedroom. Jay Burt-Smale lived in Charminster. It would be hard to find a more deliciously normal place than there. The biggest shop in Charminster sold fish. It wasn't clear if it was a shop or a hobby that had gone haywire. The front of the shop was quite ordinary looking, but it went on and on and the fish got weirder as you went deeper inside, just like the sea. There was definitely someone with a big need for fish behind it, like an alcoholic pub landlord. It was a bit out of anyone's control, bursting at the seams and brilliant.

We were fifteen and also bursting at the seams, sitting there in Jay's bedroom, surrounded by traffic cones and flashing lights from the roadworks outside. Jay's mum had recently started going out with a bass player. She was pretty cool. She said we could smoke in Jay's room, but Jay wouldn't let us. Her new boyfriend had given Jay an electric guitar. Jay plugged it into his stereo and showed me how to play 'Whole Lotta Love' by Led Zeppelin; or maybe it was the theme music from *Top of the Pops*, it was hard to tell which. He could also play the line from the middle of 'The Chain' by Fleetwood Mac, which his mum had a copy of. He was working on 'Sunday Bloody Sunday' by U2 as well, but he could only get the first five notes. It didn't matter. Learning the rest of it was a mere formality. We knew then that we would start a band and be brilliant. It would be easy. He'd only been playing the guitar a week and he could nearly do U2. I'd only just started, and I could already nearly do *Top of the Pops* and Led Zeppelin, and he was supposed to be one of the best guitarists around.

We formed the band there and then. I decided I would play keyboards. Synthesizers had arrived from the future. They had the same kind of appeal as spaceships and everybody wanted one. Mark Pepin, my new best friend, was going to play drums and 'Rutter the Nutter' was going to play a bass guitar. Nobody was certain at that stage exactly what a bass guitar was, but bands all seemed to have one.

I had spent a long time listening to 'Blue Monday' by New Order. It was so grey and beautiful. I went to a keyboard demonstration at a big hotel down the road with my dad. They had all the latest synthesizers there and they were excited about a new technology called MIDI. Everyone kept saying 'MIDI'. It was very important, this midi business. I just liked all the buttons and the lights and the noises. They had synchronized all the keyboards together with a MIDI so that they all played 'Blue Monday' at the same time. It was too much for me. So was the keyboard: it was six hundred quid. I decided to play bass instead.

Mark got his drumkit, a Trixon. I got the bass for my sixteenth birthday in November, but I had to wait until Christmas for an amplifier. Then I wasn't allowed to have it for another week for bad behaviour. I managed to find it, though, in the loft. Jay and Rut the Nut didn't seem to be taking the band very seriously, but Mark and I played together in the cellar. We were getting pretty good at 'The Chain' and 'Whole Lotta Love', and 'Blue Monday' was coming along quite nicely.

Mark arrived one Sunday and told me he'd invited Dominic White to come round with his guitar. I was furious. Dom White, who I'd known since playschool, was a hippie with no social skills. I couldn't believe Mark had invited him round to my house. Dom had quite a low opinion of me, too. He thought I was a grinning, middle-class twat. His mum dropped him off in her Mini. It was very full of amplifiers and guitars. We lugged everything downstairs. Dom said, 'My mum wrremembers your mum.' He had a bit of trouble with his 'r's. 'Yourww mum says wot, wot, wot, I'm so middle class.' I offered him a gin and tonic, but he ignored me. He was fiddling around with a soldering iron and a huge box that said 'Vox' on it. Mark and I went upstairs. Mum said, 'Is that Dominic White? You used to be such good little friends at playgroup. He was such a good-looking little boy.' Suddenly from up the stairs came a very loud 'FUCK!', three 'SHIT's and a number of quieter, broken, little 'fuck's. Mum was straight to the top of the stairs. 'Dominic, I will not tolerate bad language in this house.' It was very quiet. We went downstairs. Dom was flat on his back. He'd miscalculated on the soldering and connected himself to two hundred and forty volts. He and my mum made their peace and he decided to use one of his other amps.

In all the time I have been making music, nothing quite so fantastic as what happened in the next five minutes has ever happened again. Mark and I started playing 'Whole Lotta Love' and Dom joined in. He was quite loud, much louder than a stereo, louder than the drums. It was the loudest, best noise I'd ever heard and I was helping to make it. Dom was brilliant. I was just pedalling around the riff, and he was all over the place, high, low, fast, slow, rhythm, melody, harmony, it was shocking. I was in a band, an amazing band. I began to think that maybe Dom was the coolest man in the world.

Mark, Dom and I played together and smoked together and went to Pokesdown to look at guitars together. It was good but we didn't have a singer. Singers weren't that important in the sort of music we were listening to, or making, but to do gigs we needed a singer. We were at Mark's house, near school, for a rehearsal. There were two drumkits in the bedroom he shared with his older brother, who was learning the drums as well. Mark said, 'I saw Pete Arnold in town yesterday, he's got a keyboard and some lyrics. I told him to come.' 'Arnold!' said Dom and me, 'Eew!' Pete Arnold was the dribbly one who used to get the 17 bus with me. He didn't get the bus any more. He'd moved house. As far as I knew, he was a grebo these days – a greasy headbanger. He arrived from the other direction, but still on a 17 bus, with his keyboard, which was large. He'd gone goth, big black spiky hair and an overcoat. He was, touchingly, very proud of his keyboard. He kept calling it a 'synthesizer', which was unfortunate, because it involved a lot of lisping and saliva. We played him what we'd been doing, but he wasn't that impressed.

He started playing the chords of 'Blue Monday' at which point I started to think he might be all right. After all, we had spent all those bus journeys talking about music and I had thought Dom was a retard until I'd played music with him. Maybe it was worth letting him join in. Dom and Mark never wanted to play 'Blue Monday'.

He wasn't bashful. He said, 'Mark, play a rock pattern. Dom, you play the chords on the second and fourth beats, to give it a reggae feel, bass should just follow the chords.' We did exactly what he said and he played a melody on the keyboard with one finger. It was brilliant. We were writing our own songs, or rather Pete was.

Really, no band is ever any more sophisticated an arrangement than that: a group of people who enjoy making a loud noise together, despite their differences.

There were a lot of bands in Bournemouth and a scene. The nightclubs – and there were loads of them – were full in the summer and at weekends, but during the week they were empty. Some of them were really plush. Some were sticky. On weekdays they were host to dozens of bands who all played for each other and to each other, constantly splitting up and re-forming with new allegiances. It was great to have a reason to be in these places, other than looking at girls. Those nightclubs looked great when they were empty, all the lasers and spotlights blazing at the unemployable outsiders on the stage.

Odd Jobs

The first celebrity I ever met was the headmaster's daughter. Being nobly born and also quite pretty had given her unshakeable confidence. Everybody fancied her and she wore her adulation like haute couture; it really made her look good. She thrived on it. Some of it didn't fit her or suit her, but it was all precious stuff and she kept it safe. She was a star and she knew it.

I got to know her when I started working after school and at weekends at The Roysdean. The Roysdean announced itself as 'a Methodist Holiday Hotel'. It was in Derby Road, just around the corner from home. Derby Road is all largish two-star hotels and prostitutes. The buildings are quite grand, laid to garden squares with avenues of mature pines. It's really quite beautiful. Sandbanks, five miles to the west, is one of the most expensive neighbourhoods in the whole world: it's pricier than most of Tokyo and Manhattan. It's hard to say what makes that part of town so expensive and the Derby Road part such a bargain. From the air you can see that the whole of Bournemouth sits on a river plain. There's definitely not one part that's any more special than another; you'd expect to pay a bit more for a house near the sublime beach, but it's hard to fathom the fiftyfold price difference between the fading Regency elegance of Derby Road and the East Cliff at the low end of the market, and the chintz territory of Canford Cliffs and Sandbanks, the super-expensive end. All the worst bands were from Canford Cliffs and Sandbanks, bad funksters with highlighted hair.

There were a dozen kids from school who worked at The Roysdean, including the headmaster's kids and their gangs. We were all united in our disdain for Methodists, the hotel and its management. We were quite good at pretending to behave ourselves, and the jobs did get done, but there was a lot of larking around. You can't pay people ninety pence an hour and expect them to give everything.

I was mainly in the kitchens, washing up and mopping. It smelled pretty rank in there, a mixture of slops, cabbage and disinfectant, but the tea was excellent. It's one thing that hotels full of old people really excel at, tea. They fed us, too. People who work in hotels always get fed. People who are hungry and handling food just tend to eat it. It's very hard to stop them. It was lowly work, but I was happy. I was in love with most of the girls who worked there.

I loved girls, music and France. I fell for France on holiday and on French exchanges. I went to Germany, too, but they just wanted to play table tennis. In France everything was exotic, erotic, dangerous and fabulous. Cool women on mopeds smoked cool cigarettes and knew about cheese and poetry.

I liked reading too, but writers themselves didn't seem to be very appealing people until I turned over a school copy of *L'Etranger* by Albert Camus in the first year of the sixth form. There was a picture of Albert on the back: Gitane glowing from the corner of a sulky pout, long skinny mac and James Dean hair. It said on the flap that he played football, in goal, for Algiers.

Everything about that book resonated. It ding-donged with adolescent feelings of pointlessness. I bought a long mac with pockets big enough to carry books in. Books and records were the great sources of truth.

Green Road

My 'A' level results weren't just bad, they were astonishing. I had been a model student throughout school, I'd been encouraged to sit entrance exams for Oxford in French and in Chemistry just a few months before, but things had gone downhill rapidly. A succession of girlfriends and late nights in empty nightclubs had taken their toll. Life is not wide enough for Sex and Drugs and Rock and Roll, and French and Chemistry. I had been expected to get A grades, but I'd dive-bombed out of the system. It was very scary all of a sudden.

I'd missed my second-choice college as well, and even failed to match what was basically an unconditional offer from a grubby college called Goldsmiths in south-east London. In three very clear letters the flimsy piece of paper spelt out doom. I went round to my girlfriend's house.

She'd got two As and a B and so had her friend, who was there. They were ecstatic. They were both going to Bristol. The fragile veil of young love was shaken hard by the spectre of failure. I was pretty much dumped there and then. I went home to sleep it off. It was pretty rough at home, too. My mum was despairing. I wrote things down a lot and listened to Joy Division.

I got a job at Safeway, stacking shelves. Nothing could be as horrible as working in that supermarket. Everything about it was off. The management team were all bullied and all bullies. I had to wear a bow tie and a bright green apron. There were quite a lot of staff, but there was no camaraderie or joy. I started at the bottom. The further up the chain you got the more horrible you had to be to stay there. I found it hard to hang on to that job and I was broken-hearted and bandless. The Rising, my first group, had disintegrated, but I was playing the old piano more than ever.

All the bands used to go to Circles coffee shop on the top

floor of Dingles, the department store. It was the daytime headquarters of the Bournemouth music scene. I used to meet my friends there, too, and that was where I first laid eyes on Justine. Everybody knew Justine. Justine Andrew was the prettiest girl in Bournemouth and she was going out with the bass player in the best band in town.

A few years ago I was looking through some photographs of a backstage party at the Beastie Boys' 'Free Tibet' concert in New York. There were photos of all the New York models, and the photographer had done a little book. They were all in it – Helena Christensen, Stella Tennant, Liberty Ross, Jasmine Guinness. I turned over another leaf and there was a full-page photograph of Justine: she was quite at home in the pretty girls' big league with her green eyes, pointy nose and huge open smile, a smile that melted rocks.

I remember very clearly that the first time I saw her she was wearing a poncho and eating a toasted teacake, which seemed quite extravagant.

Duncan Collier, from Mulberry Phut, the band with the seventeen guitarists, who used to get the 17 bus with me, was moving to Ireland and the house in Charminster, where he lived with other members of the Phut, was available to rent. Justine was going to live there with the keyboard player from the now defunct Reader's Wives. They, too, had been torn apart by the university system. The drummer with the ten A grade 'O' levels had left to study accountancy. I was offered a room in the house.

I worked more at the supermarket, to pay the deposit, but it was worth it. Things turned around pretty quickly. We moved in on New Year's Day and I soon forgot about all the other girls I'd known before. Justine and I spent hours doing nothing in particular. Some girls might have been put off by the bow tie and bright green apron, but Justine thought it was hilarious. She had a crap job as well, running a hotel.

I handed in my notice at Safeway and got another job at a

scaffolding depot, putting blobs of purple paint on everything. If it belonged to the yard, it had to have some purple paint on it. It was nasty stuff that paint, took my skin off, but I liked working there. Pretty soon I was labouring for scaffolders on building sites. Scaffolders pride themselves on being the wild men of construction. I worked with a murderer called Bill. He nearly killed me a couple of times, accidentally, but he wasn't nearly as nasty as the supermarket people. He carried a revolver in the glove compartment of his horrible car, which he drove appallingly badly. We travelled all over the place together, until he had a bad fall. I was lucky to escape from that job with only a few blisters. The gangs often used to drink quite a lot at lunchtime, as much as four or five pints in an hour, and then spend the afternoon swinging from poles high above the ground.

There was a big job at the nuclear power station at Winfrith, rebuilding the main reactor. That went on for weeks. It was spooky in that place, all underground corridors and restricted zones. When we were building the scaffold tower around the core of the reactor we had to wear white suits and Geiger counters. It was still not as bad as Safeway.

2

goldsmiths college

Camberwell

Goldsmiths College said they'd have me after all, despite my recent lack of form, and I set off for London a year late to start a French degree. Someone else was getting his stuff out of his parents' car when I arrived at the student halls of residence with my own parents. I saw him unload a guitar. He was covered in paint, but even if he hadn't been it would have been obvious that he was an art student: pale and skinny; National Health specs; huge trousers and a stripy, baggy jumper. It's a moment that I remember very clearly. I liked him from the instant I saw him and I had the certain feeling that one of the main characters in my life had just walked on to the stage. His name was Graham Coxon and he had the room above me, but I didn't see him again for a few weeks. He had friends who were in their final year, and he spent his time with them.

Camberwell is a far cry from Bournemouth. It's in the most populous square mile of Europe, in the borough of Southwark, just south of the Thames. Stannard Hall, where we lived, was a rotten eyesore in an otherwise beautiful street that ran around a park with plane trees, tennis courts and a bandstand. It was a leafy enclave in a squalid neighbourhood where civilisation was permanently on the brink of collapse. It really wasn't safe after dark, or even in the daytime. There were a lot of muggings. In the broad daylight of a Saturday afternoon, a couple of weeks after we all arrived, a gang plundered the hall. There was a high fence around the building and grilles on the windows, but they smashed the doors down and grabbed everyone's stereos and cameras.

We were encouraged not to look too much like students, especially in October, when the marauding gangs were on the lookout for bewildered-looking, easy targets. A stick-thin, big-brained, benevolent psychology don lived there in the hall with Laura, his Alsatian. He gave us all hope. He drove a VW camper van and he seemed to enjoy sleeping out on the front line. You went to see him when you got mugged or menaced and he made you tea. I never needed to go and see him. When I got to know Graham he told me that there was dog poo in the lounge when he went in sometimes.

Paul Hodgson was the first person I really connected with at college. He was always getting mugged. He still is. I ran into him in the street a few months ago and he had a black eye from a thief. He was set upon by rogues even before he started at Goldsmiths, on his way to the interview. He's quite a dandy dresser. Maybe that's what it is. Paul talked a lot about Shelley and Byron. He was doing Fine Art and he made me laugh. The people who did art at my school weren't that clever, or funny. The clever people did physics and chemistry. Paul was very perceptive and inquisitive. His dad, Ken, was a plumber and Paul manipulated high-falutin' art concepts in a west London drawl, with a mild stutter. 'Owls!' – he called me Als – 'Maaate, have a word with Brownlee, he's s-pouting Were-Were-Wittgenstein; the wanger.' Jason Brownlee was another artist. He had the room opposite me. He had fallen for Wittgenstein, utterly. He hadn't properly grasped Joy Division lyrics yet; he was straight in the deep end wallowing in a big morass of intellectual spaghetti. Possibly he was looking down the wrong end of his mind, like when you look through a telescope backwards and fall over.

The Fine Art reading list was all pretty chewy. The undergraduates were encouraged to launch themselves into the wits of the great thinkers and ransack what they needed, like they were trawling through a skip. Paul was dipping his toe into some Nietzsche. He always referred to figures he was engaging with by their Christian names, as a nod to his intimacy with them. It's a good system. It humanises the mythical characters of human history. When Paul called anyone by their surname, it was a dis. 'Ner-ner-Nietzsche's n-not funny at all. No jokes in there, mate,' he said with a grin.

It was through Jason and Paul that I got to know Graham. The art department was a member's club, really. The artists didn't mix with the rest of the college. I got to know Paul in the kitchen. He was on first-name terms with the abstract expressionists but he had no idea how to feed himself. I had a year of low-budget culinary experimentation behind me. He'd come straight from his mum's. He didn't know how pasta worked and was quite spellbound by tomato purée. He had an artist's fascination with the mundane. There was something magical for him in a tube of tomato purée, a tomato being transformed into its essence and re-presented as a packaged consumer product. Was it more of a tomato or less now? Was it art? Was it good on toast? Jason waded around in the primary flavours like they were huge splashes of bold colour. He always put too much garlic in. His drawings were very dense, too.

Paul and Jason said I should meet Gra. It rhymed with car, Gra. We went up for some pasta sandwiches. Graham's door was open and there was loud music. He was a bit drunk. His room was completely full of junk; we'd only been there for three weeks and he'd managed to give the impression that he'd been born there and never tidied up. There were piles of clothes from the flea market, a lot of paintings and posters, some of which were still attached to hoardings. There was a huge fan lying on the floor taking up most of the middle of the room. I'd seen that fan on a skip outside. Stuff was spilling out of cupboards, quite a few records and cassettes but mainly clothes. There was a charm about the magpie clutter. It didn't look like anyone else's room, except maybe Paul's. Paul had a neat little row of books as well, though. Graham only had one book, *Thérèse Raquin* by Emile Zola. It looked like he'd read it a few times. It was dog-eared and the spine was all cracked. I was glad Graham had a French book. I had a lot of them.

The first thing he said was, 'How long have you been playing the guit?'

Graham

Graham was as brilliant as he looked like he would be. He was excellent at drawing things – faces, girls, monsters. The morning after we met he dangled the flex from his standard issue student Anglepoise lamp out of his bedroom window so that it banged on the glass of mine. I stuck my head out of the window. 'Brekkers, cheers? Nice.' He communicated mainly with facial expressions and in his own language. He was always playing with words. The linguistics department at college would have been fascinated.

There was a student demonstration taking place that day, to protest against the abolition of grants. College was cancelled, and we were to march on Westminster. We had breakfast at the Camberwell Grill in Camberwell Green. There isn't much green in Camberwell. It's grey, mainly. The café was all red and yellow plastic. We didn't ever have enough money to go out for dinner, but breakfast was cheap. There were the four of us – Paul, Graham, myself and Jason. Paul was still interested in tomato sauces. So was Graham. Graham squirted ketchup all over his food. Paul and Graham both saw the possibilities of tomatoes as art, but they were different types of artist. Paul wanted to create the essence of tomato and Graham wanted to make pretty patterns.

It was quite rowdy when we got to Waterloo. There was a good turnout, thousands of students. All the colleges in London had closed for the day. There were placards and banners and people were chanting, and singing, 'The students united will never be defeated.' The march came to a standstill. We couldn't work out why. The tense and menacing atmosphere was gradually building into a physical uprising. Everyone was shouting and jeering. It was very noisy and exciting. We pushed our way down to the front, like at a concert. There was a line of police defending the end of Waterloo Bridge. They didn't want thousands of rebelling students going anywhere near the Houses of Parliament on the other side of the river. A police helmet was being thrown high in the air around the crowd. Every time it soared there was a huge round of applause and cheering. Down at the front it was a perilous crush with everyone shoving from behind. I reached out and grabbed a helmet and flung it in the air. There was a big cheer from behind as I felt the hands of many police officers seize me. As I was wrenched bodily from the mob a dozen more hands from the crowd grabbed my arms to pull me back in. I was on my back on top of a sea of people with the police on my feet and the students on the other end playing tug-of-war with my body. I kicked my feet, got one leg free and lost a shoe as I hauled the other leg from the arms of the law. I disappeared back into the throng with the police swearing and the students cheering. You needed two shoes that day, especially when the riot police arrived. The riot police are like a branch of the army, really. You can't fight them. It's time to go home when they arrive. Nobody did, though. The police were on horseback and they galloped at the crowd. People were crushed and some were quite badly hurt. Speccy girls reading botany at Bedford New College or anyone who happened to be in the way got charged and flattened. A few people hung around throwing things but it had certainly broken the crowd up. I couldn't find my shoe, or Graham. It was a big day, though, and we were mates after that. I'd liked Graham from the moment I saw him. He was cool. Everyone doing art was cool, but Graham was the coolest and he floated around college.

He was listening to the Pixies a lot and he had their lyrics pinned up on his walls. He was really good at guitar. He could play anything, even the Smiths. I still find those guitar parts tricky. He was in a few bands. One was called Idle Vice. The songs were mainly about beer, but some were about vodka. He played the drums as well, but there were no drums around so he played on his knees, with air cymbals. There was a piano in the hall and we used to sing 'Blue Moon' a lot. Graham only knew how to play 'October' by U2 on the piano, so we sang that a lot as well. We were friends. We were interested in each other's record collections and we both had guitars; we connected through music, but it went beyond that. We were happy in each other's company just waiting for a bus or sharing a packet of cigarettes and making up words. I liked him because he was instantly brilliantly artistic, but vulnerable; strikingly stylish, but quite awkwardly shy. Why he liked me, I don't know. Maybe it was mainly because I liked him. Still, when you do know exactly why someone likes you, that's not really a friend. That's a fan.

We didn't often go anywhere apart from college and places that sold breakfast. We didn't have any money so we just sat in each other's rooms listening to each other's records, me, Graham and often Paul as well. Jason got involved with Jo from English and drama and disappeared.

One of Graham's proudest possessions was a half-drunk bottle of tequila in a sealed plastic bag with a 'police evidence' sticker on it. He was planning on keeping it forever, but that was patently never going to happen. We did get drunk and run out of booze quite a few times before it went, though, and we'd try and persuade him to open it. Then one morning the bottle was empty and Paul and I were quite disappointed he'd drunk it without us.

Paul loved the Beatles, but not as much as Graham. Graham's dad, who was a clarinet teacher, had brought him up on the Beatles and Beethoven. Paul's sister was friends with Captain Sensible, the singer, so he had the final say in all conversations about punk rock, but Graham was the authority on the Beatles. I had some quite odd records. Papa's, mainly: he was a big-band man. I worked my way through them all keeping the ones I liked and selling the ones I didn't to Ray's Jazz in Covent Garden.

Occasionally Graham would disappear to a studio in Euston, where he was recording with a band. I was insanely jealous. I'd messed around with four-track recorders a lot, but I'd never been inside a studio.

Goldsmiths

Goldsmiths College is a wonderful place. It's taken over most of New Cross. It's spilled out of the original building into the surrounding Victorian terraces and municipal buildings. There are new additions too, the latest in library chic and all sorts of departments, faculties and facilities. It's really thriving. The university buildings are bisected by the flooding A2, but to turn into one of the little side streets is to enter a world of studious calm.

Most of the French department was in a neat little antique cul-de-sac called Laurie Grove. London SE14 doesn't have the grandeur of Oxford: more screaming tyres than dreaming spires. It's very much a feet-on-the-ground part of town. It's quite bewildering how many things are happening at once around there. New Cross manages to be part campus, part ghetto, part middle-class suburb and part motorway, with a lot of pubs. There are always all kinds of people striding around. It is easy to spot the students, especially in October. It doesn't conform to the traditional image of a hallowed seat of learning but you'd learn more about the world in a couple of terms at Goldsmiths than you would in ten years of eating crumpets and punting around Cambridge.

I do like Oxford and Cambridge; Goldsmiths just happened to be the best place to be in the world at that time. I'd under-achieved my way into the right place and dallied on my way to arrive at the perfect time. The cataclysmic big bang that kick-started the ultimate decade of the last millennium can be traced back to a small area of the bar at the Student Union at Goldsmiths College in 1988. Somehow or other the drunkest people in that bar went on to instigate a British cultural revolution that reverberated in everything from football to rocket science. There were music students, too, and drama courses, but the art department was where the nineties started.

I had trouble getting up on Wednesdays and kept missing language laboratory, which was at nine o'clock. I took a 36 bus from Camberwell to New Cross. It is not a glamour run that route, through Peckham and the cheap end of the Old Kent Road, but it never felt like I was in the wrong place, like it did at the supermarket.

I didn't miss lingo lab on purpose, but it did gall me a little bit that Brownlee was free to ingest yet more of Wittgenstein's axioms in the bath when he rose at midday, that Graham would go on skip trawls with Paul, while I listened carefully and repeated, but I enjoyed French. There wasn't one of the lecturers that I didn't like. They were all terribly clever. It was a very thorough course. It got reality right up on the jacks and had a good look at the underneath. In cosy classrooms we learned about the birth of language, the dawn of civilisation and the first stories, civilisation's collapse and the onset of the Dark Ages, architecture, art, and archaic and extant forms of music and verse through the ages. The staff all wrote books with long titles: analyses of the principles of linguistic transference; guides to the medieval romances and the works of the great authors of antiquity.

The books that we read in the first couple of terms of French were carefully selected to blow our tiny minds. Many of them attacked the core of the cosy existence we led. We loved that. We embarked upon an intellectual cruise; took a tour through the twisted, terrifying thoughtscapes of André Gide. We took a ramble through Rabelais' ribaldry. We dabbled in Dadaism, supped on surrealism, ripped through Romanticism and embraced existentialism. There was plenty to talk about.

The college library had very tight security. There must have been millions of pounds' worth of books in there. They could probably have left the door open, though. Books are the most unlikely things to get stolen in New Cross. Street lamps and traffic lights are more at risk of theft than academic treatises. I didn't go to the library. I made a point of not going to France and not going to the library while I was there. I think I had an attitude problem. The head of the first year said she wanted to see me about my essays. She seemed quite well connected and I assumed she had found a publisher. I was quite excited when I arrived at her study. Maybe she wanted to discuss some of my new ideas. She was, in fact, appalled, she said, at the standard of my French, and how, she wanted to know, could I hope to express ideas, however original I thought they were, without a grasp of a language? I still thought she was wrong. Conceit is vital.

While working at Safeway I'd got quite good at copying the illustrations out of *Winnie the Pooh* and brushing on the watercolour, but my sister Debs has always had much more in the way of visual acuity than me. She can do jigsaws faster than anyone. We knew that she was destined for greatness when she won the Regatta Week pavement drawing competition in Bournemouth when she was five.

Art was bound to take on a new importance in the environment at Goldsmiths. I'd aligned my on-board compasses with the books and records that I liked, but I didn't know much about art. There was art going on everywhere – on the upper floors of the main building, in an old car showroom opposite. People were talking about abstract expressionism in the canteen, Fluxus in the bar. There was sculpture, film, installation, photography, painting and drawing but absolutely no one was doing watercolours.

There were loads of big ideas flying around. Everyone was reading books, listening to records, going to Cork Street and gatecrashing first-night art openings. There were theatre trips, museum visits and gigs in the union. Paul really liked football, too.

I went to Paul's space in M.B. Motors one day, the converted garage opposite the main college building. He was working on a huge grey and black abstraction. I was very impressed. He said, 'I like this bit in the ker-corner.' The corner was a good bit, you had to admit. It had pleasing asymmetry, it had dimensionality, I said. I was way out of my depth, but so was he, probably. Paint was all over his space like engine oil in a garage. Everyone had a space, a white cubicle. The spaces were all crammed together, so that everyone interacted. The space opposite Graham's on the first floor had spots painted all over it, a pleasing array of dots. We all liked those spot paintings. They were easy on the eye. They were nice to look at. Graham said they were the work of a madman called Damien. Damien Hirst.

Minds were racing everywhere. Opposite Paul, a right geezer called Jim who had been a plumber for some years was doing something with maps. He'd pasted a London *A–Z* together and was subverting its reality in some way that I was embarrassed not to be able to grasp. He said 'Luvly-juvly' quite often. By the end of the second year, he was saying 'lubbly-bubbly' and going out with an upper-middle-class girl from French and drama.

Next door to Paul the space was vacant, though. I asked him what had happened and he said that the guy came in one day, didn't paint anything, just stared at the wall and was never seen again. 'He dried up,' said Paul, with great foreboding. It was like a horror story: like someone had died. I could tell Paul was terrified, as if they were infantrymen and the next guy in the line had bought it. For some sad reason, the unknown artist had given up. I don't think anyone ever stops having ideas. It's impossible to stop having ideas. He must have lost his bottle, or realised he wasn't good enough. It's a struggle to make art. It was a forlorn sight, that empty space, but it soon filled up with Paul's debris and spare ideas. Boundaries were being tested. It was a very competitive environment. A lot of discussion went into trying to say exactly what Fine Art is. It's a hard thing to define, art. If you can say exactly what art is, then you probably are an artist.

We went to the Tate to see the de Koonings. Paul marvelled at 'Willem's' sexy pink swirly-girly abstractions. My favourite place was the British Museum, a huge castle full of treasure. They've got everything there from Beatles' lyrics on the back of an envelope to mouldering pharaohs. I spent days in there, giggling at the clocks. The early clocks were mesmerising. I thought about those a lot.

Damon

Damon's dad is an art man. He ran the art foundation course in Colchester that Graham had attended, and he ran the art department at Essex University. I knew all this before I met him, because Graham told me. Graham had talked quite a lot about Damon. Damon is someone people talk about.

Graham and Paul and I went to the Beat Factory, a bijou, pristine studio near King's Cross. We were going to listen to what this band of Graham's had been doing. They'd just finished recording some new songs. We didn't hit it off straight away, Damon and I. He was wearing a necklace and he still had 'up' hair. No one at college was doing the 'up' hair thing any more. Hair spent most of the eighties going in the wrong direction, but things were getting back to normal again.

The first thing I can remember Damon asking me was whether I'd been in a recording studio before. I had to admit I hadn't. They played the songs, which were a bit cheesy. I was very relieved about that. We went off to Eddy's house to drink poitin, Irish moonshine made from potatoes. It's really nasty stuff. Eddy was Damon's friend. They had been to drama college together. Eddy was a huge personality squeezed into a fairly large body. He played the guitar in the band and his little mate played bass; it was a nasty Paul McCartney Beatles bass. There were quite a few people at Eddy's house. The people who ran the studio and managed Damon, Eddy's girlfriend, some other drama types and poitin sniffers. It was pretty dull and we had to listen to the songs again. They really weren't that great. They were too drama college; they needed to be more art college.

Damon asked me what I thought of them, what they sounded like to me, just, you know, as someone who had never been in a recording studio before. Damon was an instantly provocative person. I'd gone along to meet Graham's friend assuming Graham's friend would be similar to Graham, I suppose. They couldn't really have been more different. Damon had buckets of confidence and gumption and he wore sandals.

If I'd liked the songs, I would probably have burst into tears, but I told him I thought they weren't quite right, which they weren't. He kind of knew it, really, but he was obviously shocked. I didn't mince my words. It was the only stick I could possibly have bashed him with. In the Robin Hood stories, Robin likes to have a fight with everyone he meets before he becomes their friend. Damon loves Robin Hood and he loves a tussle. We said, cheerio then.

The week before the end of the first term at college, December 1988, Graham came to my room, where I was playing chess with Paul. We'd decided that chess was a fine pastime and that it would sound good in later life to be able to say, 'Well, I played a bit of chess when I was at college.' We only ever played each other, though. We were both scared of losing to anyone else. Graham said, 'Been to the Beat Fac. We've sacked the other guitarist and the bass player!' Then, after a long pause, 'And we want you to play bass.'

I was definitely up for playing in a band with Graham, and Damon, if he had the keys to a recording studio, and the other guy on drums. Dave, he was called – Dave the drummer. I went down to the payphone with Graham and we called Damon. 'Yeah, yeah, yeah, there's a bass at the studio, come down on Friday.'

So Graham and Damon and I met in the studio on the last day of the first term. Damon had the keys, as he was sort of an assistant there. There were a couple of things that Damon and Graham had been working on together that we bashed around for a while. I showed them some chords that I'd been strumming in my room. Graham started to play them on the guitar, there was a drum machine going boom whack and I started grooving along on the bass that was lying around. Damon started jumping up and down and saying, 'Brilliant, brilliant, brilliant! You're a natural!' He got his lyrics book out and started singing, 'She is so high, she is so high.'

It all happened there and then. It was instantaneous, shockingly so. Graham wrote the lyrics for the verse, over the same chords, and sang a backing vocal on the choruses. I'd never been in a band with backing vocals. The two of them sang really well together, they'd been doing it for years. We made a tape and I went home for Christmas thinking, 'I'm in the best band in the world.'

Justine was renting a room in a house in Charminster and working at The Body Shop. I'd been in London for ten weeks, but most weeks either she came to London or I went back to see her.

Graham and I went back to London a week before college started, to write some more songs with Damon. We tried one of my mates from Bournemouth on drums, but he wasn't as good as the guy who wore pyjamas and worked for Colchester council that they had already, so we stuck with him.

Damon had a job, so he had a little bit more money than we did. It was an awful job, some fast croissant hellhole at Euston Station. He was a tiny bit older than Graham and me, a fact he never let us forget. Once we were allies he was incredibly generous. He was very liberal with his hard-earned cash. I was terrified of money. Damon knew how to use it to get what he wanted. He splashed it around, gave it to tramps. We went to the Town and Country Club to see the Pixies. He bought tickets for the three of us from a tout outside for sixty quid, which was more than I got a week to live on. It was a brilliant gig. We went to see quite a few gigs, the Happy Mondays, mainly bands that were on the cover of the *NME*. Damon nearly always paid.

He was very at home in London. He'd grown up there, but he didn't come across as a cockney. He was hard to place, actually. I liked him a lot by this time – we were becoming brothers-in-arms – but I never knew what he was thinking, not like Graham. I found Graham was often thinking what I was thinking; that's one of the reasons Graham was my best friend. We went out drinking, the two of us, Damon and me, in New Cross, to get to know each other a bit better. He liked the theatre. He liked

Hermann Hesse. He loved Spain, wore sandals and he followed the cycles of the moon very closely. He said his mum could do magic.

We talked about music, but not about bands, really, more about what it was and how it worked. We both wanted to be in the best band ever shaped on earth, but all boys with guitars do. I always thought it might just happen to me. He was much more direct, full of plans, schemes and determination to make things happen. He had so much energy. That's what creativity is, really, that vigour.

We walked along Peckham High Street after midnight. Damon was full of beans. He always is. He was climbing up lamp-posts and dancing on bus-shelter roofs. He said, 'Watch this, I'm going to get arrested!' and ran off down Queen's Road with a Belisha beacon, shouting random things in a very deep voice. They threw him in the cells with a mad Gurkha, until he calmed down. Graham had been arrested at the Student Union for pissing on the stage while a reggae band was playing. He was very remorseful after that, but Damon was quite proud after his night in the cooler. 'I told you I was going to get arrested! I made it happen,' he said, eyes wide.

Seymour

The Beat Factory became our new headquarters. Paul got fed up that Graham and I were spending so much time there and always talking about it. We often stayed there all night, Damon, Graham and me. We could only use it when it was empty, and it was reasonably busy so we grabbed time whenever we could get it. Courtney Pine, the jazz man, used to record there, and loads of other people who I'd kind of heard of their old band, but not their current one. It was a good little studio, with a pretty courtyard, clean carpets, TV and video. We watched every film they had. There was tea and coffee. The fridge always had some cheese in, too. There was never any cheese in my fridge.

In Bournemouth, the Rising used to make demos at my house. We never bothered sending them to record companies, though. Damon had been left some money by a relative and spent it recording some songs at the Beat Factory. He was obviously very decisive. The people who ran the studio gave him a job as a tea boy, with the aim of moulding him into a pop product, but he was still at the tomato end of things, rather than the purée stage. We all were.

I always felt special walking into that studio. It was just what we needed. None of us had any idea how the posh mixing desk worked, but Damon had a four-track and there was a piano, a few amps and room to set up drums.

We were getting songs together. We liked being there; it was nicer than Camberwell and we spent ages just messing around, jamming into the middle of the night. We'd walk back to town at dawn and get the bus to college.

Sometimes, when the studio was booked, we'd go to Damon's parents' house for the weekend and play there, in his mum's studio. She was an artist, too, and the studio was full of intriguing papier-mâché totems. Keith and Hazel Albarn are exceptionally nice people. I was overwhelmed by the sheer tastefulness of their home. They lived in an old bakery in rural Essex. It was full of books and rugs and smooth wooden obelisks. There were always nice smells, faintly spicy, wafting around. It was quiet and the sun beat in through the windows.

Sometimes I stayed at Graham's parents' house but usually we all went to Damon's where Graham and I shared Damon's sister's vacant four-poster. Hazel Albarn's *table d'hôtesse* was exquisite and mealtimes were eagerly anticipated. We all sat round the big table, where Damon would proceed to drive his parents mad.

It was beautiful there. We wrote some good songs in Hazel's studio, including 'Sing', which was on the first album. The band was called Seymour. It was Paul's idea, after the J. D. Salinger character. We all liked *The Catcher in the Rye* and agreed that it was best to own the edition with the silver cover.

Seymour's first public appearance was at the college in the Student Union on the night that the Fine Art degree show opened. For the art students it was a big climax: the whole three years at college led up to that one show. It's quite a dramatic situation. Hearts could be broken and dreams come true as tutors and suitors – galleries, dealers and buyers – decreed who would have a future.

We looked at everything. Damien Hirst's work was obviously good. It stood out. He'd done some medicine cabinets full of cute little phials. If their meaning was obscure, they were certainly nice to look at. They were only five hundred quid, his degree-show pieces. I wanted one. I'd never ever had five hundred quid, though.

Charles Saatchi was very clever. He scoured all the degree shows and bought the work that he liked. He didn't invest in art by established names, like most rich people. He invested in artists. He bought Damien's work. He could pick out the good stuff. Choosing the right option, ticking the right box, knowing the good from the bad is about the cleverest thing anyone ever has to do. No one's right all the time, but some people have a knack for picking winners, and they become winners themselves.

The Union was packed, and we deafened everybody.

Strait is the Gate

At the end of the first year, the start of the summer, we had to vacate the halls of residence in Camberwell. Graham's friend Ads had just graduated. He knew some people who were squatting in a building right next to the college in New Cross. They, too, had sat their finals and were leaving. I went back to

Bournemouth for a couple of weeks to see Justine and take the sunshine, but really I needed to be in London. The band was gathering momentum. Graham said I could stay in the squat. He'd saved me a room.

It was a horrible room. It's hard to imagine anything more horrible. Noisy and toxic from the A2, which it overlooked, busted up and broken down and filthy, but it was free. The squat was just somewhere we could stay while things developed musically. There was no college and nothing else to do. Dave the drummer quit his day job and the four of us spent the whole time rehearsing, songwriting, getting to know each other and dreaming about what might happen next. All we wanted to do was to make music. Music never yet heard, music so powerful and beautiful that people would stop what they were doing and forget everything else.

We had no money at all. Graham's mum sent him twenty pounds on Thursdays but he always went straight to the Co-op and spent it on Tennent's Super. The whole building was empty to begin with, but it soon filled up with mad people, mainly Adam's friends. It was summer and all the windows were open. I lived out of a very small bag. I always had a notebook, and some French vocabulary to learn. It was getting difficult at this stage, as I wasn't even sure what some of the words meant in English.

There were a lot of people with no money in their pockets in New Cross. On the other side of the A2, down Clifton Rise past the cool off-licence, there was a largish park, all laid to grass. An endless game of cricket took place, all summer long. We went and played, some days. There was a pub in the park, the Dew Drop Inn. It stood as a monument to a more beautiful era, dwarfed now by the cold-blooded scale of dozens of modern high rises obscuring the horizon. I'd been to the Dewie a few times with some of the sassier girls from French, and got drunk on Newcastle Brown, listening to the Joy Division songs on the jukebox. It was the best pub in New Cross.

We took my dad there when he came to stay at the squat. He stayed in London a fair bit. He only stayed with us once, though. He had a good time. My mum wouldn't have liked it. There were a lot of flies in that flat. Adam used to catch them with a beer glass and put them in the freezer. When you freeze flies, they don't die. They just go into cryogenic suspension. They come back to life when they warm up again. While they were unconscious he tied bits of cotton on to their legs. The other end of the cotton he stuck to the wall with Sellotape so that they flew around in circles when they woke up. Others bombed around the flat slowly trailing their cotton tails.

There were a lot of mouth organs in the house at that time, too. Everybody had one, and we took them everywhere with us. They really sound best one at a time, mouth organs, but we all learned 'My Old Man's a Dustman' and played it for my dad. That was when he said, 'Shall we go to the pub?'

People are very friendly in that corner of town. There are a few maniacs wherever you go, but it never got hairy in the Dew Drop. There were tattooed bikers, squat punks, goths, art students, Jamaican cricket players, my dad and a few of the old boys you get in every London watering hole. The pubs in Bournemouth often had quite aggressive, unfriendly atmospheres. In London, pubs are wonderful places. You just never know what might change when you walk into a pub in London. They're the synapses of the city, full of connections and paths that lead in all directions.

There was a street market in Deptford on Wednesdays and Fridays. We got all our things from there – records, books, clothes. I could buy as much as I could carry for about five pounds. Everything was so cheap I always felt like a rich man when I arrived. One could afford to speculate. I bought a copy of *Abba's Greatest Hits* for ten pence. I wouldn't have paid much more, but it turned out to be incredibly good. Probably the best ten pence I ever spent. Graham bought armfuls of clothes every week, and he was accumulating large numbers of shoes, particularly big boots. We all had suits from Deptford Market. Ads and I bought dresses one week. We put them on and went straight to the nastiest pub that we could think of. Nobody cared.

It was good to pass the time with Adam. He was very handsome, pursued by beautiful women, but often he just hung around with the down and outs by the big anchor at the end of Deptford High Street. He was a young man who lived without fear. He wasn't afraid of being beaten up, or arrested, or laughed at, or of not being able to get the last bus home. He didn't need rhododendron branches or the soft sea to catch him. It was a new kind of freedom, his company. Most people worry about something or other, but he didn't. He left for New Orleans at the end of the summer. All he took with him was his sketchbook and a hammock.

I spent my time at college surrounded by women in the matriarchy of the French department. It was a far cry from the threatening, all-pervading manliness of the building sites, but other girls just reminded me of Justine. Towards the end of the summer, just before the second year of college began, she moved to London.

Justine was bold and stylish and she was a winner. She could run faster than anyone in Bournemouth – she'd been the town junior sprint champion. Everybody wants to run the fastest. I think that it was being the best at something at an early age that had given her absolute confidence and wisdom. She'd been naturally gifted with good looks and athleticism, which had always made her popular. She didn't have to learn how to do anything to win anyone over. She had nothing to prove to anybody.

We took over the flat downstairs. Flat 2, 302A New Cross Road, was lying empty because the building was condemned. There was no heating, we had to boil the kettle to have a bath, and even though there were only ever a few inches of water in there, it took all day to empty. The kitchen had a collapsing, rotten floor and was infested with slugs. They left their goo on the lino. They weren't there all the time, but occasionally there were invasions. I didn't mind the slugs. They were slow and quite interesting. There were nasty white ratty things in the cellar, though, and dripping pipes. It was precarious. The next building along the terrace burned down. Someone knocked on the door and said, 'You're on fire.' Outside there were flames roaring out of all the windows and high into the sky from the roof like a huge incinerator.

Living in that flat was like camping. There was a little walled garden overgrown with honeysuckle and ivy and the sun came through all the windows. A hostile motorbike beardy lived in the building behind the wall, but one day it was demolished and he was gone. That left us with half an acre of space, through a door in the garden wall. I became quite absorbed by the garden and planted anything that might grow. I threw old vegetables over the wall and they sprouted. The potatoes did really well. Graham came round and we made chips with them. We mainly cooked on a fire in the garden, using all the demolition debris. We were cavemen really.

Ours was the only flat that had electricity by that time, all the others having been disconnected as bills went unpaid. Adam had gone to the States and the rest of the crowd moved on. Graham went to live in a cupboard in a house in Lewisham but one of his friends from Colchester called Mad Paul still lived upstairs. He was a sculptor and the main theme of his work was death. He wanted his degree-show exhibit to be his head in a box. He dribbled when he got excited, but he was an enigmatic presence on the whole. We gave him candles and he crept around in the dark alone with his mad thoughts.

Justine packed her bags regularly but never left. It was tough to start with. The flat wasn't safe. The whole neighbourhood was insecure. She didn't know anybody and there was no money.

In the band I had acquired a new family, plus I was at college during the day. She got a job in The Body Shop in Oxford Street. She'd been sacked from the Bournemouth Body Shop for messing around. She had an endless capacity for messing around. That was why I liked her. Oxford Street didn't seem to mind either and she worked on the cosmetics stand giving makeovers.

When we were together it was always wonderful. We brought bicycles up from Bournemouth and rode or walked all over town. Sometimes we took vows of silence. Sometimes we stayed up all night talking. We were young and in love and all we really needed was each other.

We went to the Natural History Museum on my twenty-first birthday, Justine, the band, Paul and some old friends from Bournemouth. Then there was a party at the flat. Large numbers arrived. Adam's girlfriend, Raych, set fire to a pile of debris behind the wall and it burst dangerously out of control. Someone fell through the kitchen window. Damon climbed on to the roof of Deptford Town Hall next door and changed the time on the big clock, which stayed at the wrong time for several years. Dave locked himself in the bathroom. Graham passed out early on the sofa. My mum and dad arrived in the morning; they were flying back from Hong Kong, and came into town from Heathrow to say Happy Birthday. We put the fires out and mopped up a bit before they arrived. The flat had been trashed, burned, soaked and soiled and it stank. I could see my mum was shocked at our circumstances.

Early Performances

The flat was right next to college, but my course work was suffering. I wasn't concentrating on French. Seymour was starting to get interesting. We did a gig at a place called Dingwalls in Camden, supporting a band from Manchester. When we arrived for the soundcheck with our entourage the headline act were quite unpleasant towards us. They were really nasty, and they were rubbish. Adam was quite drunk. He was going through a phase of contorting his face with sticky tape, so that he looked like a monster. He had stuck his lips back so that you could see his gums, that day. He'd spent a long time with a tampon taped to his forehead at college, but moved on to looking disfigured when he graduated with a 2:1, quite a good degree. He had sold one of his sculptures to a rich aristocrat lady who lived off Regent's Park and he was feeling invincible.

The second time the singer from the other band said something Adam walked over and punched him in the face. He could handle himself with the Deptford vagabonds: he wasn't going to tolerate any nonsense from that poodle.

The gig went well. We had written a few good songs by then. We played 'She's So High', 'Sing', some short, fast songs and crazy instrumentals, and ended with a very long, very fast one. I went home with Justine on the last tube and after I left it got really nasty. Graham was sprayed with Mace by Dingwalls' security and Adam had to go to hospital. But there was a review the next week in *Music Week* magazine, a bone-dry music industry paper, about a new band called 'the Feymour'. It said that they were good. We did more gigs around Camden and New Cross. People from college came and flailed about down at the front.

I thought it was kind of the people who ran the Beat Factory to let us use the studio and eat all their cheese. It seemed very generous of them. They wanted to manage the band. They sent demo tapes and a copy of the Dingwalls *Music Week* review to all the record labels. Andy Ross, who had a record company called Food, was the only one who liked the demo enough to come and see us. He bought us beers. He was nice and we appreciated the drinks. Bands don't get paid for those support slots.

The hottest new bands all played in the back room of a pub in

Camden Town called the Falcon. Andy said he'd bring his business partner to see us when we played there. We were the second support band at the tiniest venue in London, but it was the glimmer of an opportunity and we pulled out all the stops to get as many people to that show as possible. Graham designed flyers with a man eating himself and we stuck them up around college. We made certain that all the nutters and freakers came. There was one guy, a posh American kid, who would go into a completely wigged-out trance. That always looked good. He was confirmed to attend and give it everything on the night. He was in love with Adam's Amazonian sister Jo, who was rumoured to have lived in a graveyard in Islington. She was coming too. We pulled a crowd of about thirty committed arty outsiders for the big night.

All the early shows were shambolic. We poured wine all over each other before we went on and during the set, and usually smashed up the drums on the last song. Occasionally, when it was going really well, we'd smash them up before the end. That used to annoy Dave. There were gaps where things came unplugged and amps fell over as we bundled around the stage. It was carnage, and very loud. It was great fun.

Some of the songs were supposed to hurt. Andy's partner, Dave Balfe, didn't like those very much, he said at the bar afterwards. He asked lots of questions and said we were mainly rubbish, but very occasionally brilliant. All that we knew about Dave Balfe was that he had been the keyboard player in the Teardrop Explodes. He was in his mid-thirties and he talked and looked like a mad headmaster. I liked him straight away. I loved the Teardrop Explodes.

They took us out for lunch, a pizza, near their office in Soho. A month later we had signed to them, with the proviso that the drummer wouldn't wear pyjamas and that we changed our name.

I went to see the head of second-year French. She was a nice lady. She conducted the Old French Literature module. It was all books about knights and witches. I told her I had been offered a record deal. I was supposed to be going to live in France for a year. She was genuinely quite excited. She said she'd been to see Eric Clapton the night before and that I could sit my end-of-year exams the following month, then take a year out and come back if things didn't work out. I didn't go back to college after that except to sit the exams, and I missed one of those. My best result was in Eighteenth-Century Literature, which was surprising because I hadn't read any eighteenth-century literature. Not going to France had been a mistake. I only got 3 per cent in French Language. There was a lot of red pen on the exam paper. I'd really appalled whoever marked it, you could tell. There were lots of crossings out and exclamation marks, question marks and exasperated triple underlinings. The signing off remark was 'Is the candidate lucid?'

The day I got my exam results was the day I got on a tour bus for the first time.

There was no going back.

3

food ltd

Contracts

We were living in squalor with the slugs and Mad Paul creeping around with his candle upstairs, but I had the thing I wanted, a record deal. It was an incredibly mean record deal and once we'd paid the lawyers there was just enough to buy a new bass.

A recording contract is a hefty, confusing document. In the past, as one of the many formalities of business law, all contracts had to be written in Latin. It's quite hard to say what language they're written in now. There's still quite a lot of Latin in there. There wasn't a single paragraph that made sense to any of us, apart from the bit about if the drummer performed in pyjamas he was in breach. They put that in for a joke. We didn't mind him wearing pyjamas, but we agreed to it because we understood it. We had to go to the lawyer's three evenings in a row to have it all explained to us. It was very dull. The lawyer said it was the worst fucking deal he'd ever seen. He swore quite a lot. They do that, lawyers. We thought we were going to be catapulted into a new stratosphere and live happily ever after since we were about to become professional recording artists, and that we wouldn't have to worry about anything. All there was to start with was hours and hours of things to think about. In fact, the more successful we became the more we had to deal with lawyers and accountants and management. That is the stratosphere of success. How I wish we'd listened. I'm still in that same recording contract now.

Eventually we signed the deal, the only one going, and chinked champagne glasses with our new record company at their lawyer's office. The two lawyers, ours, and the record company's, had a good old ho-ho-ho about the pyjama clause and said things like 'Whatever happened to old Dickie?' They all know the same people, music lawyers.

Throughout contract negotiations, which weren't negotiations so much as 'take-it-or-leave-it's, the record company was referred to as 'Food Ltd'. The Ltd bit wasn't very sexy. On the radio they never said, 'Now, on Food Ltd here's Jesus Jones with "Info Freako",' they just said Food, or Food Records. It said 'Food Ltd' on the buzzer of their offices in Soho, too. As a business entity, Food was an independently owned company, but it was plugged into the marketing, sales and international distribution mechanism of EMI Records.

Food was two people and a cute receptionist in an office on Brewer Street. It was a tiny label. They only had three other acts, but one of them, Jesus Jones, had the number one song in America. Being number one in America is the ultimate goal of all record companies on the planet and morale was high. In the mornings Andy Ross was usually working hard on *The Times* crossword. Dave Balfe was always cross about something on the phone in the other room.

Food wanted to change our minds about some things. They particularly hated the name Seymour and insisted we come up with a list of ten other suggestions. They made a list of ten suggestions too. Blur was on both lists, so we changed our name to Blur.

It was actually really valuable to have somebody at the record company going to great lengths to point out precisely how crap he thought we were at all times. All artists need someone to argue with. In the initial meetings, Balfe ripped everything to shreds, like a college don with a bad essay. It was devastating. He flew into rants, made taunts and offered delicate torments. This was art-wank; that was dull; this was stupid; that was commercial suicide! 'YOU'RE SHIT! You wankers' was his vital message and he really enjoyed himself. He had worked with a lot of bands and had great skill in the art of disabusing cocky layabouts who thought they were the Second Coming. He was a total bully. I really liked him, and hero-worshipped him a bit because he'd been in the Teardrop Explodes. He wasn't always right, but it was all quite necessary. We had to learn to fight our corner. He was just toughening us up a bit before we got thrown to the press.

Andy liked to do business in the pub. There was never anyone more at home in a pub. He could empty the quiz machine every time, because he could get all the sport questions. He was also an expert at darts, pool, the *Racing Post* and crosswords. He always had a new joke to tell me, and he had a huge appetite for new music, forever brimming with a brilliant band he'd seen last night or how crap something everybody said was great was. He was somehow a man of leisure, or he'd managed to incorporate everything he liked into his job.

It was great to spend an afternoon in the pub with Andy after Balfe had kicked us all around the office. We spent happy hours dreaming and scheming. They hadn't given us much money, but they did give us all their attention. Balfe was a megalomaniac and wanted us to be the biggest band in the world. Andy just loved pop music and emptying the quiz machine.

London Shows

We thought we were ready for everything, but maybe everything wasn't quite ready for us. The few shows that we had done had been very chaotic. Taking to the stage was an opportunity to make as much noise and mess as possible. There were long pauses as drums were reassembled, guitars came off their straps and we decided what song to do next. It seemed important to react to situations with as much creative spontaneity as we could muster.

'No, no, no. Decide what it is you're going to do and deliver it,' said Balfe. He got so angry about one onstage bundle that he had saliva in his beard after the show. He made us go and watch Jesus Jones. Jesus Jones did everything he told them to do. They appeared to go mental, but no leads came unplugged, nothing broke and there were no long gaps while the guitarist tried to find the plectrum he'd dropped. They had spare guitars, too, and someone who passed them the spare guitars. A roadie. We couldn't fit any more in the drummer's car. There was just enough room for drums, amps and two guitars. The practicalities of being a drummer in an unfamous band are harsh. Drummers always have estate cars, so they usually get lumbered with all the other gear as well. Singers don't have any gear to think about at all, so they tend to fixate on their hair and clothes. I used to like carrying my guitar around. It made me feel cool.

There aren't many nice places to play in London. Even when I lived in a condemned building, venues seemed sticky, unpleasant places. Andy was at home in these dives; he always knew which beer to get and which was the best pool cue. Anything threatening about those places was removed by his sense of belonging there and being at home. They were nasty, but we were able to make them our own. London is highly civilised. There was always a slight risk of being beaten up in central Bournemouth pubs and clubs, which were all a lot smarter looking. Places that have live music tend to attract pretty nice people, so after the initial shock of sticky floors and niffiness, the rock music venue became our natural habitat.

We played all over London, dragging our faithful entourage of freakouts and crazies around town with us. Some people lost interest now that we'd sold out and signed to a label, but we picked up more people as we went. We played twelfth on the bill at all-day marathons and headlined in empty pubs. The Alice Owen, a spit-and-sawdust joint in Islington, had a light in the ceiling that came on if the music got too loud. If it stayed on for more than five seconds, it automatically cut the power. In a bar in a shopping centre in Shepherd's Bush, Damon climbed up the PA and hid in the ceiling. A booking agent came to see us and took us on. Then we started getting support slots at proper concert halls. The first one was opening for the Cramps at Brixton Academy.

I think Brixton Academy is probably the perfect venue for loud music. It's all standing downstairs and it's pretty big, about eight thousand people. The balcony rocks up and down when things get going. You can put a proper show on there with explosions and a full choir. It seemed like a scary, horrible place that night, though. Backstage areas were all new to us. Most of the places that we'd played didn't have dressing rooms. Here there were long corridors of them with names on the doors: dozens of rough-looking people loitered around, farting and swearing. It was like being in a hospital, only everyone looked a bit iller than they do in hospitals. There was food, too, a buffet, a hot food menu, free drinks and bowls of sweets everywhere. We sat in the strange restaurant eating sweets and staring. Someone came over to our table and said, 'Don't talk to the band, guys, OK? And when you've eaten go to your dressing room. Right?'

You wouldn't want to lose your plectrum on a stage that big. We didn't have a soundcheck because it would have interfered with the Cramps' vibes. We went on as the doors opened and eight thousand goths arrived. I was very pleased to be holding on to a bass guitar. It's hard to wear a bass and not look cool. It's like sitting in an Aston Martin. You can be sure you look good and that people will stare. Damon fiddled with his hair. Graham turned his amp right up but it still sounded too small for that room. Even kicking over the drums would have been quite a futile gesture. We ripped through the set. A Cramps crowd has really come to see the Cramps, and not four twerps in second-hand clothes. It wasn't easy. At that stage we were fragile. Our future was riding precariously on every gig. It could have been disastrous. We grew up in half an hour on that stage. When we came off we went to the Cramps' dressing room and said hi.

Studioland

We were getting the hang of playing live, but we'd yet to try making a record. Recording studios are complex. We'd never really used any of the equipment in the Beat Factory, apart from the fridge. We used it as a place to rehearse, mainly, and just recorded everything on cassette, so we didn't forget it. We left the Beat Factory when we signed to Food. It had been a luxury having a place to hang out and play. In Bournemouth, too, band practices had been enjoyable semi-social events, but there's nowhere a band can play for free in central London. It's pay by the hour. Cheap rehearsal rooms are depressing places. They have all the grime and sleaze of a gig, but no girls and no beer. There was a bunch of sad hopefuls making a suffocating din behind every door. We tried a few places before we found somewhere we could bear to be at all. The Premises, behind a café on Hackney Road in Shoreditch, was clean and bright and pleasant. The café was really quite nice. It was more of a jazzy scene there. The clientele tended to be workaday jobbing musicians, rather than hopefuls with day jobs. There was no one trying to be cool or intimidating. We were quite focused when we were there, and it worked well. It was good to be surrounded by other kinds of music. There were photos of famous accordion players and tin whistle men on the walls in the café. There was a seventeen-year-old, called Jason, who worked there. He was cool. He drove a VW van that belonged to the Premises and offered to take our gear to gigs and help set up. The label thought it was important to create a bit of a stir about Blur before we released any records, so it was a while before we got into a recording studio. When we finally did, it was like dying and going to heaven. In the sixties, studios were like laboratories, utilitarian and staffed by men in white coats. In the seventies bands made records in converted castles and manor houses. During the eighties studios began to look like custom-built luxury yachts inside. They competed for trade by outswanking each other. They could do this because the cost of making a record is quite small compared to the cost of making videos and marketing budgets. The expense of a posh studio doesn't make much difference when it comes to the bottom line. Where venues were grotty, studios were smart. They boasted brasseries, bars, video games, nice pool tables, magazines and expense accounts. There was always an appealing girl on reception. There is no grime or stickiness in the studio environment. Record producers are all quite particular about washing their hands.

We went to Battery in Willesden, to record two songs, 'She's So High' and 'I Know', with a production duo from Liverpool called Steven Lovell and Steve Power. It is hard to say what a producer does. He's sort of in charge, like an architect on a building site, but he's your architect and you have to make sure he's building your castle and not his.

In a recording studio, there is also someone called an engineer. He is always asking the producer about microphones and levels. Then there is an assistant who sits quietly in the corner trying not to look bored, and who asks you if you would like anything every half an hour.

Battery was huge. There was loads of complicated gear in

racks in the control room and a colossal mixing desk. There must have been hundreds of buttons and thousands of knobs in that room, a sea of switches and little lights. A long, tall, wide window in the wall behind the mix console looked over a church-like live room, a vast space with pine floors and carpet going up the walls; a grand piano as long as a barge sat in the middle. There were anterooms with tape machines; soundproof booths for guitar amps; echo chambers; cupboards full of looms and wires and huge fridges containing power supplies. All the rooms had double doors. The restaurant and leisure facilities were down a long corridor.

It was intimidating to start with, but all studios are pretty much the same. Once you're at home in one, you're at home in them all.

We didn't have much gear. Jason, the kid from the rehearsal studio, brought it all down in the van. I was playing a Fender Jazz copy through an amplifier that cost sixty quid. It was good, that amp. I showed it to the producers and they looked at each other and I could tell they didn't like it. Graham kept breaking his guitars, and he was down to his last one, an Aria, but there was an affiliated hire company next door to the studio.

It was a painstaking process, making a record. We'd written the songs we were going to record and we could play them fine. It took all day to set up the drums with microphones, so that they sounded good. They just sounded like drums to me. By the evening we were playing through the first song, 'She's So High'. We played it so many times it was impossible to tell whether it was good any more. That does happen in studios. You get lost inside things. You often can't tell if anything is good until you've had a cup of tea and listened back to it later. Sometimes getting it right is a joy; sometimes it's a chore. It depends on the producer, too. Some producers like to do everything a hundred times, some like to use the first take.

We were all wearing headphones, which had a clicking metronome coming through them that was louder than anything else. It was very offputting. Lovell said we had to get the tempo exactly right. I knew what a tempo was, but I'd never heard anyone say it before. We persevered, trying it slightly faster, then a bit slower, then in between. Then he said, 'That's brilliant, guys, we'll record the drums in the morning', and I was driven back to my hovel in a limousine.

We spent the whole of the next morning recording the drums and the whole of the afternoon listening to them, just the drums on their own. Again and again, considering the sound of the hi-hat, the steadiness of the rhythm itself, whether any bits needed patching up, was the tempo definitely exactly right? It's the usual procedure these days, to start by recording the drums. When the drums are spot on, all the other instruments are overdubbed one at a time. Sometimes a song sounds better if everything is recorded at once, but it's usually easier to concentrate on one thing at a time.

After dinner we checked the drums one last time and started on the bass. 'I Know' was a song based on a metronomic groove and the producers thought it would be more mesmerising if we looped the bass. I hadn't done that before. Looping is used a lot in dance music, rap and hip-hop.

The fundamental unit of groove is the riff. If the riff is good, the groove is good. A groove is usually the same riff played again and again with subtle variations. With a looped groove, you're actually hearing *exactly* the same thing over and over. The bass player jams along with the drums and a small section of the performance, usually eight beats long, is cut and pasted together to make the bassline for the whole track. Computers make this easier to do, but bands had been using tape loops before computers arrived. The Bee Gees used a tape loop for the rock-solid drums on 'Stayin' Alive'. I'm pretty sure they used that exact same drum loop for some of their other big hits, too.

There is something very earcatching about the same thing repeating, a hypnotic perfection. Eight beats is quite a small amount of time, but it is actually long enough to change the course of popular history, if you get it exactly right. Making good loops is no easier than playing well through the whole song. In fact, it puts even more emphasis on the 'feel'. 'Feel' is the subtle quality that separates the great players from the ordinary ones. It's largely innate, like a person's way of walking or talking. A hundred different guitarists will all play the same riff in exactly one hundred slightly different ways. The subtle pushing and pulling at the rhythm, the exact length of the notes and how hard the strings are hit and bent, mean that no riff is ever quite the same in different hands. Things played with clinical accuracy often sound quite lifeless and mechanical. If it feels good, it is good.

Knowing what is really good and what isn't quite so hot is the key to making a good record. I played the riff over and over and listened to it again and again until we found 'the one'. It had a slightly lazy lilt and, boy, it made the drums sound good. It was a crap guitar but it was a great bassline.

The record, a double A-side featuring both tracks, sounded amazing. It sounded like a record. It was all shiny and shimmering and it floated. We got the tempo spot on. We got the feel spot on. We listened to it a hundred times and played it to all our friends, and also, and especially, to people we didn't like. We were In Business. We were best friends. It was very exciting, but we began to separate from the lives we'd lived before. All our friends were either unable to relate to what we were so excited about, or slightly envious. We went up to Manchester Square to meet everyone at EMI. There were a lot of people to meet: a product manager, a press lady, a TV promotions man, a radio plugger, lots of people behind desks and fax machines, the marketing department, the head of the label, the head of international sales, the chairman. It was a five-storey office building full of people who worked for us.

We still had to make a video. Balfe wanted to do something weird. He said, 'Lets build a really mental flashing doughnut and wobble it around in the dark. It'll be brilliant.'

When we got to Pinewood Film Studios, the light wasn't quite as mental as we'd been led to believe it would be. It was a bunch of neon hoops. There were problems with wobbling it, too. It flashed quite nicely, though. There were dozens of people running around, speaking into walkie-talkies, smoking and sipping coffee out of plastic cups. It was very cold on the hangar-sized set, but glamorous women strutted around saying 'OK, darling?' and kissing everybody, even the scary looking light wobblers and grumpy focus pullers. There was make-up, there was hair, there was wardrobe, there was catering, cameras, playback, riggers, grips, lampies, sparkies, producers, commissioners, runners and drivers. No wonder film stars have trouble with the real world. This seemed like a much nicer place. All that fuss over the song we'd written before we went home for the Christmas holidays a year ago, the chords I'd sat up in bed playing when I should have been reading eighteenth-century French literature.

Daytime radio would have trouble with the word 'high', they said at the label. Really it was just too slow and too indie and not quite brilliant enough for daytime radio. It got played a bit in the evenings, on Mark Goodier's show, and the BBC offered us a session at Maida Vale.

Graham wasn't phased about going to the BBC. He'd been on *Blue Peter*, twice, playing his clarinet. Dave's dad had worked at Maida Vale and Damon took everything in his stride. The BBC reminded me a bit of college. They do things properly at the BBC and Maida Vale was even more impressive than Battery, a titanic complex of sound studios, from huge rooms for recording orchestras to little voiceover cubicles. It's steeped in history, and you couldn't move for sitting somewhere Jimi Hendrix had sat, or standing where a Beatle had farted. It's quite serious at the

Beeb. I suppose it has to be. Everyone there knew exactly what they were doing. The staff are all cherry-picked from the best of the best, and it was all so illustrious it made me want to scream. It's hard to rebel against. You can't really have a career in music unless you can interface successfully with the BBC, and you sort of have to do it on the BBC's terms, which are reasonable enough. You've just got to do what you do; if enough people like it, pretty soon they're knocking on your door.

Food really liked 'There's No Other Way', one of the new songs we recorded on that session. We all thought it was a B-side but were pleased they were nice about something. Most radio is broadcast live. It's more exciting to do things live, but it does take a while to get the hang of talking on the radio. There are only really two rules in broadcasting: no swearing and no silence. Silence does not broadcast well. People who haven't been on the radio very much tend to think that the few words they are about to say are what they're going to be remembered for, and they tie themselves up in knots trying to say too much. In my experience no one can remember much about what I've said on the radio, just odd lines here and there. It's like trying to recall what someone on the bus was talking about. It is quite scary, though, to start with. It's a knack, like swimming. When you relax, there's nothing to it. You can do it all day.

Images

Being in a band embraces a lot of things. There are your thoughts, which you are constantly expressing in your music, and being probed about by journalists and presenters. There are your clothes, which have to say who you are, too. Hair is cheap but hard to get right. You have to be able to think of things to say that are worth repeating, or at least repeat things that are worth repeating. You've got to be able to play an instrument, or sing, if you want to get any satisfaction out of it. You need to enjoy travelling, because there's a lot of it. Stage design, record sleeve design, videos, photo shoots . . . There is always an expert to hand, but you need to know what you want or it all just looks like everyone else's.

It takes a while to get the hang of everything. None of the early photo shoots were that spectacular. We didn't look like a band. We still weren't really, yet. We had written some songs and hung around together, but we hadn't played more than a couple of dozen shows. Some touring was planned around the first single.

We went to meet with a design company in a mews in Paddington. It was the sort of place at which everyone who did art at school would have dreamed about working. They'd designed the covers of all the greatest records ever made, by the looks of things, and there were gold discs all over the walls in reception. The offices were bright and sunny, and hip-looking people were 'just working on ideas' at big draughtsman's boards. The idea they'd had for 'She's So High' was a naked bubblegum queen astride a hippopotamus. It was a painting by a San Franciscan artist called Mel Ramos. We all agreed it was brilliant, even Balfe, who said it was important to break minor taboos. It was just a good picture, I thought.

Andy Ross thought it would be a good idea for Damon and me to go and be nice to everyone at the EMI annual sales conference, which was taking place in a hotel near Gatwick airport.

It was the start of the nineties. It was a glittering affair and things got interesting after dinner. It was the tail end of the good old days in the record business. Record companies were still expanding and setting up film divisions. They'd made a fortune from rereleasing everything on CD. Record sales were higher than ever. British artists outsold American stars and it was a good time to be in the music business. It must have been quite an expensive event. There were hundreds of people there, including some proper pop stars. The boss of the company, Rupert Perry,

Aged four months

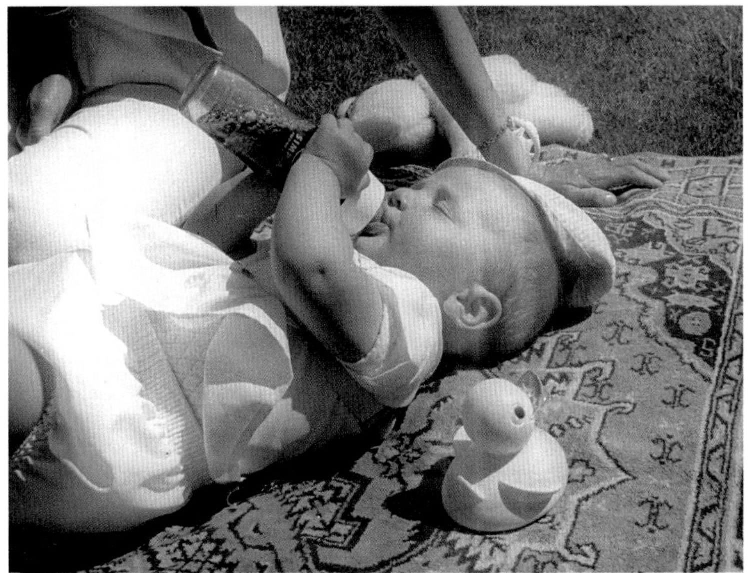

Poole harbour
with Mummy

At home with Daddy

Cheese!

Above left: Aged twelve

Above Right: Me and Debs, shortly after her triumph in the pavement drawing competition

Left: In the cellar at Glenview aged fifteen. I wore that suit to school

Clearly not cut out for scaffolding

In the cellar again, probably trying to play 'Blue Monday'

1988, having a cigarette before leaving Bournemouth for Goldsmiths, about two hours before I met Graham

Seymour, 1989

Early Blur press shot

British Image 1. Nobody ran this picture – it was seen as xenophobic. Now part of the iconography of Britpop™, I suppose

Coming home from Ritz rehearsal studios in Putney on the District line, 1992

Osaka, waiting for the bullet train, 1993

Watch out for spiders!

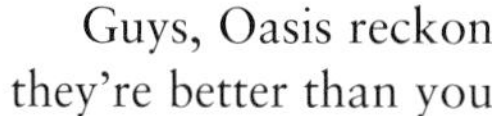

Guys, Oasis reckon
they're better than you

Smash Hits photo shoot

Tokyo. With Lexington Queen hangovers

© Paul Postle

The tie was a birthday present from Graham

made a speech on a little stage and said he wanted to introduce some special guests. Iron Maiden drove on to the stage in a bubble car and started swearing at everybody. Damon had a funny turn and ran outside. I was having an excellent time. There was a party in every room in the hotel. Nigel Kennedy, a strange kind of violin-playing arch-yobbo and the biggest-selling artist in the world at the time, was trying to throw a television out of the window of the first room I went into. A lot of men in suits were laughing. He fell in a heap on top of the telly before he got to the window. It was good in that room. I sat on the bed sharing a bottle of Scotch with a guy with a silvery beard who seemed quite interested in everything I had to say. We shot the breeze for ages. He knew all kinds of things. I liked that guy. We drank all the whisky. Eventually I said I'd better go and find Damon, who had last been spotted in a field trying to talk to some horses. Andy Ross said, 'What the hell were you talking to Andrew Prior about for an hour?' I said, 'Who the hell is Andrew Prior? I've been drinking whisky with my mate over there!' He said, 'That's Andrew Prior, you berk. He's the head of the label. I'm lucky if I get thirty seconds!'

I suddenly had a feeling that I might be able to do all right in the music industry.

I enlisted my next new friend, who was spectacularly pissed, to help me find Damon. We got into his car and put on Marianne Faithfull, really loud. It had never sounded so good, her voice. My new friend just wanted to drive his car over the golf course; it was good fun, but I was a bit worried about Damon. I found him in Balfe's room having an argument with the singer from Jesus Jones. Singers never agree with each other about anything. I was really drunk by that point and I went down to the bar to have a fight. Bruce Dickinson was at the bar. I hate Iron Maiden. They're devil-worshipping ponces. I said, 'The devil can suck my cock and you can kiss his arse, you fucking poodle.' He got me in a headlock and sucked the end of my nose really hard. I was laughing quite a lot, not really resisting. We left it at that.

In the morning, the pretty girl who was organising everything asked me if I would mind sharing a car back to London with Adam Ant. There is always a pretty girl who organises everything at record companies. 'Kings of the Wild Frontier', by Adam and the Ants, was the first album I'd bought. I said, 'That would be great, actually', and she winked at me. He was really nice and we talked about music all the way, just like I had done on the bus to school. He sent me *Ogden's Nut Gone Flake* by the Small Faces a few days later.

I got home, back to the squat, and Justine said, 'Has anyone seen you this morning?' I said, 'Only Adam Ant.' She said, 'Aren't you clever! Did he mention your nose, darling?' I looked in the mirror and it was bright red on the end. It took days to go back to being the right colour.

The record was finally released and the video was on *Juke Box Jury*. Jonathan Ross, quite an important voice, said it was crap and I swore to hate him forever. A soul singer called Kym Mazelle, who had stayed in a hotel Damon had been working in, The Portobello, gave it the raspberry too. He said it was because she'd put the moves on him when he took her up a sandwich in the middle of the night and he'd shunned her advances, which may or may not have been true. It was voted a miss, but it went into the charts at number forty-eight, which we thought was massive.

Telescope

Existence was still hand to mouth. We didn't have much money, but a cheque for three hundred and twenty-five pounds from the musicians' union came through the door, quite unexpectedly. I went straight out and bought the thing I wanted the most, a telescope. Along with the notion that I might be able to do what I'd always wanted came an all-pervading rush of optimism. I started to feel more and more alive. The more alive I felt, the more interested I became in absolutely everything. My natural curiosity burned like a bonfire. All of a sudden, the sky was the limit, and that too seemed limitlessly beautiful and benign.

I also bought a book, *Foundations of Astronomy* by Michael A. Seeds. I spent the next five years reading that book, over and over again. I took it everywhere with me. Even through binoculars, the moon is a staggering sight. I'd never looked through a telescope before, but soon I was lugging it all over the place on tour. I gazed at Jupiter, Saturn and Venus and wondered what they were doing there.

We still didn't have a manager and we needed one. A good manager understands how record companies work. He knows a good sync licence fee from a bad one and he is always on the phone bollocking someone about mechanical royalties in the minor territories. That's what a manager should be doing. Fighting battles you don't understand so that you can float around getting drunk and shagging. A management company is similar to a record company. They work alongside each other. They generally get along great and help each other. The rub is always with someone in 'Business affairs' at the label. That's the record company's legal department. No one in the world cares about business affairs departments, except for managers. Managers care about them all day. As an artist you would hope never to meet anyone from business affairs. Life is too short. That's why you pay your manager 20 per cent of everything, to deal with them. Most people who work in record companies are pretty cool. They all love music. You'd have to.

Even the largest record company is quite a simple organisation. A relationship with a label starts with the department called 'Artiste and Repertoire'. An A&R man is a fancy name for someone who was desperate to be in a band, but couldn't get his hair right. A junior member of the A&R department will see three or four bands a night, every night, more if he can. He loves it. Very occasionally he'll see a band that he really likes and tell his boss, who will sign them and take all the credit. The senior guys don't want to be drinking cider at the Falcon in Camden every night, but occasionally, they'll check out a band because they've been sent an outstandingly good demo. It really would have to be brilliant, though.

A&R departments often get nervous about acting alone. They're much happier about going to see bands that there is 'a real buzz' on. 'A real buzz' means whatever their mate who is an A&R man at another company was talking about last night, or something that has been mentioned in the *NME*. Then they all go down together and make a group decision about whether a band are any good or not. Usually every label wants them or no label wants them. Everybody passed on Blur apart from Andy 'Magic Ears' Ross. Even Balfe didn't want to sign us.

Managers like to get involved with bands before they sign to record companies; then they can put their 20 per cent commission on the signing advance. It's easier to get record companies to see you if you've got a manager they know. We went to see a lot of managers. Most of them bought us lunch. We went for the one who bought us the nicest lunch. As a rule of thumb, it's best to sign to the guy who hasn't got time to take you to lunch. There's no way you could ever make anyone in a band listen to advice like that, though.

Mike Collins took us to Fred's, a member's club in Soho Square. We'd never been to a member's club before. We hadn't been out to lunch much before. We stayed there all day drinking brandy, and Mike Collins told us how brilliant we were, and how charming. He liked my telescope. He liked the idea of the telescope. He liked it all. It was special. It was amazing.

The anticipation of success is the sweetest thing of all. It's never absolute, success, except when you're dreaming about it. This was success, really, having lunch bought for us in a member's club, and being flattered in the sunshine. It's an endless chase, succeeding. It's never over, but we were enjoying the chase. The brandies and the cigars kept coming. It was a good day.

We Hit the Road

The flat was behind a vegetarian wholefood paradise called Cross Currants. I'd tiptoe around there in my socks to get a pint of milk in the mornings. It was Dezzie's business. He was a fresh-looking Asian with infinite calm in his eyes. I liked old Dezzie. He was interested in the band. He was always talking about Barbara Gaskin, who somehow he knew. She'd had a number one record, a Motown cover. It was tantalising, not to have had any hits. I wondered whether one day he'd be telling people he knew me, and we joked about it. He was a good egg. He bought the burned-out house next door, which I thought was an impressive gamble. New Cross was another place that was right on the brink of chaos. The bank down the road took the cash machine away because too many people were getting mugged using it. Des had to put up with all kinds of loonies and whackos as he plied his Fairtrade coffee, organic vegetables and Sosmix. He was spreading his message of goodness and hope to the people of SE14. That flat was the worst place anyone could possibly live in the late twentieth century in the Western world, a polluted, condemned inner-city slum, and yet I was surrounded by kinder hearts there than anywhere else since. Justine was finding her feet, but I worried about leaving her alone in that flat. Des kept an eye on things when we went out on the road.

It was hard to know what was going to happen when we got in the van in the early days. Big gigs are all the same, but the small ones are all very different. As support act, we might be playing in quite a big venue or a tiny little place. We didn't know until we arrived. Maybe they'd love us or they might throw pints of body fluids at us; we wouldn't find out until we walked onstage. We hired a van and drove to Birmingham to support the Railway Children. They had a huge sleeper coach, and they were rather pleased with themselves. There weren't many people there, though. It seemed ridiculous to be in Birmingham on a Sunday evening. We went down quite well. The next time we went to Birmingham was to play at the University Ball, in Aston. There were half a dozen other bands playing, including Voice of the Beehive, who were managed by our record label. They were nice, those Voice of the Beehive girls. They invited us to their dressing room. No one had ever done that before. A dressing room is a member's club and a party and a home from home all rolled into one. We had some port with them and watched their show.

It was a huge end-of-term celebration party. There were thousands of kids our age there. In some rooms there were bands playing, in others there were people getting friendly. There were bars everywhere, and a huge buffet, a bouncy castle and a bleep-bleep zone with mad lights, full of people I'd never seen before and would never see again, all having the best time of their lives. Just to be there for one night made everything very simple. We were free agents.

I didn't need any encouragement to go on tour. When the record came out we were booked for three shows over a weekend – Birmingham, Cambridge and Keele University. Jason, the kid from the rehearsal studios, had been sacked for spending too much time with us. He refused to give them their van back straightaway and we got him to drive us. We were playing in Dudley, Birmingham, at a venue called JB's. It was our first out-of-town headline slot. It was dark when we arrived because we'd got lost, as usual. We soundchecked and a friendly guy, who seemed too scruffy and nice to be in charge of anything, gave us a crate of Newcastle Brown Ale and showed us the dressing room. It was one of those ones with scrawling all over the walls and a couple of knackered but comfy sofas. We left the door open and sat in there necking the Newcastle Browns. Miraculously, the place started to fill up. Soon it was heaving. The guy came back with another crate of beer. We took it onstage with us. There was a huge cheer. These people had come to enjoy themselves. So had we.

Of all the shows we've ever played, that was the most memorable. They just got it, the audience, right there and then. They got the whole thing. Over the last few shows, we'd tightened everything up, rubbed off the edges and cut out the boring bits, but that was the first time we brought the house down. The audience invaded the stage. They went crazy, every last one of them. The dressing room was packed afterwards, and more crates of Newcastle Brown kept arriving. Someone said that I was the fastest bass player he'd ever seen. Graham was holding court with a couple of girls. They were gazing at him and laughing at everything he said. People wanted plectrums, people wanted photos, people wanted records signing and all of a sudden we were giving our first autographs. It all happened in a flash, right there in Dudley. The friendly guy gave Jason a huge wedge of cash. We split it between us. There was ninety quid each, a fortune. Jason drove through the night to Colchester, where we stayed, at Damon's folks. Colchester's not that far from Cambridge, which was the next gig.

We went to bed insensible and woke up invincible. Cambridge was a town completely different in every detail from the one where we'd spent the previous day. It was very odd, perpetually being somewhere new, and with some money in my pocket. The following day we were on a university campus in Staffordshire, playing football with a band called the Family Cat. Jason was our star player. He'd had a trial for West Ham. We were bottom of the bill that night, but there was a bit of a rumpus going on about the picture of the girl on the hippo on the record sleeve. It was degrading to women in the opinion of some of the young ladies at the college, and they mounted a protest and tried to stop us from playing. It seemed ridiculous, but it was in the newspapers the next day. Quite why that was in the news over everything else that was happening in the world that day was hard to fathom. Maybe it was just a good picture.

Difficult Second Single Syndrome

The really great thing about the band was that it was just that, a band: four people. Together, we were greater than the sum of our parts. Damon was dynamic, an initiator. The whole thing was driven by his energy, but he and Graham were childhood best friends and complemented each other perfectly, musically. Graham was simply the best guitar player of his generation. He was consumed by music; listening to it, playing it, whistling or tapping his fingers the whole time. He was biologically a guitar player in the same way that Damon was a born frontman. The bass guitar was my instrument. Unlike the others, I hadn't had any formal training. I learned by listening and actually playing in bands. I was in a band from that moment I'd played my first lick in Jay Burt-Smale's bedroom.

I played in quite an unconventional way with no respect for the boundaries of the instrument. It was more like having someone playing a second lead guitar in the basement. The sparse mechanical precision of Dave's drumming was well suited to two guitarists both going at it hammer and tongs. It was uncanny how, with very little discussion, whenever we were all in a room together with our instruments, it all usually just seemed to work.

It didn't always. The second recording session was a disaster. We needed to make another record. Steven Lovell wasn't around, but we went back to the studio with Steve Power. Nothing went right. He even got Graham to try playing bass, which didn't work. It was the worst session I've ever been on. We chose the wrong songs, and we made them worse than they were already. It all sounded crap. The guys from EMI came down and stroked their chins. Even with more experience a bad session always feels like the end of the world. There aren't many really bad days, but they're certain to happen, sometimes. At this embryonic stage it felt catastrophic, spending all that time and money making something that was lifeless and worthless. It was Christmas, so we all went home for a rest.

It was nice going back to Bournemouth and being signed to EMI. I had a sense that I was changing, still growing and leaving Bournemouth behind. In the pub on Christmas Eve I ran into Jackie who I'd had a crush on at an early age that I thought I'd never recover from. She suddenly seemed like quite a small and ordinary person. She was still going out with the drummer with ten A grade 'O' levels. Now he was back from college, training to be an accountant. She was standing at the bar, when I went to get a drink. I said, 'Oooooh, hello.'

'What are you doing now?' she asked, barely disguising her boredom. I said, 'I'm an accountant.' I talked about how happy I was doing accounts. It was really quite interesting when you got into it. I was up for promotion, and maybe a car, I said, and started to quite enjoy myself. I said I had to go now, though, because I had to work on Christmas Day.

A couple of years in London had given me a whole new outlook. It was something of a reunion in the pub on Christmas Eve, but you could already tell which people had spent time in London. Poor old Jackie hadn't made it.

Despite going home and showing off, the band were actually sliding right down slippery shitstrasse. The first record, despite reaching number forty-eight and being featured on *Juke Box Jury*, did not seem to impress EMI as much as it impressed our friends, and the abortive session before Christmas hung heavy. We needed a hit. Very early in the New Year, out of the blue,

Balfe got a phone call asking if Blur needed a producer. It was Stephen Street.

We all got the next train back to London and met him at Food in Soho. It was good to get back to London. It was home, now. I knew it was home as the train rolled into Waterloo and it all rose up around my ears and I thrilled in my stomach. I felt it that day, more than ever. Stephen Street needed no introduction. He's about the only record producer whose name I knew. He produced the Smiths.

He's a handsome devil, Streetie. He'd actually been a teen mag cover star, on the back of his role as the Artful Dodger, in a stage production of *Oliver!*. We only found that out later, though, when his mum brought all her scrapbooks to his fortieth birthday party. We all instantly liked him. He said he'd never chased a band before – bands usually called him – but he had a good feeling about this one. He had a few days free the following week and suggested we try something. He liked to work at Maison Rouge, a proper eighties ocean liner of a studio, tucked in a little mews in Fulham. The eighties were just starting to founder, but it was still immaculate in there. I arrived one morning and Debbie Harry was standing in the brasserie having a coffee at the bar. I ordered a crème de menthe as I knew it was all they had left, and she laughed at me. It all seemed quite normal.

Streetie is good with drums. He once said to me that a hit record is nearly all about the drums and a bit about the vocal. He said everyone else could do whatever they liked, really, if you got the drums and the voice right. Some producers would say that in a way that would make a bass player feel a bit redundant. He said it in a way that made me feel I had total freedom to groove my pants off. He's a great diplomat, a statesman. I can say without any hesitation or doubt that he is the nicest man in pop. He's one of the nicest men in the world and I still always get a birthday card from him.

He really liked a song we had called 'There's No Other Way', but we'd stopped playing it live. He said it was too fast, and that it would sound better at this speed. He pushed some buttons, which played a drum loop he'd made at home, in his shed. It was true about drums. It sounded like a hit already. I put the bass down in about ten minutes, and Graham had done the guitar before lunch. No one had said 'tempo' once. We came back after lunch and listened to it on the big speakers, as Damon sang the melody into my ear. It was heart-stopping. It made me shiver. Damon put a new keyboard line at the beginning. Dave added some drum fills. We turned the tape over so that the track played backwards and Graham played a guitar solo, so that when the tape was back up the right way, the solo played backwards. Balfe came down and went mental. He said 'Top ten! Top ten!' and dribbled all over his beard, and then he played the keyboard line from 'Reward' on our synth.

There was a club called Syndrome in a basement in Oxford Street. All the indie bands used to go there on Thursdays. I think we started it, but everybody else thinks they did too. I first went there with Terry Bickers; he played guitar in the House of Love and he was a proper mad-eyed genius. Everyone in his new band, Levitation, had the mad-eye thing, especially the drummer. It was Neil's night, really, Syndrome. Neil was the DJ at Syndrome on Thursdays and the number one indie fan in the whole of London. I'm sure A&R men took his opinions more seriously than their own. Neil just liked listening to music. He had no agenda whatsoever other than the fact that he particularly loved scruffy outsider guitar bands, and he hitched around the country seeing them. He came on our bus sometimes. We'd get really worried if he didn't like something, or if he stopped stalking us. We thought it meant we'd lost our touch. Syndrome became the official headquarters of the London music underground. It didn't get going till about midnight in there, so people who had to get up on Friday mornings weren't likely to go. It wasn't like it was anything worth seeing, if you weren't in a band or an indie music journalist, although towards the end quite a lot of Japanese girls started to show up. We didn't mind, because they wanted to buy us Pernod.

At Syndrome it was fashionable to drink Pernod with everything and, as the drinks flowed, all the bands got to know each other. It was a scene. As soon as we'd finished recording 'There's No Other Way', we took it straight to Neil's night at Syndrome, like all the other bands did. Neil used to put the records on and dance madly to them, on the empty dance floor. He was really talented at picking good songs. Someone should have given him a record company to run, or a radio station, but all he really wanted to do was flap his arms around to new music all night. We stood at the bar waiting for the reaction of the test audience of die-hard, late-night indie kids. Lush were at the bar, so were Ride: they were eager to hear if our new record was as good as theirs. It was much more nerve-racking than *Juke Box Jury*. Chapterhouse, who were supposed to be better than all of us, that week, were listening carefully, and Moose, who Graham really liked, and Spitfire, and Slowdive and Suede and an unassuming American guy called Kurt and his girlfriend Courtney.

The dance floor was full when the record started. It was still full at the end of the record. It didn't really mean anything. It was two o'clock in the morning. It was when we were getting on the tour bus the next week and it unexpectedly came on the radio that we knew something different was happening.

4

the beginnings of success

A Glimmer of Glamour

'There's No Other Way' was a bona fide hit. It sold more and more copies each week and crept into the top ten. People knew all the words and sang along at the concerts, which were getting bigger and madder. More dates were booked. We started to appear on television. After shows I noticed that sometimes when I met people their hands were shaking.

We were just beginning to taste something new and extraordinary: a cocktail of adulation and freedom. Balfe called us into his office for a meeting and said, 'Watch out, guys, success can fuck you up more than failure.' He was an expert bubble-burster. Andy Ross kept referring to our 'career'. Career was a dirty word. It suggested work and conformity. I was an outlaw, a rebel. I didn't want a career. I wanted to cause havoc. I was a hedonist. I wanted to get drunk and be irresponsible.

I was quite resolute about that. I saw life merely as an opportunity to have as much fun as possible. All young people do, I think. Up until now excess had been limited by lack of funds, by having to get up in the morning and go to language laboratory and having to behave reasonably at college. Bands are quite exceptional in having absolutely no one to answer to. Once we'd made a good record, we could all do whatever we liked, whenever we liked, for as long as we liked. If I rationalised my decadence, I'd tell myself it was the duty of rock stars to indulge themselves beyond reasonable limits. If I couldn't be reckless and extreme, I wasn't doing my job properly.

For me drink and drugs weren't about escapism; they brought me more into the world, made me feel more alive, gave me the same stir of giddy, weightless acceleration as jumping off the cliffs at Fisherman's Walk in Bournemouth. Making music, on the other hand, does take me right out of the world. It is a supreme feeling, touches ecstasy. It's actually much the same sensation no matter how modestly or grandiosely I'm doing it – whether just sitting alone with a guitar or standing on the Pyramid Stage at Glastonbury. It's quite possible to get from one to the other in a very short space of time, but however large the audience may be, the feeling I get from making music is basically the same.

Big hits all start life as tiny little ideas. Damon is left-handed, but he plays the guitar right-handed. He's developed a unique technique that doesn't use any of the normal chord shapes. He made demos on his four-track at home, and almost everything started with those. They usually consisted of a drum machine playing a preset pattern, an acoustic guitar playing the chords and him singing. They were short, unstructured, rough sketches, but they contained the vocal melodies that everything was ultimately built around. Graham didn't often have to be told what the chords were and was usually playing along before the end of the tape.

Usually we were all pulling in the same direction. Damon and Graham's strengths complemented each other well and I added an element of groove to their architecture. The four of us had good musical chemistry. We were still developing, but we sounded like a unit.

The distilled bold precision of a well-rehearsed four-piece letting fly can be as dynamic and complete, sonically, as a symphony orchestra. Playing with the band was utterly exhilarating and there wasn't much to argue about. Chart success had given us all confidence and we were united. When Damon was unhappy about something he tended to become very animated. When Graham was unhappy, he became very withdrawn. Dave was just happy he didn't have to drive the gear around any more.

The material we recorded for the first album, *Leisure*, had been well honed over the course of the live shows, and in the studio there wasn't a lot of writing left to be done. It was just a question of playing the songs well.

Hotels

Leisure came out to lukewarm reviews, but it made the top ten in the album charts. We released a new single, 'Bang'. It got stinker of the week in *Smash Hits*. It snuck into the top thirty, but it didn't catch fire. The disappointment was cushioned by a sold-out national tour to promote the album.

We lived in hotels roughly half the time. Hotels fall into two categories: slightly decrepit, formerly grand places in city centres and newfangled execu-centres on ring roads with little hedges and leisure facilities. They both have their merits. We were quite at home in the venues, among the graffiti, the stickiness and the bad smells, so we didn't turn our noses up at hotels. They are less sticky and smelly on the whole.

Dave became fascinated by Corby trouser presses, which are a feature of every hotel room in the land. He said you could tell if they would keep the bar open all night by whether the trouser press was wall-mounted or free-standing. He could tell you exactly how good breakfast was going to be, just by looking at the trouser press. Having worked in a hotel, I knew exactly how demanding guests could be and I set about making myself a nuisance, calling reception and asking for more pillows, more towels, more bubble bath, some matches, board games, books, whether they served Ricicles at breakfast and if they knew anywhere I could get Golden Nuggets.

Life on the road had a physical impact on all of us. One of Graham's front teeth fell out while he was crawling around the corridors of The Swallow, a five-star hotel in Birmingham. I had heard him go past my room, pretending to be a dog again. He didn't seem to be causing any more bother than usual but we were banned, which was a pity as it was a nice hotel. I'd developed a large boil on my chest. It really hurt when it popped, and the goo that came out smelled really nasty.

Damon was holding it together, apart from his hernia, but no one really knew what Dave got up to. One day his nose was smashed all over his face and he was very quiet. Even when we weren't on tour he seemed to suffer. Another time he'd caught fire and Damon had had to put him out. They lived next door to each other in Greenwich. A lot of hotels won't take bands. There are only a handful of travel agents and they deal with all the bands on tour at any one time, so quite often there'd be another band staying at the hotel.

We stumbled back to the Ramada Jarvis in Leicester, the willing, worn and comfy seat of many a travelling rock circus. We'd been playing at the university. The Darling Buds were in the bar, a pop band from Newport, South Wales. They'd played at the De Montfort Hall.

I always seemed to have a lot to talk about with Graham and we sat at the bar inventing cocktails. He was interested in combinations of port and brandy. We were trying to make them catch fire. It was wonderful suddenly to be staying in places where the bar never shut and the other people there were some nice doctors having a medical conference and bands we liked.

The first time I was unfaithful to Justine was about halfway through the first year at Goldsmiths. I was in London. She was in Bournemouth. I was drunk. It wasn't premeditated. It was a brief pornographic fantasy scenario with someone I'd never seen before, never saw again. I regretted it terribly and confessed. Justine was devastated, more hurt than angry. We both cried a lot and I knew I'd never do it again. Of course, there were pretty girls at college. I flirted with one or two of them, but I never had any intention of getting involved. I suppose, if I'm brutally honest, if I'd fallen in love with somebody else, I would have been a bit stupid to stay with Justine, but I didn't. I wanted to be with her.

The second time was a real disgrace. I snogged Raych. She wasn't going out with Adam any more, but he still loved her, I think. He was long gone, but when I thought about it afterwards it seemed like a double whammy of treachery against him and against Justine. It was only a quick affectionate snog, but I definitely fancied Raych, which made it a worse crime. I didn't tell Jus about that.

Andrea, the singer from the Darling Buds, was a pin-up platinum blonde and that was the third time.

The world had started to open up to us and it appeared there was no town that didn't have beautiful women I could have married or interesting people I could have quite happily spent my life with.

Home

I loved staying in hotels, and going everywhere, but I wanted to live in Soho. It's an enticing place. I found it surprising that more people didn't want to live there. Soho is a constant carnival. It's where people go to enjoy themselves and there is something there to please everybody. It has glitz and it has grime. Immeasurable wealth and absolute destitution rub along side by side. The overwhelming rush of chic sophistication, theatres, restaurants, neon, and the crude sexiness of people drunk en masse made my heart beat faster. Soho has a fairy-tale history and a future that's open wide. The present moment always holds more possibilities in Soho than anywhere else in the kingdom, thousands of faces behind thousands of open doors, countless things about to happen. It's alive and you never know what it's going to do next.

I loved it. It seemed infinite and I just wanted to hurl myself into the chaos. After much searching and disappointment, viewings of dingy bedsits that shared bathrooms with prostitutes, and portered blocks that smelled of gravy, Justine and I discovered an unfurnished one-bedroom flat above a shop in Covent Garden on the corner of Endell Street and Shaftesbury Avenue. It had a tiny loo, a lounge with an open fire, and people thronging past in the street below. The bedroom was sunny, the kitchen was slug-free and there was hot water in the bathroom. It was being refurbished; it was still a building site but it was perfect.

I've never wanted to live anywhere quite as much as I wanted to live there, the moment that I walked in. It was on the first floor of a four-storey building between a church and an enormous hostel for the homeless and the entrance to the flat was down a little alley where the drunk ones staggered to urinate and vomit. It's rare that you get to choose exactly where you live. There's usually some practicality or other to consider, but once we'd tiptoed through the puddles, that was the perfect spot.

I paid the support band's roadie to help move all our crap up from New Cross. Everything we owned fitted into his van quite easily and it all looked revoltingly dirty in the pristine new flat. There was an old tapestry screen that had seemed quite exotic in the borough of Lewisham; it looked like junk in Covent Garden. We didn't have a fridge and there was no furniture, but it didn't matter. I quite liked not having anything. Having nothing is quite relaxing. Being alive and in the middle of the chase was all that mattered. You can live without chairs, but you can't live without dreams.

Dreams were all I had when I met Justine. I was a romantic at heart, full of indefinable yearning and impossible schemes. I didn't have ruthless ambition, but I'd stumbled into something that was beginning to find a momentum of its own.

She loved me when I was a write-off, an unqualified supermarket no-hoper. As the band started to become successful the new friends that I started to make liked me partly just because I was a part of something successful. It became a part of me. But Justine and I always had a natural, easy-going magnetism for each other. We had no television. We played board games and walked the streets together, read to each other. We both loved music. I expressed myself through it and she expressed herself to it. She was effortlessly elegant, a natural dancer. She listened and she laughed and she was always surprising me. She understood me in ways that I couldn't. I loved her.

The tragedy of getting what you want is that when you do actually get it, you always lose what you had.

Canada

The practicalities of the big time started to take over. The band's growing popularity meant that I could afford to live in the flat in Covent Garden, but when we weren't in Maison Rouge finishing the album we were on the road touring or doing promotion. Despite mediocre album sales, the success of 'There's No Other Way' catapulted the band into the international arena. The day after we moved to Covent Garden, the first North American tour kicked off. The first date was in Toronto. For some reason there was no direct flight, and we had to keep getting on smaller planes.

It was quite all right to fly back then; planes were like flying pubs. You could smoke and you didn't have to pay for anything. I was happy getting drunk with Graham, wherever it was. You have to get used to being on planes if you want to sell records, anyway.

None of us had crossed the Atlantic before. I don't know what I was expecting. I imagined the mustard in America would be hotter than it is at home, that America would be somehow more intense than England. It's quite nice, American mustard, but it's rather mild. Japan has got the really hot stuff.

My passport came under close scrutiny at immigration control. I'd jumped in a fountain after a show in Lille a couple of weeks earlier, and it had been in my pocket. The official was quite appalled by this. The Canadians, particularly, like to have a really good look at everyone before they let them come into the country. We were taken into little booths and questioned. They want to make sure that you're not going to try and overthrow the established order. I ticked a box on the immigration form that said this was not the purpose of my visit, but the official was suspicious. And I suppose she was right. As I stood outside the airport, waiting for the next thing to happen, I started to feel that travel is the great adventure. I was glimpsing the world beyond the one that I knew and getting a sense of how big it might be.

A sense of vastness looms in Canada. We mainly have towns in the British Isles. Even London gives the impression of being a town. It's built on the human scale. In North America they mainly have cities. Even places that could really be quite small are built along supergalactic dimensions; skyscrapers and ten-lane road networks with flyover systems that look like scribble. I'd never thought of Toronto, particularly, and here it was, enormous, in an enormous country.

I went down to the hotel restaurant for breakfast, alone. I was trying to work out what an English muffin was, and whether to have that, or an omelette. It was nice to be ordering breakfast in Canada. I was quite content there, alone, studying the menu.

Someone was looking at me. He came over and said he was from the record company and hi there. I said oh, hello, I was thinking I might just have a look around the city today, and wouldn't that be nice? He straightened up and said, 'Well, sure thing. Perhaps we could do that after dinner and before the show.' And gave me a list and said, 'Here's your promo.' It said something like:

ALEX JAMES PROMO SCHEDULE, TORONTO, OCTOBER 1991

Press
0930 *Scenester*, music glossy – 45,000 readers
1000 *Toronto Sun*, daily broadsheet –1 million readers
1030 HMV *In-store* magazine – record store giveaway
1100 *Glitz n Bitz*, women's glossy – 120,000 readers
1130 Break
1145 Phoner with *Halifax Echo*, regional daily –100,000 readers

Radio
1200 Alex and Damon to CFNY, syndicated national radio I/V

TV
1330 Meet Dave and Graham at MTV for acoustic set
1500 Arrive venue Lee's Palace for soundcheck

At Venue
1700 Meet and greet with competition winners
1800 Dinner
2100 Showtime

After Show
Meet and greet with EMI staff and key media.

It was only 0900 so I went back to my room and called Cousin Dick, who lived in Halifax, Nova Scotia, a couple of hundred miles away. I hadn't spoken to him since I'd sat on his knee and watched *Tom and Jerry*. I said, 'Dick, it's Alex James, Jason's son. I'm in Toronto!' He said, 'I know, it's in the paper.' We were evidently quite famous in Canada. That didn't make any sense at all. We'd never been there or anything. I went upstairs to be hot-wired to the media main.

Journalists are all quite clever, often cleverer than I am, I find. When they don't like me it really annoys them that they are clever and they are getting fifty pence a word and I'm an idiot with a fancy haircut and getting all the money and all the girls. It's best not to talk to those ones. Generally the cleverest ones work for the papers with the stupidest readers. These papers have the biggest circulations, so they can afford to pay the most. That's how it works.

There is a knack to doing interviews. It's mainly a knack thing, the interview, like playing the bass is. We didn't quite have the knack, yet. It takes a while to come. For addressing the press there was a big suite on the top floor of the hotel, The Plaza on Bloor Street. I like that hotel. It's a tall building and the sun screeches in. The first interview was with a music journalist, and we talked about the Undertones for ages. He loved the album, and couldn't believe he was being paid to talk to me. I ordered some Bloody Marys for us. It was nice.

The man from the *Toronto Sun* was interested in our controversial artwork. I said it wasn't controversial, it was a pair of tits. He wrote that down. I ordered six Bloody Marys and he wrote that down as well. I knew he would. It seemed easy, being in the paper. I launched into a kind of acceptance speech, thanking the Canadian people for everything and said a big hello to my relations, the Vines, in Halifax, Nova Scotia. That didn't seem to get to him, though. He was getting bored. He was probably off to talk to the Prime Minister next. It seemed to be quite a serious newspaper. I was on my fourth Bloody Mary and showing him my handstand when the *Glitz n Bitz* lady came in. Graham and I had been doing a lot of handstands.

Justine was in another world a long, long way away. The *Glitz n Bitz* lady was attractive and intelligent. We lay on the bed. She had a Bloody Mary, and reached inside my trousers and gave me a handjob. My moral cloth was degenerating further. That definitely was my biggest crime so far. But, good God, I was enjoying myself.

There was a jam of people clamouring outside the radio station when we arrived, and at the gig for soundcheck. They were much more enthusiastic than people had been at home. They were crazy about the record, and some of them started to get hysterical. Things were already well past weird when Glenn Tilbrook from the band Squeeze appeared in the dressing room. He was quite drunk, and very happy. Graham was beside himself. Some men with natty suits appeared and said hi they were from our American record company and that they'd flown up from New York wasn't everything *in*-credible and grinned and gave pumping handshakes. One of them had a penetrating stare and a breath-freshener atomiser that he kept dosing himself with. Graham and Glenn were drinking a bottle of brandy and doing handstands and knocking everything over. Squirt-squirt went the atomiser. The *Glitz n Bitz* lady came in and started snogging me. Squirt. No one could find Dave or the lighting guy. Squirt-stare-squirt.

Dave finally arrived in great spirits. The show was raucous and the man from the American record company's eyes were popping by the time we'd finished. He shook his head and said it was too loud.

We drove around the shores of Lake Ontario, stopping at Niagara Falls for lunch on our way to the USA. On the road the same things repeat themselves every day – the travelling, service stations, interviews, soundchecks and shows. We launched ourselves at everything with missionary zeal, but there is a steady rhythm beneath the apparent total chaos, although the barometer was still rising all the time. Things were getting more spectacular and happening faster.

Touring had changed a bit from the days of playing to thirty people in York and driving back in the middle of the night in Jason's VW, taking it in turns to sit next to him and pinch him when he looked sleepy. Being on tour is a hard feeling to explain or even remember, a gale of constant accelerations and stimulations and no time to dwell on anything.

All our petty wishes were granted – sex on tap, bars that never closed and where we didn't have to worry too much about the bill. It was a constantly unfolding escapade. I loved it, but I felt crap the majority of the time. The part of my brain that makes sense of everything was having a great time, but the part of me on the ground was having trouble functioning on not enough sleep, excess alcohol intake and travel fatigue.

There was more friction on tour than in the studio, naturally. We couldn't escape each other's irritating behaviour. Damon and his stupid love beads, Graham and his stupid skateboard collection, Dave's overall lack of panache and my own annoying habit of pointing these things out to them; but disputes were short-lived. We were brought back together nightly, in the rapture of playing loud music.

By now we had a road crew and these were the people we spent our days with. The road crew live on a bus and wear free T-shirts and smelly jeans. They are men of vast experience. They do tend to be quite nice people, despite appearances and reputations. The front-of-house sound man is usually the most sophisticated member of the crew; he's generally a bit less sticky looking than everyone else. Sound men are always fiddling about with soldering irons. You know you've got a good one when he shows you a strange-looking box he's made for making guitars louder.

The front-of-house sound man is the senior member of the

sound crew. The backline guys deal with the stuff that's on the stage, the instruments and amplifiers. They are the rock gentleman's gentlemen. I inherited my roadie from Motorhead. He'd given many years' service and knew every bassline, hotel, service station and rock venue in the Western world. He was always polishing my guitar and twiddling screws on it and asking me to stop throwing it in the drums. He loved guitars. He really cared about them. I used them a bit like biros, chewing them up and losing them.

You can't have a show without lights so there has to be a lighting crew. Lampies are often maniacs so they have an affinity with drummers. They are feral creatures, modern-day pirates. They sail the land seeking only drugs, women and free T-shirts.

There is a tour manager, too. He has to stop fights, get everyone on the bus and look after the money. Tour management is acknowledged to be the toughest job in all showbusiness. We seemed to get through a lot of tour managers.

New York

After the first American show in Boston, Damon and I flew down to New York for promo, just the two of us. We were a four-piece band and I was always slightly piqued when I was left out of things. We were all constantly jockeying for position – that's what gave the group its dynamism – but lately the other two were unbroadcastable, so they were happy to stay in bed.

There was a white stretch limo waiting for us at the airport. It was full of booze and televisions and phones. I called my mum. I said, 'It's all fine, I've moved out of the squat. I'm in New York, in a limousine.'

Two of my mother's aunts were hoofers, and my father's uncle was a jazz pianist. There were showbusiness genes on both sides of the family, but as far as my parents were concerned I might as well have told them I was joining the circus when I left college. They were always supportive, but the music industry was quite beyond their experience – theirs and almost everyone in Bournemouth. It would have been impudent to tell the careers officer at school that I wanted to be in a band. For a start I hadn't studied music. But it was just there in my blood and in my racing heart.

We sailed over Brooklyn Bridge and landed at The Paramount Hotel in Times Square. There aren't many places that overwhelm quite like New York. It was hard for someone who'd been living in a squat until a week before to accept just quite how wonderful The Paramount was. It was the first great hotel of the nineties, the monumental vision of Ian Schrager, one of the people behind Studio 54, the most legendary nightclub in history. Studio 54 was where Andy Warhol and Truman Capote danced with Liz Taylor and Audrey Hepburn, while Chic and Debbie Harry drank cocktails.

The Paramount was almost as glamorous. The staff were all hired from modelling agencies and wore designer costume; the cavernous reception area was a kind of ark in which all the best things in the world had been tastefully assembled.

I opened the door to my room. It was dark apart from a single spot-lit rose in a ceramic phial. I've never seen a rose look that good, not in an English country garden. It was exhilarating just to be in that hotel. The rooms were exceptionally small but, from the pencil on the bedside bureau to the power plumbing, exquisitely starched bedding and huge fluffy towels, absolutely perfect. Everything that's good eventually finds its way to New York. It has such immense gravity that nothing that is truly wonderful can avoid it for long. All the supermodels have homes in New York; all the great artists have shows there; film stars; rock stars; writers and the cavalry of wannabes, hangers-on and shagnasties that pursues the moving member's club of the successful, the beautiful and the fabulous. You name it. It's there. It's the best place in the world to go for a drink.

There is always one place that's the one cool place in New York, and that's where all the famous people who are in the city that night want to go. They all want to meet each other. It's difficult to get in to the one cool place, but once you're in you're in, and you can't actually get out. By then it's impossible not to meet these people. A brief residence in Manhattan is a clamouring, yammering public appearance from the moment you arrive. I've stayed under a false name. The phone still didn't stop ringing. I didn't answer the phone. Famous people came and banged on the door. It's full on and non-stop and there's nowhere to hide. To be in New York is to be on display.

Still, at this stage we weren't very well known in America, but the gig was quite a hot ticket. The guest list was a roll-call of all the English people in bands in New York on that day. There are always plenty of those, a remarkable number. It would be hard to avoid spotting one in the street or in the hotel. It was quite creepy, the number of times the singer from Del Amitri kept appearing, never at our shows, just randomly around the world. 'Graham! I saw him again! I saw him again!' Soon, we started to look out for him.

It was packed at the Marquee. I went out to the bar in the front of house with Damon. We quickly got thrashed to bits on vodkas and limes; told everyone to fuck off; snogged each other and then had a fight on the floor. We destroyed the venue in the course of the show. All the record company cheeses were sitting at tables on the balcony, staring. Damon got on the balcony and danced on the tables and spilled their sparkling mineral waters. Graham had a fight with his guitar. I tried to high-jump the drumkit and had a fight with Dave, quite a bad one. I felt we'd given a pretty good account of ourselves, but the record company weren't impressed. No one from the label came backstage, but a message was sent requesting a breakfast meeting at the hotel.

I left the venue with a model, and went back to her warehouse in SoHo. She was on the cover of *Vogue*. It was on the coffee table.

Another one-night stand. It wasn't like I pursued these women. It was suddenly as simple as not resisting. Still, I was more than willing and it was the same act of betrayal. There were so many reasons to say yes and only one reason to say no, and she was an ocean away.

When I woke up it was gone breakfast time and I scarpered back to the hotel. The manager was waiting outside the door. He was red. He said, 'Where the hell have you been?' I said, 'I've been to the top!' He said, 'Go and clean your teeth and get back down here, to the bottom. The record company want to have words.'

The man from the record company obviously had something difficult to say. I don't think he had encountered drunkenness on the scale that he had seen last night, and he was disappointed. His job was probably on the line. He said we needed to 'seize a golden ring of opportunity', and other half-baked motivational hocus-pocus. We stayed very quiet.

I wanted to buy a guitar. Graham came with me. We walked out of the meeting into the lobby. Sitting on one of the architectural sofas, like a holy apparition, was Kevin Shields from My Bloody Valentine. They were one of five bands that we namechecked in interviews. The other four bands had either split up or died. He nodded to us, so we walked over, nudging each other. He said he'd been to the show and it was great. He told me where to go to get a good acoustic guitar. Any psychiatrist will tell you that the respect of your peers is more valuable than any amount of record company bollocks.

Then we went to New Jersey.

London

We got back from that tour the day before my twenty-third birthday, back to a new life in the West End. There is rumoured to be treasure buried beneath Trafalgar Square. I'm sure there is. Even if it's just a rumour, a big proportion of all the wealth in the country is within about half an hour's walk of Nelson's Column and every day I woke up in the middle of it and felt it all around me.

I picked my way around town, never happier than when I had nothing in particular to do apart from maybe buy some rope and a piece of cheese. The very first flush of success was the most enjoyable, the initial paradigm shift from wanting something to actually getting it, but by then it was already too late. Success is the most addictive commodity in the cosmos.

My heroes were an old bastard called Jeffrey Bernard, a reprobate drunkard and writer of columns of great wit, and a fictional prostitute called Aunt Augusta from Graham Greene's *Travels with my Aunt*. I decided to concentrate on being an alcoholic genius.

I'd seen how the record company arranged things while we were in America. They'd call wherever it was they wanted to take us and say something like, 'Hiii, this is SPUD FENSTER from EMI RECORDS, I've got the GUYS FROM BLUR in town, they'd love to come around. CAN YOU PUT THEM ON THE LIST?' It never failed in America. It's an expensive business, being a man-about-town. I thought I'd try my luck, and got the phone book out. Justine called and said the magic words EMI, Blur and guest list. It worked nearly everywhere. Ronnie Scott's, the jazz club in Frith Street, was about the only place where it wouldn't wash. I got through to Ronnie. He said, 'Blur? Never heard of 'em. They'll have to pay like everyone else.' It was towards the end of the evening, and I started arguing with him. The last thing I remember saying was 'wanker' and the next thing I heard, a couple of weeks later, was that he was dead. I felt bad about that.

I was systematically working my way through all places of revelry in the whole of the West End, but what I really needed to set myself up in business as a practising alcoholic genius was an HQ.

Freud's was a subterranean cocktail bar on Shaftesbury Avenue. I'd been there once, as it was near the house. The barman had mad dreadlocks, and I saw him at a party after a Jesus Jones gig a couple of weeks later. His name was Mark, and he said, 'Come down, I'll make you a cocktail.' I went there the next night. It was a tasteful room, all slate and plaster with mood lighting around the tables and tracklights on the bar, which was very well appointed. There were hundreds of bottles of different spirits and liqueurs on shelves, sticks of celery, bowls of lemons and limes, whizzers, twizzlers, whirlers and shakers, juicers, a coffee machine and a sandwich toaster. You could buy the art on the walls if you got drunk enough. There were pretty girls there, too.

I'd never drunk cocktails really properly. We were still Newcastle Brown men at heart. To start with, Mark made me one called a Long Island Iced Tea. It's all the clear spirits shaken with ice in a large tumbler and topped to the brim with orange juice. It tasted like lollipops. It was very good indeed. He was an expert. We had some B52s next. They're on fire and you have to drink them through a straw. Then he made margaritas, very dry, with the glass dipped in salt so that you tasted it on the rim. I said that I was going to come here every day. He said, 'You should, you've got your own entrance!' There was an iron staircase at the back of the room behind the piano. It went straight into our alleyway. It was true. It was my own entrance. He said we'd better have a beer. He said you needed to drink a fizzy one after every three cocktails. The bubbles help your body absorb the spirits, otherwise they build up in your stomach and you drink more than you can manage. I love the nuggets of advice shared by seasoned booze guzzlers. The best one ever was to have one day off drinking every week. That's the vital one. Then bills got paid, I phoned my mum and I learned how to say no. A door that I'd lived next to for three months had suddenly opened on to what became an extra room of the flat. A city is just a whole lot of doors, and if you walk through the right ones anything can happen.

It didn't seem to matter which direction I walked from Covent Garden; there was a lot to see and I did a lot of wandering. It was part of my broader research. The Inns of Court and the eerie shanty town of mad, masturbating down and outs at Lincoln's Inn Fields. The river: Cleopatra's Needle with its inexplicable consort of sphinx and unthinkable Second World War blast damage. There were few overt reminders of the ravages of war in London. It was fundamentally a city at peace. I wandered through the parks, the alleys and thoroughfares feeling a part of it all and gradually finding myself at home.

Justine left The Body Shop and started doing make-up for photo shoots; she usually got a couple of jobs a week, but it meant we were poor again. Despite my infidelity, we were closer then than ever. We'd been together for four years by that time. She was the first woman I'd ever been able to be myself with. She gave me confidence and banished doubt.

Until then the band had all lived within walking distance of each other. But around the time *Leisure* came out we balkanised. Graham moved to Marylebone, which was still in walking distance, but he went to the pubs there mainly. We'd always gone to the same places before. Damon went west, to Kensington, where the pubs weren't very nice, and Dave went north to Archway, where they were really horrible.

Trouble

There are all kinds of deals to be done when people start to like your music. A record deal is the obvious one; that's for the records. Publishing is for the songs. They're different things, records and songs, so if Blur recorded a song written by someone else, Blur would get a recording royalty and whoever wrote the song would get a publishing royalty. It's called publishing because it goes back to the days of sheet music, when songwriters had their music physically published. We did a publishing deal, which should have put some money in our pockets, but Balfe had persuaded us to spend the money on some more mental crazy amazing lights for the live shows. But they were a flop and he bought them back from us, cheaply. Come to think of it, I never saw the 'She's So High' lights again, either.

Mike Smith was Blur's publisher and he moved into a bachelor bedsit on Rupert Street. Rupert Street was about the sleaziest, nastiest, low-downest corner of Soho. I went round to see him with Justine. It wasn't the sort of flat that you could entertain in, or even really stay in for very long. It just had a bed in it and approximately a million records. We went to the Crown, Brewer Street, and played darts even though he wasn't drinking and I was having a day off. He was one of the best people to go out for a few drinks with, or go without a few drinks with. At that particular moment he was trying to sign Teenage Fan Club. He was always trying to sign someone. That was his job: deciding which bunch of drunk idiots he should give a big slice of corporate cash to next. We were the first ones he'd signed.

I always liked listening to the demos Mike got sent. We were both big fans of the Keatons. They were a twelve-piece sonic terrorism outfit. One of them didn't play an instrument. Instead he did things with honey. It got sticky at Keatons' gigs. He wasn't sure whether to sign them or not. For me, the Keatons were a no-brainer. He played a song called 'Creep' by a new band called

Radiohead. We quite liked it. It was a bit depressing though. He said that they hardly drank at all. I passed on them. He couldn't afford them. The Cranberries took us all by surprise. He was really miffed about not spotting the Cranberries, they were a bargain.

I was living the good life, but I wasn't really making any money. It didn't bother me. Accumulating wealth wasn't the purpose of the band. I did start to notice that bills weren't always paid. Sometimes we couldn't use a particular hire company any more. Quite often people would ask us how we got on with our manager, and whether it was working out.

Some of the big retailers stock records on a sale or return basis. The album had stopped selling and Woolworths returned quite a lot of copies. Then a really big bill came from the VAT man and we couldn't afford to pay it. It was serious. I had no idea what VAT was. I was good at playing the bass and showing off. That was my job. We trusted our manager to make sure that those kinds of unpleasantnesses were taken care of. It turned out that quite a lot of bills remained unpaid. We owed everybody money. We brought in new accountants, who told us we were staring bankruptcy in the face and facing prison if we couldn't come up with the cash to pay the VAT. Whenever this happens it's time to start looking for a new manager.

We went back to see Chris Morrison, the manager who hadn't taken us for lunch the first time. He had spent the whole meeting talking about business and Ultravox and Thin Lizzy and laughing like Basil Brush occasionally. He took us on. He said, 'You're going to have to go back to America to get some cash.' He loves doing deals. He did a deal with a T-shirt company and signed us up for a thirteen-week American extravaganza, so that we could sell some T-shirts and posters and pay off our debts. It was the only way to get money. Fortunately Jesus Jones, our label mates at Food, had the number one album there, and the American record company really had no choice but to finance the tour.

We'd lose about a quarter of a million dollars on a thirteen-week stint, but we'd just owe that to the record company, which is what record companies are for. The main thing was we'd get some instant cash from selling T-shirts. We were ready for another American odyssey. We thought.

5

the genesis of britpop

Grunge

The music media moved to a weekly rhythm. The seven-day cycle of charts, playlists, the *NME*, *Melody Maker*, *Sounds* and *Record Mirror* meant that scenes and styles came and went quickly. It was around the end of baggy and the start of shoegazing when we left London to go and sell our T-shirts.

Thirteen weeks, a quarter of a year, is quite a long time however you look at it. The day we arrived in New York was a noteworthy one in the annals of pop. It was the exact day, in September 1991, that Nirvana released their masterpiece, *Nevermind*. It's no exaggeration to say that *Nevermind* was the most significant American record of the decade and that the world changed that day.

American rock music had been quite dull for as long as anyone could remember: squeaky-clean and faintly ridiculous. Suddenly here was a sound, a look, an attitude and a record that united all disaffected young white Americans. Right up until then, British music had been selling well in America. A succession of pop acts like EMF and Jesus Jones had number one singles in the *Billboard* charts and a string of Manchester bands, the Stone Roses, the Charlatans, the Happy Mondays, had staged a British invasion of college radio stations.

Until Nirvana there was no subversive American music to compete with the stuff that was being made in England. American radio stations were crying out for bands from Manchester, like you or I might insist on having some cheese from France or chocolate from Belgium. A&R men gave huge sums of money to bands like Northside, and the High on the basis that Manchester was an enchanted place where great music comes from. Of course it is, but it very quickly became yesterday's news. It shouldn't have affected us, because we weren't from there. The trouble was that everyone assumed we were. They said we had that Manchester sound. Manchester was dead and buried by the end of the week. The only place it was reasonable to come from if you wanted to make records at that time was Seattle.

SBK Records was on the forty-second floor of a skyscraper on the Avenue of the Americas, slap in the middle of Manhattan. A peculiarly tidy workplace and more like our accountants' offices than the EMI building, it had zero glamour, a stiff atmosphere. Nobody laughed or had a hangover or called us darling. The company had already requested we make a different video for 'There's No Other Way' which we had done, and it was soon clear that they were keen for us to make other changes; drink less; smarten up our act generally: don't stay out late; don't fool around with women – it was like we'd got married to them.

For the American record company the ideal band would all be sober, constantly grinning, nice about everybody and happy to let the label make the records and videos. We were used to record company pressure from Food. It's a healthy thing. Ultimately, Food's idea of what a great rock and roll band sounded like and behaved like was quite similar to our own, that's partly why we signed to them – that and the fact that nobody else liked us. The rub is always that bands are trying to express themselves, which is satisfying, creative and worthwhile; record companies are trying to please everybody, which is pointless, vacuous and not what art is.

There were piles and piles of Blur promotional CDs around the office, which were in the process of being mailed to radio stations. We didn't know anything about these records. What were they? The artwork on the cover was weak, a 'blurred' image. The colours were not strong either. The title was also bad, 'Blur-ti-go'.

The man with the oral hygiene spray called us into his big office and gave us all the thrusting handshake. He said he was '*toad*ally pumped' about the remix. We said, 'What remix?'

He explained that our record hadn't been quite right, but they'd managed to fix that. 'These remixer guys, they're *reee*lly, *reee*lly haat.' It took him a long time to say each 'really', and 'hot' came out with a wallop. It had about five exclamation marks. He put a lot of himself into the statement and we all felt his pain. He played the remix at low volume and tapped his foot and shook his head around. He was burning. He believed in energy.

The mix, which was of 'Bang', was exceptionally bad. The band had been removed and replaced by a mixture of the High and Northside with a baggy beat. It was a disaster, an embarrassment, and it was already being sent to radio stations. The worst thing that could happen would be that radio stations played it. He said, 'Guys! You gotta trust me on this one', and he showed us his pain again.

I woke up in The Paramount with a girl called Mary, who I met at a Dinosaur Jr gig. We had some strawberries for breakfast and I went to Boston.

Bands always go to Boston after New York. There's probably nothing wrong with it but leaving New York is a wrench every time and I always arrive in Boston and wonder what the hell I'm doing there. Record companies are terrified of Boston just like indie bands were terrified of Neil at Syndrome. There are so many college kids there that it's become a sort of test market. If the radio station in Boston starts to play a record, dozens of others across the USA follow the lead.

It's still about the most important thing for a record, radio play. If the record gets on the radio, then you're in business. So Boston is important.

The gig in Boston was part of a radio festival spectacular. The station had put a lot of oomph behind the event and the record company saw it as a vital building block. We'd discovered a new drink called Jägermeister. It tasted a lot like cough medicine. I'd spent the previous night at a bar on Lansdowne Street drinking those. There are half a dozen clubs on Lansdowne and if you're playing at one of them you get a pass for all of them. I left Graham at the one that was playing Dinosaur Jr records and went to the one that was playing Sister Sledge. It had girls dancing in cages. The Sugarcubes were on an American tour as well and I'd seen Einar the night before in New York. He was a poet sort of person. He was having a lot of fun dancing to Sister Sledge with Björk. He was so happy. We had some Jägermeister and he said, 'I'm gay', pinched a girl's bum and fell over laughing.

It's easy to meet people in America, especially if you're English. I asked the girls in the cages if they wanted to come back to the hotel for a game of cricket. The hotel lobby was deserted as everyone goes to bed at eleven o'clock in Boston. The cricket got out of control when Graham arrived and insisted on fast bowling. The girls didn't have a clue what cricket was, anyway.

Riots, Fights, Guns

There were a lot of bands playing at the festival and there was a girl dressed up as a cowboy dobbing out Jägermeister, which we didn't have to pay for because we had special badges. We went onstage really late and by that time we had drunk all the Jägermeister.

It was one of the times when the band was drunk and better for it. It was a tiny club and it was packed. There were people outside who couldn't get in. Everybody was drunk. The sound man had been warned not to turn the PA up too loud. I'd heard him scream, 'FUCK OFF!' to the man from the record company. Inspired, we all turned everything up to maximum and let it rip.

The crowd went totally berserk: a mob of moshing, surfing, stage diving and screaming. All the crap with the remix and the manager and the people who thought we were from Manchester flew out the window and we played better than we'd ever played before. We could all play really well by then. We knew exactly what we were doing and we were brilliant.

It was the perfect recipe. A pissed-off and pissed-up, passionately anticipated band with a lot to prove playing in a packed venue. We whipped up a frenzy. It was everything you'd hope for if you were in a band or in the audience, but it was absolutely out of control and the venue cut the power after the third song. The crowd started to riot. They were destroying the place and we had to run for it. We got out before the police arrived, but a lot of people were arrested.

The radio station had never seen anything like it and washed their hands of us. The record company were aghast and they sent a bossy lady down to keep an eye on things. They were threatening to pull the finance for the tour, which would have meant no T-shirt money and big trouble. The bossy lady kept putting her hand on my knee and looking into my eyes.

The next show was in Ithaca, New York State, in a small bar. Jim Merlis, our American publicist, had fast become a friend. He was always asking me to say, 'Cheers.' He really liked the way I said 'Cheers'. I really liked the way he said, 'Coffee.' 'Corfee.'

His girlfriend's parents lived in Ithaca. We were invited to dinner at their home. They are physicists working at Cornell University. Bob Richardson won the Nobel Prize for Physics when he discovered superfluidity. He said he was as surprised as anybody that he'd found it. He stumbled across it when he was cooling some helium down to a very low temperature and the helium started doing weird things. He said that if you stir a superfluid, it spins forever. 'Forever?' I said. He smiled and nodded. It was during the asparagus hollandaise that I realised I really liked these people. They were both highly intelligent. I asked them questions all night. We talked about cosmology a bit. I didn't get to talk about those things very often, and my mind was full of it, from the astronomy book.

We went along to the local radio station in the morning. The DJ instantly identified himself as a buffoon. He had appalling coiffure and perfect teeth. It was a disaster from the moment he opened his mouth and introduced us as 'the Blur'. From Manschester. He asked Graham what he thought about the new Seattle sound. Graham said he fucking hated it. Our hapless host put a record on straight away and flew into a rage. Radio stations can be fined for broadcasting swearing on the airwaves, but it was Graham's flat refusal to engage in platitudes that had really riled him. After the adverts we were back on air, but someone accidentally said 'shit' again and that was the end of it. We were hauled up before the director of programmes to apologise. He seemed like quite a nice bloke. He said, 'Just don't fucking swear on my airwaves.'

The tour staggered slowly along the East Coast. In the taxi on the way to the 9.30 club in Washington, DC, I felt Damon bristling next to me. He must have been pulling faces at the dudes in the next car, because as I looked up one of them had pulled a gun out and was pointing it at him.

By the time we got down to Atlanta for a couple of days off, I was the only man standing. The Beastie Boys were staying at the hotel, which was on Peachtree Street. Everything in Atlanta is on Peachtree Street.

I asked to be put through to a Beastie and said, 'Hey, I'm Alex from Manschester, what's up?' He didn't want to come drinking. I went to a bar on my own and met a girl called Michelle. She had an Alfa Romeo Spider and she took me on a tour of the city. There are a lot of people who want to have a good time in Atlanta. We went to a gay bar, a lesbian bar, a college bar. We went everywhere. It was a great city and a great car. She drove fast while slugging tequila from a bottle. She said she had another car and the B52s had used it in the video for 'Love Shack'. They were friends of hers. As I try to recall the weekend we spent together it feels like I spent it inside that video. She personified everything about the song and I wondered at the time if it had been written about her. She was a singularly striking presence. Everywhere we went everyone seemed to know her. She was from Athens, where R.E.M. are from. She told me she had been Michael Stipe's girlfriend. Much later on, I mentioned her to him and he said, 'Uh-oh!'

It was unusual to meet anyone beautiful who hadn't been involved with another musician. I discovered that I'd shared the model from New York with Jesus Jones' keyboard player, who I'd met in Freud's a few weeks earlier.

Michelle gave me her address in Athens and the next time the band were in Atlanta I got someone to drive me to Athens to look for her, but I never found her again.

We wound all around the South, through Texas and back up north to Chicago and Minneapolis. The gigs were going brilliantly, but the organs of the mass media were focused on Seattle. I was in an alcoholic stupor and drank beer for breakfast. I had two black eyes, one from Dave, the other from Graham.

Graham became very lively in drink. Dave just got on with it quietly. I can't remember why Graham punched me, but I was always annoying him. He became very distressed when Audrey Hepburn died and listened to loud, doomy music in the front lounge on his own for days. Even though we fought, we were united. There was never any question of us not wanting to be in a band together.

It takes three days to drive from Minneapolis to Vancouver, a terrifying thought. Dave asked if I wanted to learn bridge and we dealt the first hand as the bus pulled away. We were still playing when we arrived in Vancouver.

We'd stopped halfway in a place called Miles City, Montana. Cities everywhere have similarities, and tiny places do, too. We could have been in a village in the African bush. It was hot and dusty and there was a prefab supermarket that never closed, a motel, a few houses and car parks. A local approached one of the crew for their autograph; they'd never met anyone from England before.

I went for a walk with Damon. When I was wandering around somewhere I'd never been before, as I often was, I found it hard not to get lost. I usually walked in a straight line. It served me well, the straight-line principle. I never get lost heading in a constant direction. We walked out of Miles City and kept on walking, and pretty soon we were out on the searing plains. It was sweltering and hazy and ever so quiet. I spotted a squashed snake in the road, and all of a sudden noticed another. Then there were squashed snakes everywhere I looked. I was wearing shorts and plimsolls, and I didn't have my cricket bat with me. Damon is never scared of anything. He said, 'Just watch where you're going. They're just snakes, they're not going to bite you.'

I recognised that I was in one of those situations that I only seemed to get in with Damon. A similar thing had happened in Alabama when the bus had stopped in a lay-by. We sprang from the bus and ran as fast as we could through the fields until we were out of breath. I found myself standing next to a waist-high, muddy tower. I said, 'Look at this! Strange! Looks like a nest.' I peeked in the top, and there was a huge spider as big as a fist in there. I said, 'Good job we spotted that!', then we realised that the whole swampy field was high-density spider accommodation. They were huge, and they were everywhere. The bus driver had been winding us up about them. He'd said if you get bitten by one of those critters, all you have time to say is 'I've been bitten by a f—' before you died. He was definitely lying, but we weren't in a good place. There were flies landing on us, and a lot of whirry bugs bombing around, the sort that really big spiders like to eat. The whole place was humming, really noisily. It was only when I stood still that I realised I was sinking into a bog. It was unpleasant, and we crept out of there very carefully.

But we had wandered into snake territory this time. Damon was wearing sandals. He'd found a stick that he was whacking and swishing around in front of him. My strategy was more the creeping-along-quietly approach. He walloped a big cactus and said, 'Don't be a poof!' I said, 'Well, why are you trying to fight them, they'll get out of your way if you give them time.' We'd seen quite a lot of live ones by now. They were rattlesnakes, and if you listened carefully you could hear the odd rattle and hiss. A man with a rifle appeared on top of the hill we were headed towards. He was in full survival nutter gear: big boots, fatigues, ammo belt, combat jacket, peaked cap and mirror shades. He was performing some kind of drill or ritual. He'd take a few paces then drop on one knee and take aim with his rifle. It would still have been alarming even if every time he took aim he hadn't been pointing his gun directly at us. His movements were jerky and insane. He was definitely trying to scare us; whether he was going to shoot us remained to be seen. I thought probably not, but when you're in the desert and a particularly strange man is pointing his gun at you, you can't be sure. Damon is the only person I've ever known who would use a bent stick to front up a man with a gun. It was the second time that fortnight that someone had a gun on him and I'd been right beside him. There was no cover. I thought it was best to ignore them both and concentrate on not standing on a snake.

America had been frustrating in many ways. We didn't fit in. We weren't from Manchester, or Seattle. The remix greeted us everywhere we went. Graham was beside himself about Audrey, Dave was very quiet. People kept pointing guns at Damon. I had two black eyes. We crossed the Canadian border and it felt like someone had flicked a switch that made everything all right again. We'd been playing in bars, mainly, in America, but the venue in Vancouver was huge. We went along to the radio station, and 'There's No Other Way' was number one in their chart. Everybody was really pleased to see us. The presenter knew that I was from Bournemouth and liked cheese. He knew that Damon liked Hermann Hesse; that Graham was a painter and Dave was the quiet one. They were all asking about 'the Boston Riot', enthralled and laughing about the bad remix. The station had been playing the album cut of the track. The presenter said that the Seattle sound sucked. Seattle is the next town south down the coast. We were being hailed as the saviours of music. We were fêted. It was Damon's birthday, too.

The venue was on the waterfront and there were speedboats for hire. Graham and I didn't have any ID but the speedboat man recognised us and let us take one. I was just opening up the throttle when our record came on the onboard radio. We opened her up and spent the afternoon zooming around the harbour.

Back at the venue, things weren't going so well. The dressing room was the smartest, newest, cleanest one we'd had on the whole tour and Damon and Dave had demolished it. They'd taken the ceiling down and were starting on the walls. At some time previously there had evidently been a food fight and a beer-throwing contest. The people from the radio station had come along to hang out and thought it was brilliant. I went out to the bar with Damon. We were celebrating his birthday and being number one in Canada. There was a bottle of Tabasco on the bar, for Bloody Marys. He said, 'Watch this!' and necked the whole thing. Temporarily, he went into convulsions and was sick. Then the hiccups started. They were the biggest hiccups I've ever seen. There was an element of sneeze in each hiccup, and each one possessed his entire body. It wasn't deadly serious, but we were supposed to be onstage in twenty minutes. We went on late. I smashed a guitar and a few drums. Having destroyed backstage, Damon tore into the front of house. Dave swan-dived into the crowd and was devoured, so I finished the drums off. We hadn't done that for a while. It is very satisfying to make a lot of noise and break stuff.

I bought a flute in Seattle the next day. All the kids had sold their flutes and violins and were taking up guitar and heroin. The flute was a real bargain, solid silver. We worked our way down the West Coast, playing on a boat in San Francisco. That's a great city. Playing on a boat doesn't work, though. When we came onstage, everyone rushed to the front and the thing practically capsized. The captain stopped the show and we had to wait until the boat was moored alongside the quay to start playing again.

It struck me once more that there are so many places I could live and be happy, and so many people I could do it with. A little success gives a perspective on life's *embarras de richesse*, but London was home, and where the girl that I loved was.

Regroup

America had fried us. We'd thrown ourselves right in. We'd come out still standing, but we were still totally skint. EMI released another single, 'Popscene', a tougher-sounding record than anything we'd released previously. It stalled outside the top thirty. Radio weren't interested, we didn't get on *Top of the*

Pops and we were suffering quite a backlash in the press. We ignored grunge. We didn't look like anybody else or sound like anybody else.

We did a tour of the UK with the Jesus and Mary Chain, Dinosaur Jr and My Bloody Valentine. From some quarters we were perceived as quite a lightweight pop act but we could hold our own with the noise heavyweights.

The rollercoaster took further tolls on our health. I was drinking more and more. We were complete outsiders, with nothing to lose. We started dressing like we used to at college, Oxfam suits and big boots.

It was a very quiet time for British music. There seemed to be nothing happening at all. The British media were only interested in American grunge bands. We were out of favour, but we knew what we were doing at last and when you know what you're doing you just have to keep doing it.

We recorded *Modern Life Is Rubbish* at Maison Rouge, mainly with Stephen Street. There was just enough in the band's bank account to cover the rent, but when Justine didn't get any jobs we were as poor as we'd ever been. Whenever we were in the studio the owner gave us fifty quid a day. Split four ways it was enough to buy lunch and a packet of fags. There were few distractions and we were able to concentrate on the one thing that we all really wanted to do, which was to make a great record. *Modern Life Is Rubbish* is my favourite Blur record. I think it's our *magnum opus*. The scope of the album was vast. We were all listening to different music and pulling in different directions. 'Musical differences' are often cited as the reason bands disintegrate, but they are actually what make a good group great.

By now we'd spent enough time in studios to know the difference between a compressor and a limiter. We weren't bamboozled by how long it took to set the drums up or confused by click tracks and we started to become more adventurous.

The songs grew from Damon's home demos as before, but we developed most of them in the studio, rather than in rehearsal rooms, so we were able to take our ideas further. String quartets were added to some of the tracks, brass sections, oboe and orchestral percussion.

I hadn't worked with 'professional' musicians until we recorded 'Popscene', and at that time I wasn't sure how we would measure up. The brass section had given the impression of a gang of painters and decorators as they unpacked their equipment. It was as if they were unfolding stepladders and unloading brushes. They splashed their bright paint all over the song. They played mainly by ear, just like we did.

The string players had music stands and reams of manuscript paper. Their visits were more like a maiden great-aunt coming for afternoon tea. 'Quick, tidy up those drum takes, they'll be here in a minute!' We weren't really allowed physically to touch their instruments; fair enough, I suppose, but it did highlight a class division between classical musicians and rock musicians. We worked very differently from the string players. I'd never written down a single note.

The four of us rarely had to tell each other what to play, but with session players it's vital to explain very clearly exactly what's required. Working with these highly trained, accomplished musicians made me realise just how quickly the band worked together and how well we understood each other; that actually, one way or another, we had all become very good musicians ourselves. My confidence grew.

Other songs sounded better completely raw, on the bone, as it were, and the four of us recorded those live. There were mad instrumentals and psychedelic expeditions; there was music-hall melody and mosh pit madness. It didn't sound like anything else. We worked hard. Christmas was approaching, and we announced a show at the Hibernian Centre, right next door to the studio. The Salvation Army band opened the show with carols. A feminist punk collective called Huggy Bear played next and one of Damon's old friends from drama college dressed up as Santa and gave away copies of an ancient carol we used to sing in the dressing room called 'The Wassailing Song'. There were only about three hundred people at the gig, including the Salvation Army band. It didn't get reviewed – not one music editor felt our new 'British' sound was worthy of interest. Even a bad review is a thousand times better than no review. It was the first time we played most of the *Modern Life* songs and they went down very well. Santa was stampeded by the faithful and to this day 'The Wassailing Song' is Blur's most sought-after rarity.

Outside of the four of us, confidence in the band was at an all-time low. The Food guys came down to the studio the next day and stroked their chins. I was in the middle of recording the bass on a song called 'Star Shaped'. They listened to everything we'd done and shook their heads. They said there were no singles, and that it was ridiculous that a band with so much potential should be making such a doggedly British record. There was pressure from the American company for us to rerecord everything with Butch Vig, who had produced *Nevermind* for Nirvana.

Both Balfe and Andy started ranting, 'You can do it your way or you can do it our way. Either way, it's your last chance.' 'You drink too much.' 'Nobody is interested in British pop. It's not going to happen.' Balfe started playing 'Reward' on the keyboard again and everyone ignored him. I finished the bass on 'Star Shaped' and went Christmas shopping at Harrods with Graham.

Damon wrote a song called 'For Tomorrow' at his parents' house on Christmas Eve. We were supposed to have finished the recording by Christmas but it was too good to leave off the album. We went straight back to Maison Rouge in January and recorded it. It was symphonic, sophisticated, elegiac and elevating. We nailed it. Streetie said it was the best thing we'd ever done.

British Image 1

We posed for photos with a huge dog called Sherman, and scrawled 'British Image 1' on the backdrop. The photos were damned as xenophobic. Nobody wanted to play the video. The record went to number twenty-eight. The reviews said it was ambitious but anachronistic, and bade us farewell. We hit the road.

We were always a kick-arse live band. A curious thing happened as we toured *Modern Life*. The audience changed. Throughout the first record the crowd had been mainly girls, but now the front row was mostly men. Suited and scootered, like a lost cavalry, came the mods.

We kept on playing and we kept on recording.

We were right on the breadline. We went to Japan to earn some more cash, and to investigate. Quite why the Japanese love British pop music so much is open to interpretation. They do, though. They love it. We had no idea we were big in Japan, but we got to the airport and there were quite a lot of people there, with presents, cameras and pieces of card for us to sign. It was surreal to disembark from an aircraft, jetlagged, poor and struggling, and to be greeted like princes, in a strange and wonderful land. They knew all about us. We each had our own little fan club. Graham seemed to have the biggest following. We were followed everywhere we went and were provided with security guards. They were completely unnecessary, as the girls were very respectful and polite. I think the security guards were there to make the girls feel more important.

It takes a while to get the hang of Japan. There were fans in the hotel, fans at the record company, on the train, in the lift. They giggled and smiled and pointed. It was very pleasant, but interviews were difficult. There was usually an interpreter involved, and a hangover.

The best nightclub in the world is in Roppongi, Tokyo, but it serves the worst booze. It's called the Lexington Queen. It's Bill's place. If you're ever in Tokyo, go and find Bill and tell him I sent you. There are many reasons why it is the best nightclub in the world. The first is that I never had to pay for a drink. There aren't very many Western people in Japan. No one goes there on holiday, which is a shame. The majority of young Westerners in Tokyo are people in rock and roll bands, and models. Modelling is big business in Tokyo. Bill lets bands and models in for free, and doesn't charge them for drinks. It was hard to understand how an arrangement that wonderful could exist, that I could go somewhere that was full of beautiful women and the drinks were free. Models love meeting people in bands. I met two or three girls at the Lex that I'd met in other places, one in Milan, one in Atlanta and one in London. That booming basement became my office in Tokyo for many years. I don't ever remember it closing. The only drawback is that the Lexington Queen hangover is the most vicious and overwhelming of all the hangovers in the world. It is especially bad when combined with a ride on the bullet train, or a morning of interviews. It is a small price to pay. The Japanese also embrace getting absolutely smashed and smoking fags, and they have very good systems for beating hangovers. The spas are sensational, and a big bowl of noodle soup works wonders.

We still managed to mess everything up in Japan. We were late. We were rude. We didn't bow low enough. We didn't play for long enough. We weren't deliberately offensive, just naive. There is a lot of etiquette to observe in Japan and we burbled with bad protocol. I was often asked if I had any messages for my fans. I said, 'Please stop throwing cheese at me.' Cheese is very hard to get in Japan. It is so rare that it comes in tins, to preserve it. I had always expressed great interest in cheese in interviews. The fans had gone to great lengths to find cheese. A journalist reported me to the record company, and I was asked to apologise for abusing their generosity.

Fan culture is highly developed in Japan.

Festivals

When I got back from Japan Justine had gone missing. I located her, finally, staying with friends in Worthing. I walked down to Leicester Square after a couple of refreshers at Freud's, and soaked it all up. A fight broke out between a horrible thug and a little guy. I've never seen someone hit another person so hard. It was all the more shocking for coming straight after Japan's whizzing serenity. Japan was so different from anywhere else I'd been. I found my perspective had shifted, that I was seeing the country of my birth through fresh eyes.

We'd been travelling around Britain on and off for the last two years; I had a working knowledge of all the major cities and I liked every single one of them. On the whole people who live in sunny Bournemouth believe that people who live anywhere else are slightly mad. Why, they say, would anyone want to live in Coventry? It has no beach.

At first glance, Britain has all the ugliest large towns in Western Europe and the most unfathomable metropolitan geography in the world. I had Manhattan worked out in about ten seconds. It's almost impossible to get lost there. Modern cities are designed, designed around modern life. Britain's historic towns have grown madly out of control like a force of nature, gardens running wild into a space age.

In medieval Coventry all people really needed was somewhere to go to church, park their horses, swap turnips and watch Shakespeare, and no doubt it was as neat as a row of buttons back then. It underwent explosive growth during the industrial revolution and local planners must have just been getting their heads around the arrival of the 'motor car' and where to put the Rolls-Royce factory when the city was blitzed in 1940. It regenerated and expanded further to accommodate more heavy industry, which has since mostly vanished, to be replaced by technology-based businesses, and bands like the Specials. It's been a continuous success story and I wouldn't swap Coventry for Vienna. All those layers of history and transformation; it's beautiful.

I loved the brilliant chaos of our cities. The mood, as we toured the country with the new millennium slowly appearing on the horizon, had been nothing short of festive. Grunge music expressed pain, dissatisfaction and self-loathing, like the Smiths had ten years earlier, but young people in Britain had money, opportunities and each other and they were celebrating.

No matter what anyone said, we knew we were a great band. The second single from *Modern Life Is Rubbish* was called 'Chemical World' and it went to number twenty-eight, too, the same as the last record. It wasn't a smash, but there were some good signs. Eddie Izzard, my favourite comedian, mentioned in an interview that he listened to that song before he went onstage. We demoed some new tracks even though the album had only just been released. They were the best songs we'd ever written.

It was the summertime and we went to Europe to play at some festivals. Festivals were a phenomenon that exploded in the nineties. The festival transformed from a countercultural beardy bong session into a mainstream mass phenomenon, like fishing and football. I think it was because the best music attracts the prettiest girls and when the pretty girls come, everyone else soon follows. What was basically a cross between a stadium gig and going camping suddenly became very appealing once the magic ingredient of pretty girls was added.

The word 'festival' is a marketing device. It suggests a celebration, religious significance and culture. Festivals are just big gigs. There's nothing wrong with that. It's more effective to do things on a huge scale. Huge bands, huge festivals and huge numbers of people mean the media come to cover the event and pick up on new things that are happening. A band can't really operate without getting involved with festivals. These temporary cities are all built on the same model. The crowds are out the front and they stay in tents, light bonfires, get spaced out and see all their favourite bands. Backstage is a like school for bad children.

Some festivals are more like theme parks than others.

Hultsfred in Sweden is a special one. Sweden is a beautiful place. People tend to head for the sun on holiday, but the north has a wide-open beauty about it and a mystery that the packed beaches of southern Europe lost as soon as they started charging for deckchairs. There is space and wilderness and water everywhere. There is a sense of things being clean, fresh and wholesome. The Swedes are sexy and very friendly. They seem to like the English more than is rational. Hultsfred is out in the wilds. There are lakes and forests, streams and sunshine. In midsummer it doesn't get dark until after midnight, when the whole place becomes a mass of bonfires and candles. It's Utopian. For once we didn't seem to be the drunkest people. We were quite wide-eyed with wonder. Something amazing was happening.

They just got it in Sweden. They were the first people to get Britpop. They were on to it before the Brits. Maybe grunge didn't really make sense to them. Sweden is too clean for it to work there. Before we went onstage, journalists wanted to talk to us and were asking pertinent questions about what had happened to British music, and they knew our B-sides. I kept looking at Damon and he kept looking at me, and everyone kept looking at us.

We went on at midnight. It was dusk. The crowd were having a wonderful time. They were singing a song about a little frog that gets lost. It was a beautiful song, reserved for happy occasions. We took to the stage. They were ready for it. They really celebrate summer in Sweden. That's what makes Hultsfred special. All the anguish of the dark winter months is over and there is a palpable sense of joy and liberation. There were cheers and then it went very quiet. Damon started to sing the chorus of the froggy song and Dave banged the bass drum. Twenty thousand people joined in. We had decided to start the set with one of the songs we'd just demoed called 'Girls & Boys'. Dave accelerated his bass drum to the disco tempo, 120 beats per minute. There is something special about that tempo; it's supposed to make your heart beat faster. Mine was thumping. The keyboard crept in with the bass drum. I flicked my fringe and slammed in with the bass. It was the first time we'd played the song. The crowd went absolutely berserk. They went bananas. They were entranced, ecstatic, twenty thousand of them. By the last chorus they knew the words and were singing along. Our lives changed forever during those three and a half minutes. It brought the place down. There were bras flying on to the stage and grins everywhere you looked. People were shouting for B-sides and screaming our names. It was quite a short set. We finished with 'There's No Other Way' and went off. They were screaming for an encore, so we went back on and sang the frog song again and tried another new song called 'Parklife'.

Everybody I met after that was smiling at me. I realised I had a lot of new friends in Sweden.

The Besançon Balance

After Sweden we knew we were holding a couple of aces. We'd already done the UK tour around the release of *Modern Life Is Rubbish* and nothing further was planned at home. 'Sunday Sunday' was the final single to be released and it went to number twenty-eight. That made three number twenty-eights in a row, but the press were starting to come around and we got our first front cover since 'There's No Other Way'. We disappeared to Europe for a short tour.

There were a few shows in the French provinces. Word was getting around that we had some good songs. I like French people. I was wandering around Rennes on a Sunday afternoon, and some cool-looking French guys approached me and asked me, in very bad English, if I was Alex James. They were surprised when I replied in French. We tore around in their old Renault; they showed me the cathedral and we went back to their house. French people love showing you their cathedrals. They made me a soufflé and introduced me to Apollinaire, a romantic poet I'd missed. They insisted I kept the volume of poems and we went to a bar. We picked Graham up on the way. They called some girls they knew and I spent an enchanted evening playing belote, the French national card game, with the barman. There was something very comfortable about that level of celebrity. When things started to go really crazy, I lost the privilege of just bumping into people, going to their homes and having a peaceful, ordinary time, but I enjoyed that day. I was welcomed like a brother, not a rock star. These were people just like me, with the same interests; I never saw them again but it was delightful to step into their lives for a moment.

Graham had a Ventolin inhaler for his asthma. Ventolin helps oxygen to get to your brain. He'd take a few blasts and do a drawing before the feeling wore off. That's how Art Club started. Art Club was at two a.m. every day in my room. We needed constants when we were forever on the move, and I looked forward to Art Club. The other member of the club was Cara, the hired keyboard player. I loved Cara. She lived in Malvern with her husband and children, and played the piano in the local grand hotel. She was an exceptionally good card player. We played crib a lot and she was sometimes able to help with the crossword. She was a natural aristocrat. She exuded dignity and also mischief. Her musical ability was daunting. If I played her a record she could tell me what the chords were and if I sang her a melody she could play it back with an accompaniment. When everyone eventually arrived back at the hotel in the evening, the piano became the focal point. I'd say, 'Play, "The Old Man's Back Again", Cara.' She'd say, 'How does it go? Sing it, boy!' I'd sing and she'd pick it up right away. Sometimes we'd sit there all night. Everything about her was musical. I was always asking her to sing 'English Country Gardens'. I was very attracted to Cara.

The temperature was still rising all the time. Gigs, and the band itself, wherever we went, were becoming something of an event.

We had been booked to play Reading Festival. It's the last festival of the summer on the August Bank Holiday weekend. We knew it was an important one. Everyone was going to be there. We were playing in the tent. The band on the main stage, The The, were having a bad night and the tent was absolutely packed by the time we went on. We had introduced a new system of not getting too drunk before we played. It was the inevitable triumph of reason. That show was probably the most important gig we've ever played. Chris Morrison gave us all a wedge of cash afterwards and told us not to worry any more. It wasn't long since we'd recorded *Modern Life Is Rubbish* but we went back to Maison Rouge with Streetie and started recording the new album.

I hadn't sung a lead vocal before. When we got back from Sweden I'd written a song about the stars and moons that had been preoccupying me. That was one of the hardest things to get right. The rest of the album flew on to tape. 'Girls & Boys' was recorded very quickly because we'd been playing it live, and the other singles came together almost effortlessly. The demo of 'To the End' had a good feel so we worked from that, rather than starting again.

'Parklife' was quite a complete song from the first time Damon had played it to us. We'd been watching *Quadrophenia* on the tour bus and we sent the track to Phil Daniels, the lead actor, and asked if he wanted to sing the verses. He said yes, simple as that.

The only song that was a great effort was 'This Is a Low'. The backing track was recorded and sounded musically more emotive than anything we'd ever done, but Damon was struggling with the words. For Christmas I bought him a handkerchief with a map of the shipping forecast regions on it. I can't take all the credit, but maybe he was blowing his nose when the inspiration came to him. You can never tell when the muse is going to appear. It went on to become Blur's most popular song.

The company that owned Maison Rouge sold it. The brasserie shut down and there were never any balls for the table football. The toilets were horrible. Yet somehow it was easier to make music in a more realistic working environment, without the comforts, and the album was finished in no time. We'd developed a way of working, and we had a team of people that we knew and trusted around us.

We thought we'd made a great record, but we had no idea what was about to happen. Guitar bands that made great records sold maybe a hundred thousand copies. The Stone Roses had been the biggest selling guitar band of the decade so far – their album had gone platinum – but that was a couple of years earlier. Everybody was listening to rave music and celebrating. Balfe was pleased with the record too, but he obviously had no idea either. He sold Food to EMI and moved to a big house in the country. He could have got a much bigger one if he'd waited six months.

6

triumph

Smile!

We were at a photo shoot in a garage kind of place on King's Road, Chelsea, the same place we'd had our photo taken with Sherman, the big dog. There weren't that many photographic studios, just like there weren't that many recording studios, and we'd seen most of them by now. Andy Ross arrived with champagne because he'd just got the midweek chart position for 'Girls & Boys'. It was number five, which was good whichever way we thought about it, and we thought about it a lot. That was the start of the champagne and a long, long sunny day that dissolved into bubbles.

Success at home was a completely different thing from being big in Sweden, or Japan. That was like going on a strange holiday. I still came back to my old life at the end of it. Even though we were away a lot, and loving it, London was home. The more I travelled, the more I felt that. Our lives had been changing a lot, but actually the pattern of our lives changed very little when we started to sell lots of records. We played gigs, had our photos taken, did interviews, just like we did before.

The two most important things in the world when I was growing up were *Smash Hits* magazine and *Top of the Pops*.

Smash Hits was a blend of sophistication and stupidity that somehow managed to unify the whole of pop music. Its pages held the evidence that bored children needed that everything was, in fact, brilliant. Sometimes Wham! were on the cover and sometimes it was Morrissey and Pete Burns. At its peak the magazine was selling nearly a million copies a fortnight and the music industry flourished. The most popular bands made videos that cost a million pounds, while tiny independent labels thrived at the other end of the scale. That magazine spawned monsters every bit as irritating as today's celebrities, possibly more irritating, because these people considered themselves 'Artists', but *Smash Hits* made music the focal point of all youth culture and the 'ver hits' era was the golden age of the pop song. Music is not the focus of the *heat* generation. In the early twenty-first century there are more music magazines for people aged over thirty than there are for teenagers, and I wonder whether youth culture has had its fifty years in the sun, whether we'll ever see another band that absolutely everybody loves or hates. In America there's never been anything like *Smash Hits*. Maybe that's why six out of the all-time top ten records in *Rolling Stone* magazine are by British bands. In America, it seemed a band could sell a billion records but most people would still have never heard of them. *Smash Hits* would never have allowed that to happen.

The *Smash Hits* office was in Carnaby Street, just around the corner from Food Ltd, and the writers used to spend a fair amount of time in the Old Coffee House, a pub on the corner of Beak Street, one of our haunts. They were exceptionally bright, mainly female and mostly younger than us. I liked being in that magazine, but it was actually more enjoyable just getting drunk and being stupid with those girls on Monday afternoons, playing darts, arguing about haircuts and who was fanciable, before they started writing about us. That was actually more like being in the magazine than being featured on its pages.

Top of the Pops was the other fundamental force. It was more than a TV show, and it's hard to believe it's actually gone. Its final broadcast was in July 2006. It's still probably the most powerful brand name in music broadcasting. There weren't many things that were exactly as I thought they'd be, but appearing on that show was just like walking inside the television. It was almost magical. Practically everyone there seemed hardly able to believe that they were inside it. There was always a wide-eyed, open-mouthed glee about the studio audience. The acts on *TOTP* were just a part of the spectacle. Everybody mimed, which made it even more unreal and dream-like, but it was all the bit-part players and extras who made it special: a mammoth blast of bright lights, cameras, smiles and flesh.

The canteen at the studio in Borehamwood was completely surreal. It was jam-packed with the casts of *Grange Hill*, *EastEnders* and whatever top bands were in the country that week. People on telly do have faces you can just stare and stare at. It's what they get paid for. When we'd been on it in the past we'd been looking at everybody else and thinking, 'Wow! It's them.' Everybody was looking at us this time. It was a good line-up. Vic Reeves, the comedian, was performing his version of 'Born Free' with a couple of long-leggedy backing dancers and Mark and Robbie from Take That were presenting the show. The crowd were panting, hysterically screaming and throwing themselves around. All the other bands came out to watch us mime 'Girls & Boys' and the audience went berserk at four grown men pretending to play their instruments. It was brilliant.

I had a very small suitcase with a clean pair of pants and socks, the collected writings of Colette, a large bottle of gin and as many small bottles of tonic that would fit in. We'd just come back from Belgium. We seemed to go to Belgium a lot in those days. There was never a moment to sit back and enjoy the fact that we were actually going to be on *Top of the Pops*. We were too busy enjoying Belgium.

I went to drink my gin in the bar and Vic Reeves was there with his friend Jonathan Ross, who had given our first single the raspberry on *Juke Box Jury*. I changed my mind about hating him forever when he offered to buy me a drink. Then they took me to a place called the Groucho Club.

The Groucho was quite a small place. There were comfy chesterfields and good-looking staff. It reminded me of an airport lounge and most people there were probably in between flights. There were bowls of Twiglets and someone was playing the piano. That was the furniture, same as anywhere else, with Twiglets thrown in. What set it apart from everywhere else were the people who went there. All towns have one place where everybody wants to go more than everywhere else. Les Bains Douches was the top spot in Paris; in New York it was Spy; Shocking in Milan and so on, all the places I was most likely to run into Einar from the Sugarcubes again. In London, the Groucho was *the* place, the place where anybody at all might walk through the door. In fact, everybody always looked up when the door opened, to see who it was. Everyone was very friendly. They are when you're number five.

It was a long evening that ended up at Dave Stewart's house in Covent Garden: Dave, myself, a Pet Shop Boy, Vic Reeves, a billionaire and a transvestite. Dave was explaining his art collection, like a proper grown-up rich person. I spilt a drink on the fibre optic carpet. I'd been pretty well behaved up until then. I was living just around the corner, but I still didn't own much more than I had in the suitcase. Dave Stewart had lots of toys. It was a house for impressing other rich people with, a cross between an old-fashioned imperial castle and a spaceship. I wandered home as day was breaking. Jus wasn't there.

I didn't have any keys so I scaled the front of the building and climbed in through the window. There was a message on the answerphone from Justine. She was calling from Charing Cross police station to say she'd been arrested for some kind of altercation with a police officer in St James's Park and was having a night in the cells. She'd been with a booze head from another band who were also signed to Food. When the limo came in the morning, I took it round to the police station and tried to get her out, but they hauled her up before the magistrate. I had to go to Belgium. It was going crazy in Belgium, they said.

Young, Free, Single, Rich, Famous, Unbearable

Since I'd got back from Japan to an empty flat a few months before things had not been so sweet at home. Justine moved out as I became more selfish, drunk and unfaithful. It's hard for a relationship to survive one person becoming successful all of a sudden. Apart from that one arrest, she handled it very well, but I didn't. I missed her when she was gone and there was no peace.

To start with, I'd go away on tour and, basically, riot, but I always came home to her calm, stabilising influence. As *Parklife* gathered more and more momentum I slipped anchor and blew adrift on the shallow sea of a permanent backstage party. There was always one more place to go and I leapt into London's deep and dark night.

I decided to stick mostly to champagne. I'd always liked that stuff. I think it started on aeroplanes. They threw champagne at people on aeroplanes in those days, little quarter bottles. Leaving behind a grey Saturday morning at Heathrow they brought the champagne round as soon as the sunshine started crashing through the little windows. It lit up the bubbles as they rose to the top of the glass. Cheap aeroplane champagne: it was a wonderful colour in the brilliant sun. I contemplated the bubbles and measured the gold against the blue sky behind and was happy. In motion, travelling somewhere at great speed, completely serene and still as those bubbles whizzed and fizzed.

I started on the monopoles. Monopole is one-year-old plonk and good for mixing but I soon developed a taste for Taittinger. That's quite crispy and biscuit-flavoured. I found Bollinger and Moët a bit yeasty. Taittinger was just a phase and I settled on Cordon Rouge. I got three bottles of that on the rider every day for about five years, but I supplemented it with a systematic tour of all the great champagne houses, Krug, Dom Perignon, La Veuve, all colours, all sizes, all years. On special occasions, or given the choice, I went for Cristal. That was my favourite. It's in a clear bottle and has a very delicate flavour; a liquid gold that transmogrified into sizzling suds on my tongue and left me thinking about violets.

They're all marvellous. I got quite good at opening a bottle with just a gentle hiss, with one hand. It was important to get all the foil off, to avoid lacerations, and hold it at forty-five degrees, to stop it going everywhere, but the most important thing of all about champagne is that you have to eat a fresh carrot for every bottle that you drink. It's very acidic and if you guzzle it it makes your breath stink.

I was quite happy with my three bottles of Cordon Rouge and my three large carrots.

Champagne was the perfect toast to a time of hope and new beginnings in London. Whole swathes of the city were in a redevelopment boom. Social and cultural interest was rejuvenating; something was stirring in the art world; a new government was looking increasingly likely; *Parklife* knocked Pink Floyd's new album off the number one slot, to everyone at EMI's surprise. Blur weren't part of a movement; we were right out on our own musically, but we were a part of London's almost instantaneous rebirth as the world's hippest city. There were two faces on the covers of all the music magazines. One was Damon's and the other was Kurt Cobain's. And suddenly one of them was dead.

New Friends

It was the premiere of Quentin Tarantino's *Pulp Fiction*. Damon and I had been for a couple of Long Island Iced Teas and were in no mood to sit down for an hour and a half. We shouted at the screen for a while and left. We decided to go to the Groucho. I'd been telling him about it. It's a member's club, but we got in by saying we were meeting Dave Stewart. We figured he wouldn't mind.

Damon went off to argue with a guy with a ponytail and I sat at the bar staring at myself. This was a good club. There was no way of knowing what would happen next. Damon came back twenty minutes later with Helena Christensen. She was the most beautiful woman in the world. I was very interested in her face. I suppose everybody was. It was a face that made suggestions that great things might be true and pictures of it always made me feel better. I wondered how else I might have come to meet this woman. Appearing on *Top of the Pops* and being in *Smash Hits* was very satisfying, but it wasn't my ultimate aim in life. Being face to face with, in my considered opinion, the most beautiful woman in the world was an absolutely concrete result. I suddenly felt I'd arrived somewhere new. It was completely ridiculous that all I did was put my fingers on strings. I said, 'God, I think you're beautiful. Do you like cheese?' She seemed to know a fair bit about cheeses. There was one you could get in Denmark that had worms inside it. It was a lot to take on board all of a sudden.

She said, 'Come to Browns.' There was a driver waiting and Damon and I got in the car with her and Michael Hutchence.

Pass the carrots!

Mile End

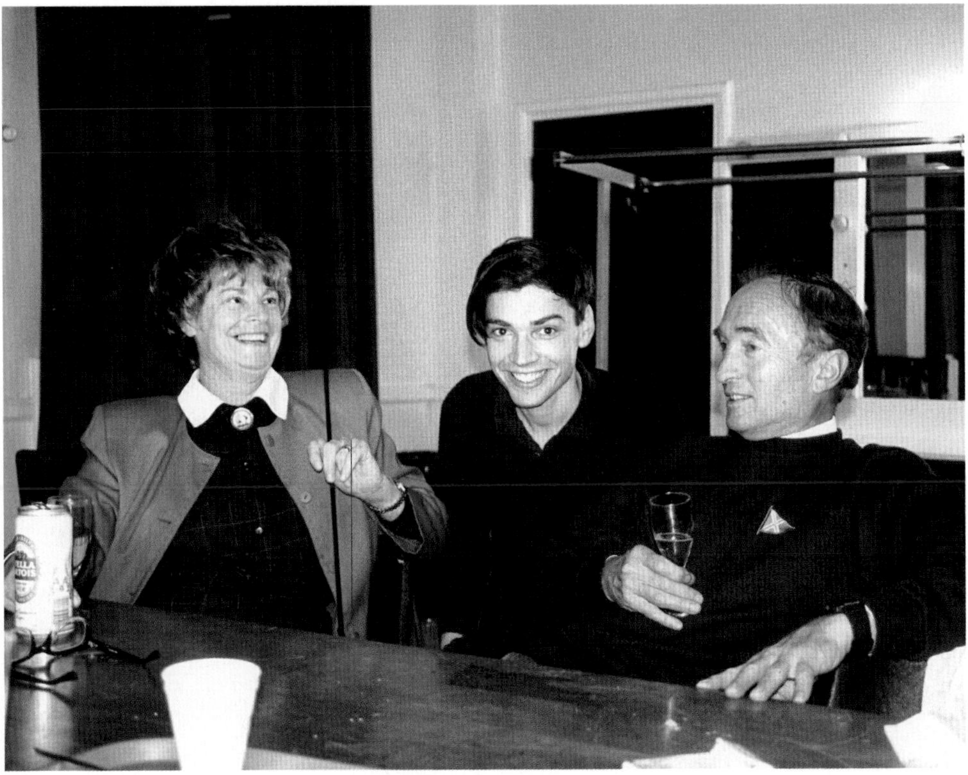

Backstage in Southampton with the Jameses, 1994

Life improved no end when I learned how to play with one hand

Still getting the hang of that one

Left: Another glorious day in showbiz!

Below: Cara and the band backstage, 1994

Shooting the video for 'Parklife', 1995

The rhythm section

More medicine

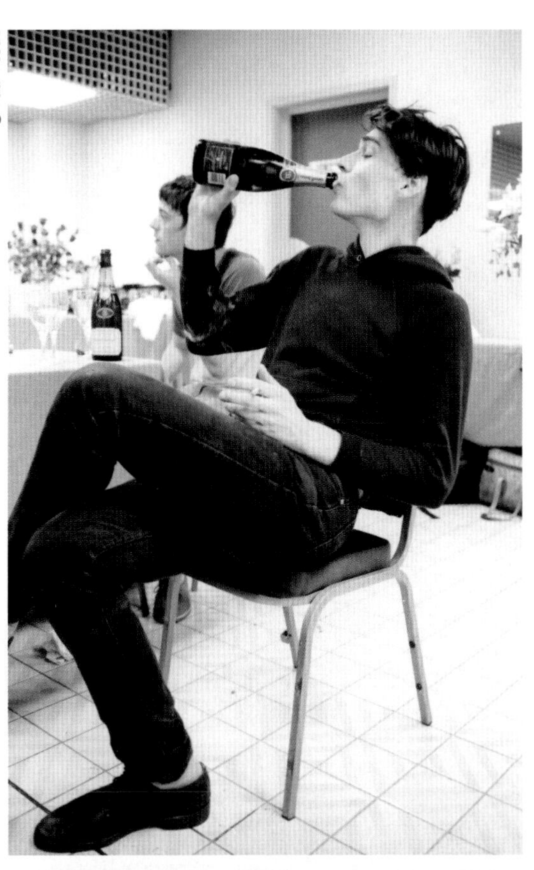

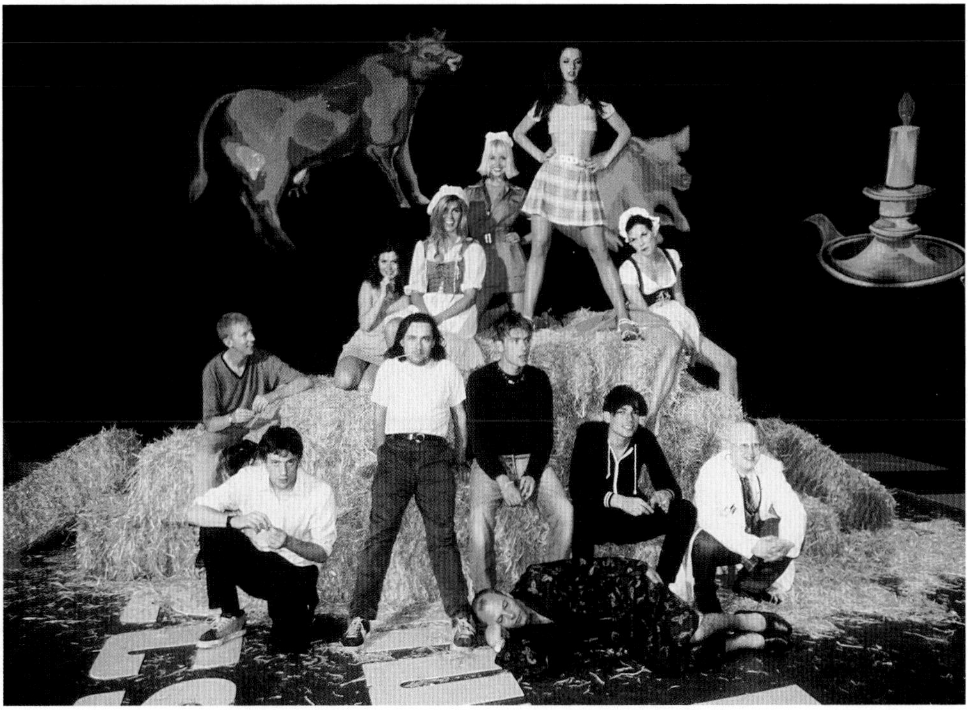

© Paul Postle

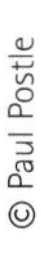

'Country House' video

Brit Awards, 1995

A man with a Barbour jacket and a bottle of champagne is invincible

Dressing room, Besançon

Westin Hotel, Tokyo

With Marianne at Mercer Street, 1996

With Peter Hook at Reading Festival, 1998

Photo shoot for the cover of *Guardian Weekend*, 1998

Browns was very glitzy, gaudier than a wedding cake. It was built on different foundations from the Groucho. It was a house made of the very finest straw. Despite most of the people in the Groucho being off their faces, it was quite an intellectual, brainy kind of a place. Huge minds set free in drink and exploring each other, quipping *bons mots* and scheming. Browns was more the bodies exploring each other kind of place and it was best to check your brain in at the door. Soap stars, boxers, footballers, princes, models and gangsters traded money, fame and sex. It was quite dark for somewhere that was made entirely from lights and mirrors. On the whole, Browns attracted a worse kind of person than anywhere else in the universe and at that point I was the worst person in the universe. Arrogant, drunk and indomitable, and yet everybody was saying come on in.

I went out every night. Film extravaganzas, magazine launches, parties in shops and bashes in museums and big houses in Chelsea and Notting Hill, gigs at the Astoria, gay discos, the Groucho, Browns, an endless circle of red carpet.

Graham had now moved to Camden and sometimes I went to see him there in the Good Mixer public house. He shunned the garish drama of the party circuit but he couldn't escape from the circus either. He had become the mad king of a strange people who all looked like him, and he held his court at the Mixer. Dave never went out. He bought an aeroplane as a means of escape and occupied himself with that. Damon moved to Notting Hill. He was starting to get pursued by paparazzi, and there were often fans and photographers outside his house. He kept on working. We all got on well with one another but nobody really liked each other's friends. We weren't so much of a gang any more. We all had our own gangs.

I was sitting at the bar in the Groucho on my own. It was pretty empty in there as it was a Saturday. I didn't recognise anybody. I was just sitting at the bar drinking a Brandy Alexander:

brandy, cream and nutmeg in a martini glass. It was nice to have a quiet drink, and a think. I was smoking a Camel filter, checking myself out in the mirror and wondering who to call and where to go next. A silly voice said 'Alex! Alex from Blur!' I ignored it. Then it said, 'I love you, Alex!' I looked up and at the end of the bar someone was pulling the funniest face I'd ever seen, puckering his lips and batting his eyelids. I laughed and said, 'I love you too, darling.' And went back to my thoughts. The voice said, 'Don't you remember me? From college? We played pool together! I'm Damien! Damien fuckin' 'irst!' I said, 'Wow, I was wondering what you looked like.' He brought his wine over. He lived in Germany and he loved the Beatles. He swore a lot. He seemed very interested in everything I said. It was unusual to meet someone so forthright and curious. He was fascinated, more fascinated than anyone had ever been by exactly what had happened with the band. He quizzed and queried, prodded and probed. It's usually dull to answer questions. People ask you questions all the time if you're in the papers and on the telly. I was beginning to recognise that celebrity status was like living a kind of perpetual interview. It's like you just sprouted another weird head in place of your old one and everybody wants to stare at it and ask it questions all of a sudden. After a while, it's too late and your old head will never grow back and you're left with the one that people point at. It's your own fault, too.

I liked Damien's questions. They were unusual. Soon I was trying to explain where Jupiter was. Damien liked the fact that it didn't have a surface. Something without a surface was very exciting to him. It was to me, too. I was drawing him a map of the solar system and he was making me laugh.

I'd done a fair bit of hobnobbing with famous people by this time. They didn't seem to have anything in common, particularly. Famous people generally seemed like everybody else, only a bit more famous. Rich people aren't particularly different from anyone else either. They've just got more money. Fame is just another kind of money. It can do things that money can't, but it's just a currency. No one ever loved anyone because they were rich. No one ever really loved anyone because they were famous, but it's an attractive quality.

Over the course of our conversation, I gradually became aware that I was talking to somebody quite exceptional. He was very, very funny. That was the first thing about him. He was an irresistible combination of rudeness and wit. The two qualities set each other off. He drew everybody in: the barman; people on either side of us; the piano player. He bought drinks for everybody. It was the kind of place where that happened. A lot of comedians drank there, too, so there was no shortage of funny people buying drinks. It was a good place to be. Damien was intensely engaging, though. He was trying to tell me something that I realised I really needed to know, and he was illustrating it with farts and stupid facial expressions.

He wasn't yet famous, but he was obviously a genius. When I woke up, my pockets were full of his drawings.

The Brits

On the day of the Brit Awards I had breakfast with Mike Smith, my publisher, as I often did. He was nursing an extra spiky headache and trying to draw me. He always had a sketchbook with him, in his satchel. He was perpetually losing that bag. He left it in Freud's so many times they had a special place behind the bar for it. You could tell if he'd had a big night by whether he had his bag with him at breakfast time. He always got it back by mid-afternoon, although sometimes it took all morning to locate, when he should really have been trying to sign the Cranberries. Quite often it turned up at the Bull and Gate, Kentish Town. That was always a good place to start looking.

He had a black taxi account so he could always trace it when he left it in his cab. It sometimes spent the night in restaurants and it did a whole run at the Astoria, Charing Cross Road. It always came back in the end, apart from once. He completely lost his old bag at the Brit Awards. He went back and checked the whole of Alexandra Palace, but he never found it. Sometimes he would become maudlin, and mourn for that bag. It was still a talking point. He was wondering whether to leave it at home altogether tonight.

The Brits was a no-holds-barred piss-up. It was a night of complete carnage every single time. It's the music industry's biggest night of the year. The music business is a succession of big nights: parties, awards and launches, openings anniversaries, presentations, big gigs and festivals, and that's just work. The Brits is the daddy of all parties. All the big guns line up for the Brit Awards. Madonna, Elton John, all the evergreens, the unsinkable battleships in the business, would be there. I'd never been before. We were probably considered a risk by the organisers, too likely to act up, and, besides that, the band had never been nominated for anything. Every year as the awards came around and we didn't feature in the line-up, there had always been time to dwell on our disappointment. This time we were up for something in practically every category and there had hardly been a moment to consider what it all meant. We were performing a couple of songs, including 'Parklife' with Phil Daniels who'd become a fifth member of the band.

It was a vast glittering spectacle, a multimillion pound trifle. America has the Oscars and we have the Brits. It's the annual showbiz party that everybody wants to go to, the one that reaches beyond the music and gossip pages and into the headlines.

In a sea of onlookers, beyond a moat of international media, the whole of Alexandra Palace was bedecked, bejewelled and lit up like a Christmas tree. Inside there was a full-sized fairground with carousels, bumper cars and a big wheel. Hundreds of waiters tended to acres of white tablecloth. Champagne flowed, cocaine snowed and a steady rain of superstars took a bow.

I invited Justine but she was too busy dancing with the bass player from Pulp and I ended up on a park bench with Keith Allen. He'd just kind of appeared and he just kept appearing from then on.

When I woke up in the morning, I knew my life had changed forever. We'd won everything going; it was a record-breaking haul. Blur had become a household name over the course of the evening. I went out to get *The Times* for the crossword. A young girl walking along the street with her mother went into hysterics and there was a picture of me on page three of *The Times*. It's always a jolt to be confronted by your own image when you're not expecting it, especially the first few times it happens. There is no image more shocking or scary than your own. I can see why some of those people who lived in the jungle thought their souls were being stolen when they had their photograph taken. It was like there was a bit of me that had gone beyond my reach. I'm sure the jungle-dwellers didn't think it was their souls being stolen anyway. It was just a bit of media vertigo as far as they were concerned, too.

We were in all the newspapers. Until the night before we'd been strictly music magazine fodder. I'd always found it slightly depressing when taxi drivers, having established that I was a musician, would ask the name of the band and then say, 'Nah, mate.' A lot of time was spent in taxis. They're one of the perks of being in a band. If you're a TV presenter, you get free clothes. If you work in a hotel, you get fed. As soon as we signed our record deal there seemed to be a taxi waiting constantly. Record companies don't perform miracles, but they do make sure bands turn up to things.

Suddenly taxi drivers had heard of us. It was much worse. Being grilled by a thrilled taxi driver trapped inside a hangover trapped inside a taxi trapped in thick traffic, first thing in the morning, was harder to bear than being obscure. I do like talking to taxi drivers, just not about those kinds of things. It's too repetitive. I started to say I was an accountant, which was usually good enough to kill it. I thought accountants probably needed to pretend they were rock stars occasionally, but I had no idea people in bands sometimes had to pretend they were accountants.

The Great Escape

Our lives were changing. Graham split up with his girlfriend and Dave married his. Dave's new wife's ex-flatmate was going out with a singer-songwriter person called Stephen Duffy. He'd been the original singer in Duran Duran and had written some good songs, mainly about girls. I met him at the wedding and we talked for a long time, mainly about girls. We decided to make a record together. I wrote some songs about girls and a month later we were on *Top of the Pops*. Damien Hirst liked one of the songs, 'Hanging Around', and used it in a film he was making. I was seeing a lot of Damien by this time. He'd moved back from Berlin to London where he was making quite a noise. He was intrigued by success and by Blur as we'd been at Goldsmiths together.

He and Keith Allen were a double act. They could really make each other laugh and the euphoria of their humour created a strong bond between them. I saw a lot of Keith, too. He was a permanent fixture in London's nightscape. He knew absolutely everybody and everybody either loved him or hated him. His younger brother is a Hollywood film director; his ex-wife is an Oscar-winning film producer; his daughter is a pop star. I can see a small part of his essence in all of them, but he was the devastating big bang from which they all evolved, a free spirit; that's what Damien really liked about him. There was always a danger that Keith might set the house on fire or be absolutely disgraceful in some way. He must have been nearly fifty. He'd just lost his hair and started wearing bad jumpers.

The final member of the Groucho squad was a chef, a Frenchman named Charles Fontaine. He was credited with inventing the fishcake, but that wasn't why I liked him. He just liked cooking and enjoying himself. He wasn't part of the fame rat race. I made records with Duffy and I made merry with Keith and Damien and Charles.

During the making of *The Great Escape* there were people outside the studio, outside all our houses. The recording process was interrupted by TV appearances, awards shows and late nights. There were journalists in the studio control room, observing the band at work, photographers taking pictures of us recording our parts and picking our noses. We all had our own circles of friends – it would have been weird if we hadn't – but we still spent more time together than with anybody else.

We got a lot of fan mail. Ninety per cent of fan mail says the same thing. The majority of letters are written by a small number of people who write lots of fan mail. They didn't just write to us, they wrote to everybody, asking for photographs, autographs, tickets, favours and so on. Then there's the other 10 per cent, from people who had something particular to say to all of us, or one of us, because we'd moved them in some peculiar way. Some of it was beautiful and lifted my heart. Some of it was very, very scary. Graham seemed to get the hairiest stuff; he showed me photographs of people maiming themselves and threatening the worst if he wouldn't help them. My weird ones tended to veer towards pornography, which I was much more comfortable with.

One of the first things we recorded for *The Great Escape* was 'Stereotypes', which we were all very excited about at the time. We thought that it would be the first single. The demo version of 'The Universal' had a calypso feel. It was a tune and a half, using Mozart-style chord suspensions and Bacharach-flavour modulation, but we couldn't get the arrangement quite right. We battled with it for two days, on and off, and were just about to give up when Damon hit upon the string figure that ultimately became the intro. After that, everything clicked into place at once. That was two good ones in the bag. There was a baroque oompah song about Balfe selling Food Ltd and running away to live in a big house in the country, but that was just a joke.

We were halfway through recording *The Great Escape* when we played a one-off gig at Mile End Stadium in east London. It was a huge outdoor show. We'd broken out of the usual circuit of arenas into the big time. I don't know how many people it held, maybe twenty-five thousand. It was a stadium. We were used to playing to large audiences at festivals, but this was a home crowd. It was a rainy day in a part of town not normally associated with rock and roll, but it was a hot ticket and it wouldn't have mattered if it had snowed.

We played 'Country House'. We'd just finished recording it and although it was an odd one, Streetie suggested it might go down well live. I had to concentrate harder than usual on what I was doing as it was the first time we'd played it. I remember looking up after making a mistake halfway through the first chorus to see if anyone had noticed and the whole crowd was bouncing as one, waving their arms in time and smiling as they squashed each other senseless. By the last chorus they were all singing it. When that happens that means it's a single.

It was a strange day overall. I was expecting it to feel like a crowning moment, but I remember being surrounded by a lot of people I didn't particularly want to see. Blur had become public property.

Battle of the Bands

The day after the show at Mile End we flew to America, where we were still playing in bars. It was a blessed relief to be incognito, free again to have random adventures with girls in red cars without it turning up in the Sunday newspapers.

We'd all suffered a bit from tabloid shame. Graham was going through a phase of getting run over by cars. Damon's ex-girlfriend, who he'd once written a sickly, sentimental ballad about, sold her story to one of the more ghastly newspapers. She looked small and plain in the photograph, not like in the song.

The stories came thick and fast. One tabloid had me dating Helena Christensen. According to the front page of the *Daily Sport* I was involved in a lesbo-slut triangle. Another tabloid had me down for a make-up artist who was servicing the whole of Browns. The *Star* printed a photo of me with a music journalist called Sylvia Patterson. None of it was true. Sylvia sued the *Daily Star* and got five hundred quid. She was thrilled about that and bought me a drink.

I discovered another bar in Endell Street: the Mars Bar. It was open for an hour longer than Freud's. I went there with the barmaids from Freud's after that shut. All the girls who worked in Freud's were pretty. It was that kind of a place. I was very at home in the Mars. It was a good building, a five-storey town house with a restaurant on the ground and first, and a mad chef in the cellar. Freddy, the Dutch owner, offered jobs to the barmaids I brought with me. He was grateful to me for bringing them round there and gave me a set of keys to say thank you. He asked me to replace what booze my friends and I drank, but we could help ourselves. It was a happy arrangement and I tried not to abuse it.

'Country House' was pencilled in for high-summer release. It seemed like more than just another record. It felt like the world was changing. The band's influence had become so noteworthy that even the Labour Party had their eye on us. Damon went to the Houses of Parliament to see Tony Blair and came to the flat with a couple of bottles of House of Commons gin afterwards. I could imagine Damon looking the future Prime Minister right in the eyes and saying, 'What?' and Tony Blair saying, 'Excuse me?' and Damon saying, 'WHAT MATE?' and making him feel uncomfortable. This was one of the times when Damon had the gun and the other guy had the little stick. People were shouting, 'Je-sus, Je-sus' at Damon, quite a lot at gigs. He didn't need a pat on the back from anybody. Mike Smith had a big new office all of a sudden. He had been trying to sign a band called Oasis. They were from Manchester. Their first album was doing well and their girlfriends were always in Browns. They were signed to Creation Records where Dave's wife worked. She called me when their single went to number one and asked if I knew where they could have a party. I was the party guy. She booked the Mars Bar and we all went along. It was just another night in the Mars Bar. I went to the Groucho and they went to Browns and I thought no more about it.

Their album was selling fast and the music press started to draw comparisons between the two acts. I didn't really have any strong feelings about them. The singer had a good voice, but the music was honky. They were quite a different thing from Blur. They seemed to have a lot to say about us. I always sniggered when they slung their muck in our direction. Both bands were in the papers quite a lot and journalists would ask us what we thought about them and no doubt they had to answer lots of questions about us. They worked themselves up into quite a froth. I always dodged questions about other bands.

Oasis kept rising to the bait, like dogs barking at cats. We seemed to be the main thing they talked about. The *NME* particularly liked to stir things up and antagonise them. They definitely wanted to see a fight. Record companies usually cooperate with each other with big releases. Not this time. Both bands were pencilled in to release the lead singles from their new albums on the same day and nobody wanted to budge.

Damien Hirst directed the video for 'Country House'. It used the language of breasts and bottoms. Graham's new girlfriend was on a crusade against that kind of thing. She had a real zeal for it. She hated the video, and us. Particularly me, I think. Graham became quite despondent. He was the only person in the whole country who wasn't interested in the record war. As the release date drew nearer, everything escalated to a full-on frenzy. Everything.

I suppose if I was trying to explain to a very old lady what I did for a living, which I do have to from time to time, I would have said, 'I'm a musician, I make records and behave appallingly. It's great.' If the old lady said, 'Do you mean like Oasis?' I would have to say, 'Yes, exactly.' There wasn't that much difference between the two bands and, when viewed from a little old lady's point of view, they were pretty much the same thing. That said, I think on the whole old ladies prefer Blur to Oasis. Oasis probably had the edge with 'geezers' and 'lads'. As the insults flew and grew, what might have been a page three, five or seven story became a matter of national interest and a front-page news item. The week the records came out I went to stay with Damien in Devon. He had bought a farmhouse on Exmoor. Phones didn't work there, but I kept up with what was happening. It was impossible to avoid. There was something in the papers every day. It was on the television news, on the radio. It was on the breeze, even. I found out we were number one in a car on the way back to London, listening to the top forty countdown like everyone else. There was a party in Soho and Graham surprised everyone by trying to jump out of the window.

Here it was, the great national success story, but I think we were all confused. Damon was trapped inside the most famous face in the country and he couldn't buy a bottle of beetroot juice without causing a sensation. Graham felt he'd gained the world and lost his soul, that the juggernaut of attainment had compromised his principles. I think he felt he'd lost control of what he wanted the band to be, and that we'd made a terrible mistake. I didn't think we'd compromised, but I had lost the thing I loved the most. Justine was still the only woman I'd had anything approaching a sophisticated emotional connection with. Everything else had been skin-deep and selfish.

Apart from Belgium, where things had inexplicably cooled off, there was hysteria across the whole of Europe. In Italy we were mobbed, we had police escorts in Portugal. Shops were closed for us. Roads were closed. We were trapped inside a radio station in Madrid and our private jet had to wait with its engines running while the Guardia Civil extricated us. Even they all wanted our autographs. There were thousands of screaming people outside. The screaming at gigs was deafening. From the end of summer to the start of Christmas, the screaming never stopped. It's really bad for your ears. Graham didn't like it at all. He wanted to play his guitar out of tune and draw monsters.

Proper Girls

We had a fortnight off for Christmas. I went to the House of Commons and got drunk. It was good in there. It was reassuring that there were so many clever people doing their best, behaving responsibly and acting for the greater good. I met Clare Short, MP, on the way out. She's my favourite politician. I kissed her and said, 'Happy Christmas, darling.' I was still enjoying my lack of responsibilities. Being able to have whatever I wanted, whenever I wanted, had made me grotesque and self-centred, but there was a huge upside to being cash rich and morally bankrupt.

I had rather a lot of girlfriends, particularly in London. There were three girls in the flat when I woke up a few days before Christmas Eve. Francesca had appeared all of a sudden a few days before and she was nice. Lisa was usually at Browns, but that had closed for Christmas. Tabitha was a catwalk model. She was astonishingly pretty. That face had catapulted her from Petersfield via Tokyo, where I met her, in the Lexington Queen, to the most exclusive enclaves of New York City and the most fabulous houses in The Hamptons. It was a ticket, her face; a skeleton key for every door there is. There was no room that wouldn't have been enhanced by her presence. She turned heads and flipped brains over. She was never that famous, but she had everything that famous people have and more. People stared and wanted to talk to her, wanted to follow her. In a way fame would have weighed her down. She didn't need to be famous. It was kind of beneath her. She had a unique quality of unaffected, lighter than anything, beauty. That was enough for everybody. It's the most precious and sought-after quality in the universe and she had it. When someone has that, they really don't need anything else. An endless stream of billionaires, singers and cool daddies sought her company.

A lorryload of clothes arrived and we all dressed up. I wanted nothing more than to go and play the trivia machine in the Crown at Seven Dials. Doing the washing up with three beautiful women is pretty riveting. Sitting in an empty pub is blissful. We had some cocktails in Freud's, as it was on the way.

Lisa was good fun, a shrewd operator. She'd had a few famous boyfriends. The gene pool of the famous is quite tiny. Everyone in the public eye seemed to be shagging the same handful of girls. Even in other countries, girls I met knew everyone I knew, or so it seemed. It was hard to break out of the circle. Lisa was as unavoidable as taxes. Streetwise, half Jamaican. She could sing and had a record deal, but that didn't come in to why anyone liked her. She just knew what boys were thinking. She always knew something that I didn't that I really needed to know. I suppose that's the definition of a beautiful woman. Making records has got nothing to do with it.

We all stayed up for a few days at my house, dancing to the Bee Gees in the Mars Bar and playing cards. I called my mum on Christmas Eve and said I was coming for Christmas and bringing a girl called Francesca with me. I didn't think she could handle all three of them. I grabbed a Stilton from the cheese shop and we jumped on the train.

It was nice to be in Bournemouth. We ran into Danny Collier, the cool kid who used to get the bus every day, and went back to his parents' house for some whisky. I'd sometimes dreamed of leaving and coming back like this from conquering the world. I did what I said I was going to do. I showed those fuckers.

Maybe my mum didn't see the all-conquering hero. She just saw a drunken buffoon, a glittering ponce with a huge grin all over his stupid face of the moment. She knew the neighbours were all dying to come round and see the famous person, and here he was singing songs about red knickers and trying to buy a horse on Christmas Day.

On Boxing Day I went back to London to get Tabitha and took her to a hotel where I'd always wanted to stay, in Corfe Castle in rural Dorset. Suddenly we were alone and it was very still and quiet. Immaculate. We walked to Kimmeridge, my favourite place, and I built a big bonfire. There's absolutely nothing to do there, just fossils and shells and rock pools. It's where you realise if you love someone or not. I felt a bit bored. It was surprising. She was possibly the most beautiful woman in the world. I thought success would be the answer to everything. I'd climbed a hill and seen a mountain in the distance. I climbed the mountain and I saw the moon. I somehow got to the moon and realised I'd left what I loved behind in another world. I missed Justine. I'd come all this way to realise I really was happiest with what I already had. It was a journey that had to be made. I wanted it all. I'd never felt I wanted to escape from Justine. I'd just lost her. I just wanted to sit and be quiet with her, listen to her thoughts and make her laugh.

People were arriving back in London. I went to the Atlantic Bar. I handed my coat in and the girl gave me ticket number 007 and winked at me. God, she was pretty. It was relentless. When I woke up on the floor in Endell Street there was someone trying to suck my cock. It was one of the staff from the Groucho. I clipped him round the ear and he scarpered.

I was woken again mid-morning. Someone was throwing stones at the window. It was Damon. He never rang the doorbell. He said he was having a bad time. I said, 'You want to hear what's just happened to me, mate.' That cheered him up a bit, but I hadn't seen him like this before. He was really suffering. Everywhere he went he was tormented by Oasis's music. The balance of power had shifted. Their album was outselling ours. We drank some tea and he told me he was going to Iceland.

Ten days later he called and he sounded like a new man. He said, 'Get yourself over. It's heaven up here.'

7

regroup

Divas

In interviews we were often asked who we wanted to meet the most. Pretty soon those people started turning up everywhere. I never expected to meet them, let alone not be able to avoid them.

Graham was quite absorbed by a French diva called Françoise Hardy. He talked about her in interviews sometimes, especially in France. Françoise liked our records, too, and wanted to record a version of the ballad 'To the End', in French. We jumbled, hungover, on to the Eurostar to have lunch with her. The French don't have a royal family. Instead of having one monarch for everybody, everybody seems to have a slightly noble quality in France. If they could have voted for a king, they probably would have had Serge Gainsbourg. He was a cross between a poet, a singer and a tramp. He made some good records and seduced all the most beautiful women in France. That's what French kings should be getting up to. He was dead, from Gitanes and pastis, and she was married to a film director, but she was a fair queen to his king.

Paris was yet another parallel universe of nice surprises and new smells. I really liked the people at the French record company. It was quite a small office in Paris. They were a bit like a band, the staff. Even the drivers seemed cool enough to have record deals themselves. They added flair and finesse to all bad traffic situations. The people who looked after us genuinely enjoyed being with us and wanted to show us the finest restaurants, the best nightclubs and all the wonderful things in life.

Madame Hardy lived in a secluded, sumptuous apartment block in Montparnasse. It was all painted black inside and full of sunshine and exquisite treasures. Serge Gainsbourg's pinball machine was in the corner of the salon. There was a cheeseboard with some very rare cheeses and exotic accompaniments – figs and dates, gooseberries, even. The first thing she said was, ''Oo like cheese?' It was practically a dream sequence. I answered, in French. None of the scenarios we had improvised at Goldsmiths' French conversation classes had been about being invited to Françoise Hardy's apartment and shown an enormous cheeseboard. I suppose it's quite unlikely. It was why I'd wanted to learn French all along, though. It all made sense now.

She explained the cheese, to break the ice. Having the cheese explained is one of life's great pleasures. It is a moment to step outside of the traffic and into the senses. Here was one from the Alsace region that was so smelly that it was illegal to take it on public transport. There was a ewe's milk variety from Corsica, rolled in spices; a sharp, hard cheese from the Pyrenees and so on. I'd never seen any of them before.

She was a truly beautiful woman, around fifty, skinny as an elf and confident, yet delicate. She looked good in that black apartment. It really set off her light poise and bearing. In her grace, she was a balancing act. Graham was chewing his fingers off and trying to smoke a cigarette on one of the huge sofas. Damon cut the nose off the Brie, which is extremely bad manners, sniffed, and said, 'Are we fackin doin' this, or what?' She really liked him straight away, you could tell. She started to talk about her husband, and how Damon reminded her of him. He was in the jungle, or something suitably swashbuckling. It was an enchanted afternoon. If there's such a thing as making it, she'd made it. She had everything money could buy and beauty could bring. She was fabulous with a fabulous life and fabulous friends. Life was all about buying cheese, large yachts, art and the freedom and great quiet of huge wealth. The security and abracadabra of immortal celebrity status throughout France was assured. It was nice being Françoise Hardy, and nice being with her.

In the early days of the band, Damon had expressed a soft spot for Martha from Martha and the Muffins, but we never heard from Martha. My favourite record was *Strange Weather*, by Marianne Faithfull. It's a collection of classy laments that she delivers in her knackered baritone. I loved that voice. I don't think I could have coped with working in a supermarket if it hadn't been for *Strange Weather*.

The very first time I'd been completely spellbound by music was watching a mechanical organ at a steam rally in Dorset when I was a toddler. My mother tells me I stood in front of it for hours in a trance. Christmas carols, Ray Conniff, Prokofiev, the songs from *Bugsy Malone*, Dexy's Midnight Runners, Mike Oldfield, New Order and countless others all held me in their spell at one time or another, but *Strange Weather* was the record that Justine and I had fallen in love to.

I went to a party in Chelsea with Keith and Helen Terry. She'd sung backing vocals in Culture Club's 'Church of the Poison Mind'. She was a television producer now. People who'd done odd things like that kept turning up in other guises, especially at the Groucho. I have no idea whose house it was. It was a big mansion and Princess Leia was alone in the dining room, unconscious. Rifat Ozbek was in the kitchen. In the next room there was Marianne, sitting on a sofa, holding court and smoking theatrically. I could tell something was going to happen.

When I used to go to Peter Robinson's house on Tuesdays, we'd play a game we called Barnes and Kidd. They were famous football players. Barnes used to run up the wing and knock the ball to Kidd who'd nod it into the goal. Every Tuesday we played that game in the alley behind the stamp shop, practising it, polishing it and fantasising. We played half in the alley and half in our imaginations. I loved football, but we were always getting thumped because ours was only a small school. We actually had a handful of good players and when the junior six-a-side tournament took place one sunny Saturday in May we got through to the quarter-finals, much to everyone's amazement. At that stage we faced a school that had thrashed us earlier in the year. We held them to a draw until the last minute, when Martyn Whittingham danced up the right flank and floated a perfect cross into the six-yard box. I was on the end of it. I'll never forget the feeling as I headed that ball home. It was my finest moment.

Ten years later I sat on the X1 bus on the way back from Salisbury to Bournemouth in the first spring sunlight of late February with Justine. It was the first time we'd gone on an outing together. I was falling in love with her, but she had a boyfriend in a band and I worked in a supermarket. I'd said, 'My breath stinks', and she'd said, 'Let me smell it.' I put my mouth up to her nose and opened it and, completely unexpectedly, she'd kissed me, for the first time. That was better than football.

Music had been so important to me for so long and Marianne had made my favourite record ever and there she was. 'Hello, Marianne,' I said, 'I'm Alex. From Blur.' She said, 'Ah, dear Alex, I'm going to roll a banger, and you're going to write me a song. Deal?' That was right up there, too.

I went to stay with her for the weekend, to record a vocal. I could really talk to Marianne. She'd been through everything, from top of the pops, to the bottom of the slops, from being the most famous daughter of the sixties to a smackhead on the streets of Soho. She'd had it all and chucked it all away. Now she lived in a cottage made of shells in the demesne of a big castle in County Kildare. She had a grand piano and a chef, but that was all. I wonder if you really need anything else.

I'd tried snogging her at her friend's house a couple of weeks before when I'd gone to play the demo to her. I'd passed out after a half-bottle of eau-de-vie and woken up on the sofa in the morning with her bending over me. I just thought I'd give it a go, you know. She said, 'You dog! Do you want some coffee?' I said, 'Oh, fuck! I've got to go to Iceland. What's the time?' She said, 'It's time to have some coffee and go to Iceland.' It certainly was.

Iceland

It's hard to stay really alive, to keep really stimulated. Hedonism is a full-time job. To keep finding new ecstasies and not get stuck in old routines takes all of a man's might and all the world's serendipity.

Iceland is somewhere else altogether. It has different geography from the rest of the world. It doesn't look that big on maps, but when I got there it was gigantic. It's got big weather, distant horizons and hundreds of miles of nothing at all. It's not really built on the human scale. Maybe that's what it is. Trees are usually there to help to put things in proportion, but there aren't any trees in Iceland. It goes straight from little bushes to huge mountains and volcanoes. It's quite a new place, geologically. Actually it's the newest land mass on earth. It burped out of a submarine volcano not long ago at all, and is still a planetary building site. It's totally topsy-turvy. The water is either frozen solid or steaming and the landscape, with its petrified lava flows, gives an impression of fluidity. Reykjavik is only about the size of Bournemouth. It's very cosy and clean. The water in the river that runs through the centre is absolutely pure and tastes delicious. There are docks with fishermen and parks with no tramps in. You can't really be homeless that far north. Damon hadn't stopped talking about it since he'd first been in January. He had stayed a few weeks, written some songs and accumulated an entourage. It was about midnight when we went out. It was still sunny though. There is one high street of shops and bars and it was thronging with people. We stood on a roof terrace and watched the good times roll. There was a semi-official welcoming committee with sausage rolls and brennivin. Brennivin is the local tipple. It's definitely got cumin in it, and alcohol. It's drunk in little snifters alongside a tall, thin, cool glass of lager.

From the terrace, everywhere I looked there was something else that caught my eye: a distant wilderness, a volcano, a silent sea, a couple snogging, a startlingly beautiful girl. It was all new and interesting. I sipped on a beer and drank the views. A few people had asked if I'd seen any pixies yet. Pixies are a thing in Iceland. People became more friendly when I said that I thought I might have seen one, actually. Thor said it was more likely an elf, when I described it to him. Thor asked me what I wanted. I was beginning to get used to that happening, recently: strangers asking me if I needed anything. I said I wanted to go horse riding, please. He said that was easy and before I had time to finish my beer we were driving up a dirt track in a large, old car. First they had to catch the ponies. A couple of Vikings ran around shouting and chasing, falling over and laughing. Pretty soon they'd caught a couple. Saddles appeared, but there was only one hat. Thor said, 'This horse is good boy, no trouble, don't need hat so much. If you want hat take this horse. Maybe this other a bit, you know, need hat.' It was two a.m. and the sun had come back after an hour's twilight. It just makes a big circle in the sky in summer. The ground was all mossy and soft. I hadn't ridden a horse before. I'd been trying to for ages. Thor said, 'Just hold on.'

The guys who had caught the horses were riding around bareback and falling off occasionally, laughing and swearing. I had a slug of brennivin and climbed on the one that didn't need a hat while everybody held it still. It was fine. It just stood there. Soon everyone who wanted a horse had one and we were cantering up a green mountain alongside a stream. Reykjavik and the sea were way down behind us. I hadn't known any of these people for more than three hours. Most of them believed in elves. It was only twelve hours since I'd woken up on a sofa in Barnes, southwest London, with Marianne bending over me. Things were happening fast. I don't think you need to be famous to find yourself riding a white horse at two o'clock in the morning, it can happen to anyone, but it was the rate at which unusual things were happening which was overwhelming.

There were quite a lot of girls outside the studio, and following us around everywhere. It's considered very bad form to have sex with girls who hang around outside. I tried it in Barcelona and it was great. I didn't always sleep with every girl that I met – it wasn't all I wanted to do – but sometimes it was all they wanted to do. I didn't seem to want sex as much when it was constantly available. Riding horses up mountains was fine.

I went with Damon to a little bar just off the high street. It was called Kaffibarrin. There and then, the owner, name of Inqvar, offered Damon a stake in the business if he drank there while we were in town. Drinks would be free. There didn't seem to be a downside. We needed an HQ. We were introduced to all the high-ranking booze heads as they arrived. Here was a poet; here was the minister for something or other; here was the singer from Fonkstrasse, Reykjavik's hottest new band. Then Einar from the Sugarcubes arrived. I'd been wondering when he'd turn up again. I greeted him like a long-lost brother. Inqvar told everyone that it was Damon's bar now. I don't know if Damon ever saw any money out of the partnership, but there was always somewhere to go. The place was rammed by the time the sun came up again and I stumbled outside to throw up. It seemed to be quite acceptable, like burping in Japan; a lot of people were doing it. It was a madhouse. It was nice outside. A long-legged elfin girl with olive skin was tittering at me. I said, 'I'm going home, do you want to come?' She said, 'Oh, OK.' That's how I met Magnea, who I suppose I nearly married.

She lived above the pet shop on the high street, had a philosophy degree from Paris and very long legs. She's the only girl I've met who could drink more than me. She liked whisky, but we tried everything. Halfway up a mountain on a horse is nothing. It's quite easy to describe geography, but Iceland really started with her, and I couldn't go back now, for all its wonders, without being overcome with thoughts of her. She was pure mischief: a pixie.

Manhattan

Damien had a show in New York. It was at the Gagosian Gallery in SoHo. Larry Gagosian, the proprietor, is the number one art dealer in the world. He's said to know the whereabouts in the world of every piece of modern art worth more than a million dollars. He's mustard.

A whole lorryload of Dolce & Gabbana catwalk couture turned up at the flat. I picked the best suit. I could see my face in it. There was a matching bodice and pointy shoes. I got dressed up, hailed a taxi and went to New York for the weekend for Damien's show. I just took my passport and my wallet. There weren't many pockets. I figured I could stay awake for three days, no problem, so I wouldn't need to worry about a hotel. Something always turns up in New York, anyway.

SoHo was the latest bit of New York to be beautiful. Initially it was great not having a bag or a hotel to worry about. I got a taxi straight to the gallery. The show was opening the next day.

Art shows are never ready until the last minute and there were lots of skinny women on mobiles and beardy kids building things. Damien had stopped swearing and had a steely kind of a vibe. All the most rich, most ghastly people who buy art live in America, and they were all coming. America has proper rich people, like it has proper famous people, and fatties. They're just richer and famouser and fatter in America.

I went to a bar called Toad Hall with a guy called Michael. As soon as you arrive in New York, you're off to some new place with some new face. Toad Hall was a proper American bar. In many ways it was similar to the Good Mixer, Graham's pub. The pockets on the pool table were bigger. The jukebox had one good song on it, 'Cool for Cats' by Squeeze. If you're at home in one bar, you're at home in them all. I bought the barman a drink, played pool with Michael and wondered what was about to happen. You can never tell in New York. It's a boom-bust economy. One minute you can be on the twenty-eighth floor of a portered apartment block in mid-town asking for fresh lemons, the next thing you know you've lost all your friends and are walking along a dark street with no shoes on. That is what happened next. I'd thrown my shoes out of the taxi window. They were really hurting. My feet aren't catwalk size. I was ejected from the apartment for saying that Blind Melon were crap. I didn't realise it was the singer's apartment. I've since come to like them, but he died shortly after my visit. I wanted to tell him I'd made a mistake, but it was too late. That's how it is in Manhattan. It all happens so fast. You just get the one shot in all your encounters. I made it back to Toad Hall but there was no one I recognised. When you've lost all your friends in New York, it's time to have a dry martini.

The New York dry martini is a bit of Western voodoo. It's the ultimate cocktail. Administered correctly, it parts the clouds of fear and the brilliant sunshine of resolve floods the darkest corners of the mind. 'Bombay Sapphire, up, with an olive!' I said to the barman. That's gin, shaken with ice and the tiniest dash of vermouth, served in a conical martini glass, with an olive. Some people like a lemon twist, or even a raspberry. Olive is best. You can tell how good a martini is by looking at it. It should be tiny, not more than a gulp, if you want to knock it straight down. There should be a mist of condensation on the glass, indicating that the contents are ice-cold. A good martini is a pure concentrated triumph of minimalism. Some bars keep their gin in the freezer so that the ice doesn't melt during the shaking; that keeps the final product as undiluted as possible. When made with very cold gin, it's called a Gibson. Not many barmen know this, though, and it's pointless trying to explain. I've tried. You just have to find a man who knows and stick with him.

The Toad Hall martinis were big and sloppy with whopping great olives. At least they were made with good gin. I sat on the barstool, sparked up a Camel and cast my clearing thoughts wide. That was when I knew I had to get some magnets. I had a really good chew over the properties of magnets, a whole martini's worth. They suddenly seemed very strange and interesting. Why did they want to stick to each other, and why did they have two ends?

I said, 'Where can I get some magnets?' to the next guy at the bar. He said, 'Canal Street, they've got all kinds. Yikes, what a nasty martini. It's too long. The gin wasn't cold enough. They should keep it in the refrigerator.'

He took some postcards out of a jacket that had a lot of pockets and began to hunt for a pen. He offered me a postcard, which I wrote to Magnea. I explained to her that I was in New York, looking for magnets. I bought the guy a beer. His name was Robert, he was an artist and his father was a scientist, and he knew a lot about magnets. We decided to get some good martinis. I called Kelly. Kelly ran Spy. In London, going out was straightforward. The Groucho was the best place to go. Everybody knew that and everybody went there. In New York, the best place to go was always changing. You'd go somewhere in February and Jasmine Guinness and Liberty Ross would be there and you'd leave with Chloë Sevigny, and then if you went back to the same spot in April it would have closed and the whole neighbourhood become completely passé and unmentionable. Spy had a good eighteen months at the top. It was a huge cave with big sofas and small martinis, low lighting, and all the most expensive and impossible women in New York.

'Kelly, it's Alex James, cheers, mate. Yeah, great, look, I'm round the corner, but I've lost my shoes. Is that going to be all right? Two of us. Of course I'm drunk! Best behaviour, promise. See you in a mo, then.'

It's most pleasing to be told by a door gorilla that there is absolutely no way you can come in without any shoes, asking for the boss and being greeted by him with open arms and escorted to a table. Robert had taken his shoes off and hung them around his neck. His hands were covered in oil, his hair was a mad frizz and he was wearing supermarket clothes. He was good-looking though.

We had a couple of martinis and went back to Toad Hall. Angela was there. She was Damien's ex-girlfriend. She'd lost everyone, too. It was getting late and the three of us went to play snooker. She was quite good at it. I crashed in her room at The Gramercy Park Hotel, woke up, got some new shoes and a toothbrush. Things always work out eventually in New York.

I managed to stay up for the rest of the weekend and took the redeye back to Heathrow, arriving Monday morning. I wasn't allowed to take any of the magnets on to the plane, though. They set off every buzzer in the airport. I got to the studio in time, but I was in pieces. I could hardly speak. Damon's face was as tightly set as Damien's had been before his show when I arrived at the session, in my ragged couture. Everything was set up and ready to go. As soon as Graham started playing the guitar I felt superhuman. I picked up the bass and music was pouring out of me. Melody had an intensity that it lacked in my everyday state of mind. The music collected and connected all the strange emotions I was brimming with. By midday we'd written 'Beetlebum'. It was a completely new sound.

Still, it was relentless. It was Dave's birthday and he wanted to go out. London was in full swing, Cool Britannia was in business and governed from its headquarters, the Groucho Club, which was getting bigger and more packed with out-of-control success stories. I took Dave there. He hated everything about it and had a really good time. The walking wounded were returning from New York and there were cheers as unaccounted-for stragglers arrived.

Mayfair

I was missing Iceland. I thought about Magnea sometimes, living in that faraway place. We had similar minds. She was as full of hedonistic abandon as I was. I wondered what life with her would be like. She was carefree, clever and pretty and it was impossible to say where life would whisk her. She had everything; she had the whole world at her fingertips and the whole world wanted to grab her and swallow her. Damon had found something in Iceland, too, not a woman but a place of sanctuary. He wanted to record all his vocals in Reykjavik.

We both couldn't wait to get back there. Graham wasn't keen on leaving Camden. The four of us laid down more backing tracks at Mayfair Studios in Primrose Hill. Maison Rouge had become too smelly.

Primrose Hill is a precious enclave of beautiful houses and beautiful people just to the north of Regent's Park, a quiet and pretty haven. A trip to the ciabatta man at lunchtime would often yield a minor celebrity encounter.

Mayfair was a new studio and a new way of working. Until

then, everything had been recorded on to tape but Streetie had a new computer-recording system. Songs and parts could be edited, slowed down, speeded up, reversed, quantised and cut and pasted together very easily. 'Essex Dogs', the last track on the album, used a lot of computer trickery. Musically, it's probably the most accomplished thing the band have done, with quite sophisticated counterpoint and cross rhythms, virtuoso playing. Those are never the ones people remember, though.

'Song 2' was about the simplest thing we've ever done, and the quickest. Dave set up two drumkits and he and Graham played them both at the same time. The loud guitar in the chorus is actually a bass going through a home-made distortion box. The whole thing was done in about fifteen minutes. I had a bad hangover and I felt horrible. It's a nasty record and it wouldn't have sounded so nasty if I'd gone to bed early the night before. We did it without thinking too much about it and felt better afterwards.

'Beetlebum' and 'Song 2', the two big singles on the *Blur* album, our fifth, were written much the same way as we'd written everything, around a chord sequence or riff or melody initiated by Damon, four guys in a room with no windows, kicking arse. Some of the other songs on that record were more individual efforts. We were all making records with other people and we didn't need each other so much as we had, but when the four of us were all on form, collaborating, was when the best music was made.

Graham and I were both the worse for wear one Friday morning and popped into the Queen, a pub on the corner of Regent's Park. For some reason we had our Ivor Novello awards with us. I guess we were showing off. They'd just been delivered to the studio as we were leaving for the pub. Among musicians, 'Ivors' are probably the most coveted of all the industry gongs. They are awarded for songwriting. Having gold and platinum discs on display at home is in bad taste. I gave those to my mum. I always find it peculiar when people have big pictures of themselves on the walls, too. It's not quite right. Most awards get lost, given away or broken on the night they are received. Even if they survive the evening, awards belong in offices, not in the home. Apart from Ivor Novellos. You can put those on your mantelpiece and people in the know will think all the better of you for it. Graham and I were sitting on stools in 'the top Queen' with the awards sitting on the bar in front of us. They are quite distinctive, a small figurine of a Muse.

The pub was quite empty. We sat there, easy in each other's company. Graham and I so often spent time in an empty pub, somewhere or other. I hadn't really seen much of him lately, because I'd been in Iceland with Damon and also because he had a new girlfriend. I could talk to Graham about anything, and he usually knew more than I did, but he needed looking after. That was part of his charm. He was very lovable. There was no one cooler than Graham. He always fucked things up more fantastically than I could ever manage, which, somehow, I respected him for. If I was drunk, he managed to make me look less ridiculous by being always a little bit drunker. If I was worried about something irrational, it usually turned out that he was slightly more worried about something slightly further fetched. I worried about a lot of things. Unsupportable anxiety was commonplace, especially in the mornings, when the gross misconduct of the night before came flooding back. Despite all our triumphs and conquests we all worried and felt just as hopeless and stupid as everybody else.

All four of us drove each other into rages occasionally but we all wore each other's company well, usually. I felt closer to Graham than anybody, though. He was my best friend; not just in the band: in the world. I would have sat next to him at school. There was nothing I ever had to hide from him, no matter how heinous it seemed. He was totally absorbed by music and had such an obviously brilliant musical mind that I don't think he ever felt the need to demonstrate anything to anybody, unless he was in the mood. Most people accept the mindless drudgery of record promotion. It was painful for him. He was only interested in playing the guitar. Music is a natural, continuous quality and it flowed from him.

I was trying to draw Magnea's nose, to show Graham exactly what it looked like. It was a good nose. An elderly gentleman came to the bar to order a drink. He said, 'I've got one of those.' I said, 'What? One of Magnea's noses?' He said, 'No, one of those – an Ivor.' We didn't believe him at all, so he went home and got it. Then he put it on the bar next to ours. His name was Sandy, and he'd got his Ivor for writing the theme music to *Upstairs, Downstairs*. It happened to be Graham's favourite song ever. They became very involved after that, and I wandered back to the studio. Damon had put his award on one of the speakers behind the mixing desk. I put mine on the other one, to make a stereo pair. Many hours later, Graham arrived back at the studio with Sandy. Damon saw them stumbling through the front door on the CCTV. He said, 'Who the FUCK has Graham dragged in now?' I said, 'Don't worry, it's a songwriter he met in the pub.' 'Songwriter?' said Damon. 'Songwriter! He's a songwriter, is he? Has he got a fucking Ivor Novello award? No. I don't think so.' At which point Sandy fell through the door clutching a figurine in an outstretched hand.

Favourite Places

We all occupied different corners of London. Dave was married in Hampstead. Graham was a confirmed Camden Town person. He spent most of his time in the Good Mixer with his entourage, like it was his dressing room. He was cock of the roost there. It was a cul-de-sac though. There was never anyone new and interesting in that pub. Damon lived in Notting Hill. I find that part of town particularly irritating. It suits him because he thrives on antagonism. All the most annoying people in the world live in Notting Hill. The people who live there think they're it because they had dinner in a restaurant and that Damon Albarn was there and he was making such a fuss, and they're on the guest list for Reading because Hugo did the sponsorship marketing. Damon is the only cool person who lives in Notting Hill. Forget about the rest of them, they don't know Jack, even if they've got his phone number.

I loved living in the West End, the fountain of everything new and wonderful. The others muttered their disapproval about the company I was keeping. It's fair to say that the Groucho Club was not a wholesome place. Damon and Graham weren't the only ones who objected to it. To some people, it was objectionable overall in every way imaginable: a proudly exclusive, sugary cocktail of celebrity, money, frocks and genius. I loved it. In 1996, forget New York: the Groucho Club was the best place in the world to go for a drink. Famous people are the worst starfuckers of everybody and there's nothing that goes down better in the Groucho than the latest new famous person, and, just for a moment, that was me.

Like a toddlers' playgroup, the place was run almost entirely by women. There were men working behind the bar, but the power and the discipline were in the hands of no-messing matriarchs. Bollockings for atrocious behaviour were meted out with terrible feminine force, usually in the cold light of day, when offenders were confronted with a laundry list of misdemeanours. Gordanna was the most feared manageress. 'Forget about what Keith was doing, I'll be talking to him about that separately, you can't keep riding that bicycle down the stairs. Someone is going to get hurt.' 'What? Well, I'm not surprised you've got a sore leg. You're a bloody idiot. Do you want another Bloody Mary? And if you want to pay the pianist five hundred pounds to play "Wichita Lineman" for an hour, get him to come round your house and do it.' 'Well, I'm not surprised you can't remember, you're a fucking idiot. Honestly, Alex.'

In the Groucho it was sometimes hard to tell whether the person next to me at the bar was someone I'd recently met, or someone I recognised vaguely from off the television. Sometimes it was both. It didn't seem to matter too much. Quite regularly now people were making that kind of mistake with my face. 'Hey, don't I know you? I'm sure we've met.' They were always mortally embarrassed when they realised. Living behind a familiar face is like driving a flash car. There are always some people who'll want to put a big scratch on it, and you have to be careful where you park. The Groucho was the right kind of car park, but the thing that made it really special was that Damien was often there. Britpop was never a scene. It was a lot of not very brilliant bands copying two or three good ones, and the good bands never really saw eye to eye. The burgeoning art explosion was exactly the opposite. The artists were unified as a group and they relied on each other but they didn't plagiarise each other.

Damien's star was rising. He'd completely charmed the entire staff of the Groucho by buying them drinks, telling them jokes and doing drawings for them. They vied for his attention and the place was never closed to him. He could delight and attract people in a way that opened doors and arms, like Tabitha's face did. Even when he was wearing Prada he had a faintly agricultural mien. His main talent, and he had many, was that he was good at getting the best out of people. He raised everyone's game.

Damien was the undisputed king of the art set. The artists in his circle were like a huge band. Their work was all highly individual, but his ambition, charisma and acumen drew them all together. He was a true catalyst, he stimulated everybody and as they all tried to outsmart each other, the range and content of their work blossomed. The art crowd's appetite for each other and for everything raged and they decorated the dives of Dean Street with their presence. Soho was fizzing. It meant staying up all night could lead to interesting encounters. There was a big mad family of extraordinary people who didn't want to go to bed yet. I was drawn into the crowd by a cocktail of sexual chemistry and intellectual magnetism. Minds raced all through the night. It was inspiring. I found new reference points, my horizons broadened.

Damien's discourse was a combination of gags, poetry, repartee and swearing and his mind raced to the top and bottom of things and made strange connections. He loved making people change their minds and was good at it. Famous faces might turn heads, but he was someone who could turn minds inside out. He was part goblin and almost insane and could so easily have been in prison; but then you could say that about most of the Groucho's cast.

The Groucho led inevitably to other glitzy places. All great artists are great cooks and maybe great cooks are all great artists. Charles Fontaine, the fourth member of the gang, was partial to tripe and prone to huge fits of temper. He had been the chef at Le Caprice.

Damien was a big fan of swanky restaurants, the swankier and more expensive, exclusive and elitist, the better. The posh restaurant is part of the natural environment of the artist. The best restaurants are the ones with the best people in. Unless you're really hungry, people are far more interesting than food. A great restaurant makes the rest of the world seem very ordinary and that sensation of glamour is a hard thing to achieve. Very few places have glamour. Glamour makes hearts beat a bit faster, luxury makes hearts beat slower and, when the balance is right, you float away. Le Caprice is so discreet that you could walk right past it without realising it was there. You wouldn't ever walk past it because it's tucked at the bottom of a dead-end street behind Piccadilly.

To eat there is to leave a clamouring world behind and spend a couple of hours in the clouds. It's the best restaurant in the world. America is great for pizza and anything you can eat with your fingers, but they can't do the fiddly, classy stuff. There are restaurants in France where the food is better and the rooms are grander, but they are often full of ghastly rich non-French people boasting to each other in loud voices. Le Caprice is chic. From the moment I walked in for the first time and caught the mellow hum of hot gossip, until the brandies arrived, nothing could have been finer.

It was a long summer Sunday evening the first time I went there. We strolled up Piccadilly. I was wearing shorts from Deptford Market. It was easy to see why Keith and Damien irritated people. Damien was going through a phase of shouting exquisite obscenities whenever it went quiet and you just never knew what Keith was going to do next. I sometimes found it excruciatingly funny and begged them to stop, and sometimes I just begged them to stop. Their girlfriends were with us, and Jay Jopling, Damien's Old Etonian art dealer. The maître d' greeted Damien warmly and professionally. Then Damien whispered something in his ear that made him practically bend in two. No matter how drunk Damien was, he never lost the ability to make people split their sides, even sometimes people he'd really been annoying. He'd go to great lengths to win people over or exasperate them further. The jokes flowed continuously. I had tears streaming down my face, and pains in my sides.

There was slapstick, wit, wordplay, anecdote, funny faces and rude noises. Because he could deliver a joke so perfectly the punchline spent most of the time waiting in the distance as he elaborated and extemporised. A regular customer on the next table made a complaint about Damien's language, and having discovered who he was complaining about, came over to say hello. I think Jay managed to sell him a painting. Ideas flew out of Damien, like they fly out of everybody, but he was a man of action. He made his dreams come true.

Infinite Returns

It was such a relief to be on a plane to Iceland again and leaving all the madness behind. Thor sent a hundred and fifty Hell's Angels to escort us from the airport into Reykjavik. I went straight to Magnea's house and they all revved their engines outside the window.

Graham and Dave weren't interested in going to Iceland. All their parts were done, so they didn't really need to be there. There's no way I wouldn't have been there, even if I'd hated the place. But it really was the top of the world.

Magnea liked going to all the bad places, bars in the docks where the fishermen had fights and the place by the bus station where the bad alcoholics and mad people drank. She had the quality of glamour and those dives emphasised her beauty. She conjured a plain, everyday situation into a vivid, whirling world of wonder.

'Bastard.'

'Well, you've got three boyfriends, you're worse than I am.'

'Wanker.'

'Do you want a drink?'

'Fucker.'

I think we probably loved each other.

To start with there were quite a lot of girls outside her flat, waiting for me. By the end of the week, there were loads of boys outside. It was her three boyfriends and all their mates. I had to leave via the bathroom window to get to the studio.

Civilisation was no longer safe anywhere and so we went on an expedition to the interior. In the magazine on the aeroplane it said that the Icelandic interior was uninhabitable. I'd been intrigued by the thought of an inhospitable landscape. Surely you could live anywhere, if you were determined?

I was wrong. No one could live there. The otherworldliness starts with an eggy smell. It's not a smell that I could ever get used to. It's constantly updating itself with new overtones and flavours of the day, a multifaceted huge and invisible smellscape. When the wind changed, it seemed to present a new view of the smell, one that I couldn't have considered from the other side, or the back of it. It lurked and it thrusted and it wouldn't leave us alone.

Once we got through the stench, we were on to the ice. The ice goes on forever. I never managed to grasp the idea of 'forever' quite so clearly as on the Vatnajökull Glacier, Europe's largest. It's not just the scale of the thing. It's the timelessness and the immeasurable silence of the place. It goes beyond geography into the realms of planetary science with its astronomical proportion, a pure, elemental realm. We zoomed around on skidoos, unaffected by the passage of time in the perpetual sunlight, mountains in the distance and the sky blue and constant.

When we emerged, I went with Magnea to visit a poet called Buppi, who lived in a cottage by a lake at the bottom of a valley, which is only right. He was a mad-eyed sprite, bald as a baby and bright and playful as a stream. He was very engaging and I couldn't help myself from getting involved with his thoughts, which were quite complicated. We walked up a big hill, which is always a good thing to do with a poet. Magnea picked camomile flowers and we sat on the prow. 'Everyone in Iceland is a poet,' he declared. 'Wherever you look, there's a distant horizon. Everyone's standing at the centre of a very big circle.' It was true. The Icelandic people are a race apart. It's a very modern society. They're exceptionally well travelled, and resilient. The women are beautiful and the men are quite fearless. There is a Viking streak in all of them. A popular sport was driving bangers at full speed up the sides of U-shaped glacial valleys to see how far up the vertical face they could get. Sometimes the cars just fell off.

The great unknown was all around and all-prevailing. They flung themselves into it with bravado. Buppi was a genuine wise man and my brain was starting to overrev.

So much ice and water. Steaming out of the ground, falling from the sky and sitting in huge lakes, streams that tasted so sweet and cool. Iceland. The Vikings called it Iceland so that no one would bother invading it, and stashed all their beautiful women there.

We stopped at a frozen lake that had thawed at the edges. A small wooden hut stood alongside. The hut was built on top of a geothermic spring. There are geysers all over the place. This was quite a steady, calm one; some of them were explosively violent and drew crowds when they were erupting, but there was no one around for miles. We stripped naked and sat in the hut, feeling the supercolossal thrum of the molten core of the earth. It was a great sauna, the very best. When we could bear the heat no longer, we took a running plunge into the frozen lake. Then we needed to get back in the hut. It made our skin prickle.

Things were pretty mental everywhere. The band were booked in for a short tour of North America. I thought I'd have a couple of weeks off the booze for the duration and take stock of everything that was going on in my life.

I was in a band. Good. I was drinking too much, but I'd stopped. Good. I was shagging too much. Hmmm. Good. Writing songs for people whose music I'd always loved. Good. It was all good, but it didn't have Justine in it anywhere. I called her and invited her out to San Francisco. She said, 'Yes.'

Even when I went to bed early, all those miles and miles and miles and never knowing where the toilet was and having a new address every day, and new friends, just took it out of me. I wouldn't have swapped places with anyone, but it was still physically exhausting.

It wasn't as much fun without the bad things, but hangovers had become ordeals that hung around for days, like bad weather, dealing out every kind of pain, psychological torment, ache and torpor.

I thought as a rock star I owed it to people to enjoy myself to the absolute limit. It was a missed opportunity for everybody if I didn't. Turpitude, extreme immorality, is the privilege of the rock star. No one else would get away with it. Even film stars and footballers have to conduct themselves with some degree of common decency. They're all answerable to somebody. Making music is a self-indulgent business and success is just more wood for the bonfire. Absolutely every proper rock star in history has gone through a phase of self-indulgence of proportions inconceivable to the rest of the population. That's kind of what a rock star is. It would be dull to just turn up and play some songs and leave. It's not what everybody wants. There's nothing profoundly evil about what goes on backstage. It's just mucky.

Damien won the Turner Prize and put it behind the bar at the Groucho, twenty grand. It was a good time to have left the country. I wondered if I knew anyone normal any more. I unwittingly came across an article about Charles Fontaine's culinary genius in the first bookshop I went into when we arrived in Toronto. He was supposed to be my most normal friend and even he seemed to be big in Canada.

8

rocket science

Cavemen

It was hard to say what was going to turn up in the loo at the Groucho. One night in those toilets I got talking to a guy who said he had a twenty-thousand-year-old flute, so I gave him my number. Rarely for the Groucho, he called me in the morning and asked if I wanted to see it. We met at a warehouse in King's Cross. There are lots of warehouses around there, but this must have been the strangest. The entrance was nondescript. A steel gate on a grubby street gave on to a loading bay with the usual pallets and forklifts. We walked through more heavy doors into great rooms full of incalculable amounts of treasure of all kinds. There were Egyptian artefacts, sculptures from ancient Greece, manuscripts, icons and jewellery in endless, neat rows – all of them priceless. It was the property of the British Museum. The museum only displays a fraction of all its assets at any particular time, and this was one of several places where the nation's surplus hoard was stored, a holding bay. Some of the pieces would be loaned to other museums, some were being studied, some were just waiting there to come back into fashion. It would have made any vulgar New York billionaire art collector weep to peek in there. The warehouse setting was a good environment to see wonders like that. I had no desire to possess any of it. It was all too precious to have a private owner. The abundance of rarities was devastating. Some of the things were in glass cases, some were packed in boxes with labels stating their contents. They were free from any kind of marketing or presentation hocus-pocus, but everything there had some historical significance, and hundreds and thousands of years after it was made still had the power to take my breath away. It made Damien's stuff look piffling and flimsy by comparison.

The ancient musical artefacts section was on the third floor. There was an expert in these matters in attendance. I recognised a flute-type thing, a clay pipe with finger holes, but she said that was relatively recent, only a few thousand years old. The oldest musical instruments do date back twenty thousand years. Archaeological findings show that there was almost nothing in the way of art until twenty thousand years ago and then suddenly there was an almost instant gush of cave paintings, tools and musical instruments. The first instruments were drums, probably mammoths' skulls, bashed with mammoths' bones. Not much has changed in the drum world.

The earliest tonal instruments were made from reindeer toe bones. They're closer to a whistle than a flute to look at, but they are technically flutes because you blow across the hole, rather than down it. You get different notes in the harmonic series depending on how hard you blow. Of all the things in that warehouse, they were among the least obviously beautiful. If one turned up in the kitchen the morning after a big night, I wouldn't have said, 'Wow, someone's left this amazing thing here.' I'd probably have thrown it away before realising what it was. It didn't look like much, I must be honest. It didn't sound great either but those little crusty bones were where it all started. A primitive musical instrument made by a primitive scientist.

Twenty thousand years later, anyone sitting down at a piano is sitting on top of a huge mountain of accumulated knowledge. When you hold even the cheapest guitar, you're wielding a very sophisticated tool. The twelve-tone scale is a triumph of scientific understanding. It's such a perfect structure that it's rarely questioned or even understood by the people who use it. All musicians know how to tune up their instruments, but very few have any idea what they are actually doing as they tune. Musicians rarely have any more of an inkling of what music is than an electrician knows what electricity is.

All the really tricky business of the evolution of music has taken place, and it's not important to know everything. It's just important to know what sounds good. All anyone needs is one little idea. It can even be someone else's idea. All you've got to be able to do is pick the good ones. There are no rules that can't be broken in music making. Confidence is all-important. Things that are completely wrong can sound new and interesting if they are done with conviction.

Sometimes we struggled with songs and it paid off; sometimes we struggled and got nowhere. Sometimes it was easy. Our most popular song was written in fifteen minutes while we were waiting for a piece of gear to turn up. We just thrashed it out. I hadn't been to bed. None of us took it very seriously; it wasn't long enough to be a single and the only words you could hear were 'Woo-hoo'.

If musicians only talked about writing songs in interviews, they would be very dull to read. It's an exhilarating process though, songwriting. Writing a new song felt better than anything else that happened with the band. It was better than a hundred thousand people screaming at us, or sex with strangers, or meeting the Queen at Buckingham Palace. It always starts off with the certain feeling that I will never be able to do it. Then something always happens. Making music isn't something you do by thinking about it or talking about it; it's something that you do by doing it. The four of us would all play together and usually it was good. You can't usefully analyse it any further. The equations of music-making chemistry are complex. Turn up to work and turn up the volume.

Astronomers

I was reading the astronomy book for about the fifth time when I joined the British Astronomical Association. They sent me a newsletter telling me where to look for meteorite showers, comets, planetary conjunctions and eclipses. The tone of their correspondence was very friendly and encouraging. I was also welcome to use their library at Burlington House, in Piccadilly. It's one of London's finest buildings, Burlington House. It's the home of the Royal Academy of Arts, as well as a number of learned societies. I love that part of town; ambling around St James's with nothing in particular to do was about my favourite daytime activity. There are people who still dress like Sherlock Holmes in St James's, south of Piccadilly.

At the desk at Burlington House I said I was a member of the British Astronomical Association and asked where the library was. I was shown into a vast, galleried, oak-panelled hall with books from floor to ceiling. It had those ladders on wheels attached to rails, to enable you to reach the books on the top shelves. There was one other person in there. He was deep in thought with a book on his lap.

I could hardly believe how brilliant that room was. It was like walking into a dream I'd been having. I wanted to stay there forever and read everything. It had to be the finest collection of books for space heads in the world. There was a huge section on the search for extraterrestrial intelligence, none of which sensationalised it in any way. It was all cold and rational and delicious. It was immensely calm in there and sun flooded through the vast windows. The Queen lived at one point in a house not far away, and I felt almost certain that she might pop in to get away from everything and perhaps consider briefly the moons of the outer planets or read the latest published papers. The photocopied monthly newsletter didn't suggest anything like this. It was an excellent deal for seventeen pounds a year. I took out a dozen books.

I didn't tell many people about that place. I liked keeping it to myself. No one would have been interested anyway. I'd been going there for quite some time when I mentioned that I hadn't received my newsletter, as I was returning some books. The librarian said, 'Newsletter? We don't publish a newsletter! Are you sure you've come to the right place?' I said, 'This *is* the Astronomical Association, isn't it?' He said, 'This is the Royal Astronomical Society. Perhaps you're looking for the British Astronomical Association? That's upstairs.' Another gentleman came over. He seemed to be in charge. He said that I was welcome to come here if I could get two other Fellows of the RAS to propose me as a member – as if that wouldn't be a problem – and they shooed me upstairs. In a tiny room at the top was an old lady sitting in front of a small bookcase. She was typing. She was very friendly and said if I wanted to borrow any of the books I was quite welcome.

I was usually the only person in that library. It was a shame.

I prefer playing music to listening to recordings of it. Maybe the Victorians had the right idea. Where there is now a plasma screen, there might once have been a piano. I'd rather sit with a guitar or at a piano with a songbook and let it all flow through me. It's like being able to get inside a painting or a dream or the mind of the person who wrote it. Graham was forever right inside some musical landscape; he always had lots of CDs with him on tour. Dave always took a computer wherever we went.

Damon usually took an acoustic guitar, herbs for making tea and a selection of magic hats. I always took a guitar, too. I worked my way through the great pop writers: Roy Orbison, who the Beatles learned a thing or two from; Holland-Dozier-Holland, who wrote a lot of the Motown classics; Jimmy Webb, for 'Up, Up and Away' and 'Wichita Lineman'; the Gibb brothers – the Bee Gees – I marvelled at their sophisticated key changes, wonderful harmonies and the best grooves of anybody; the melodies of The Mamas & the Papas written by John Phillips, and countless others besides.

A guitar is a good companion on the road. When I felt wretched, broken, guilty and disgusted with myself, it was a source of comfort. When I was feeling cheeky I dived into its mysteries. It's a good piece of furniture and every home should have one to go with the piano. Houses without musical instruments are slightly barren places.

As well as a guitar I had my trusty book, *Foundations of Astronomy*. I'd been reading it from cover to cover for years by then. As I learned more about astronomy, the less I realised I knew. The ordinary, everyday part of life is so overwhelming it's easy to forget that we're floating on a pure and beautiful blue sphere in space and that the greatest adventure is about to begin. We're on the cusp of new paradigms; shifts in our understanding of everything and things are changing fast. The astronomy book had had two revisions since I had started reading it. In the 1990 edition, no planets had been positively identified outside the solar system. Since then, they've started turning up everywhere.

My favourite place is called the Oort cloud. It's a big jumble of icy rocks way, way beyond Pluto. They float gently around the sun in endless silence. Occasionally one of them falls out of its orbit and starts hurtling towards our star, which heats it to an incandescent fireball before slinging it back where it came from. Most comets come from the Oort cloud.

The Oort cloud is too far away to get to at the moment, but Mars seemed like a reasonable place to be aiming for.

The *Idler* magazine sent me to interview Patrick Moore, the astronomer. He's also a musician and there were quite a lot of things I wanted to ask him about. His house was full of books and silence. It was a good place for thinking. He interviewed me, really, to start with. Patrick Moore is a mighty scholar; he'd written at least fifty books about astronomy. True expertise is a rare thing, a combination of flair and an almost involuntary awareness of detail. I saw it in Damien and in Graham. It's what drew me to them. Patrick Moore was self-taught, an autodidact. His tenacious, rational mind had just dragged him along with it. He had the experts' gift of making things that are complicated sound simple.

I'd been wondering what shape the universe was. I'd kind of got to thinking it was hyperspherical and I'd been drawing hyperspheres a lot, and staring at them. I asked him what sort of shape he thought it all was. He said he'd asked Einstein the same thing, and Einstein didn't know either. Personally he wouldn't be drawn to conjecture. He wasn't really a magnet man, either. Even the hot topic of magnetic monopoles didn't really stir him up. We thought about the Oort cloud for a bit before we got round to Mars. He probably knows that planet better than anybody. He's been studying it for decades and knows its geography, its geology, its weather and seasons, its chemistry and its history. He'd studied it with telescopes and spectrometers, he'd been in continuous conversation with other leading Mars authorities for decades and he was of the same opinion as me on one thing in particular. One day soon we'll live on Mars. No doubt about it. He said the first man to walk on Mars has probably already been born, which hadn't occurred to me, but it could well be true.

We considered the largest volcano in the solar system, Olympus Mons, and the kind of things that would have to happen to make Mars habitable. The idea of transforming a dead planet into a lush green paradise was such a triumphant notion for humanity. In ancient Greece, man saw himself as an all-conquering hero. I can see that very clearly in the art that survives from the period: the great thinkers, the great athletes, the great species of mankind. For the ancient Greeks, there was no doubt that the human being was the greatest thing that had ever happened. In today's deforested greenhouse, we all share a burden of guilt that we're destroying the planet we live on and it's depressing. While cooking some poached eggs, Patrick Moore said the scariest thing I've ever heard. We'd been talking about life on Mars, and it naturally led to the question of life elsewhere. Here was a man of profound learning and vastly superior understanding, I think one of the three cleverest people I've ever met. He'd quickly tired of my childish, whimsical wanderings, and really was just being kind by telling me stories. I soon know when I've met someone who's cleverer than me; it's daunting but alluring. Big minds are irresistible places, but dangerous.

'I have absolutely no doubt,' said Patrick Moore, 'that beings of far greater intelligence than ours exist and know all about us. We are as far from them as King Canute was from television.'

It was scary because I'd been thinking the same thing myself. An intellect as advanced as his would have been quite enough for one day.

'I think the toast is burning,' I said.

Hollywood, Mars

After talking to Patrick Moore, I wanted to go to Mars. I thought about it a lot. I talked about it with the others. Damon and Graham thought I was being ridiculous. Dave was my astronomy cohort in the band. He had been a keen astronomer as a boy, and knew the difference between pulsars and quasars. He was enthusiastic. We both wanted to go to Mars, but for the time being we had to go to America a lot, more than usual. Usually they couldn't wait to get rid of us with our sloppy drinking, unprofessional conduct and irrelevant Britpopping but 'Song 2' was taking off in the States. That meant we had to go to Los Angeles a lot and it also started to make me think that nothing was impossible. America was the one place we'd never really had a proper hit. As my ambitions were serendipitously fulfilled, one by one, the thing I needed most of all was a new objective. I kept thinking about Mars.

Los Angeles, where the new record company was based, is like an onion: it has many layers and there is nothing in the middle. Dealing with it was enough to make our eyes water, but it's an essential ingredient in all recipes for global success. Either nobody wants you in that city or everybody does; nowhere else deals quite so straightforwardly in human currency than the Hollywood celebrity stock market. It's more hierarchical than Japan, it's dumber than Disneyland, it's awful and it's great.

There are so many ridiculous schemes afoot in that city that a trip to Mars seemed quite a realistic prospect. Although going to another planet was a far-fetched notion, and everyone apart from Dave took it as a kind of madness, my interest in space was actually one of the things that kept me sane. It was really quite grounding. Everything makes sense in space. It's all knowable and predictable. It makes a lot more sense than Hollywood, that's for sure.

I had a reasonably thorough knowledge of physics and chemistry. I'd enjoyed science since Jimmy Stubbs and I had tried to make big explosions when we were ten, and I'd never really stopped enjoying it. I am naturally inquisitive. It's my greatest gift. Science explains how things work, so I embraced it. Music could easily be categorised as a scientific discipline. Under analysis it is a species of pure mathematics. The sound of music is the hum of the harmonic series, the number sequence 1/2, 1/3, 1/4, 1/5, 1/6 . . . You could say it's just maths with the volume turned up. I just tried to put the notes together so that they exploded.

Hollywood is a small part of a big city. It has the most transient inhabitants of anywhere on earth. People zip in for twenty-four hours, get their faces on the telly and zoom off again to spend their money. Even the people who live there don't live there. They just work there and have homes elsewhere. It's one big office, really.

From the rock and roll district of West Hollywood, the distant dolls' houses of Beverly Hills precariously and clumsily stuck on to the cliff faces give the impression of a world designed by a child, a world teetering permanently on the edge of collapse.

Everyone in Hollywood, it appeared, would have me believe that they were in some way essential to the business of superstardom, or intimately connected with it. It's a gold rush town; everyone is a prospector and anyone could get lucky.

There must be more hotels in West Hollywood than anywhere else in the world. From rent-by-the-hour sleaze holes to castles fit for mad movie stars and everything in between and, over the years we'd stayed in them all.

The Hyatt on Sunset Boulevard is the hotel where most bands stay the first couple of times they go to Los Angeles. Sunset is a long and quite ordinary road whose most valuable characteristic is that it's famous. It's famous because famous people go there. The Whisky is on sunset: The Doors played there, famously. Johnny Depp, the famous actor, has a well-known, famous nightclub called the Viper Room on Sunset. A lot of famous people do their shopping at Ralphs supermarket on Sunset. It's famous for it. In Paris no one tells you that the Eiffel Tower is famous, or that many famous French people have lived there over the years. The elegance of the boulevards is ennobling. The cartoon crappiness of Los Angeles and its insubstantial garishness are undignified and have the opposite effect. The place is as nasty and delicious as a big slice of fresh pizza and, for all its ghastliness, there are always a lot of people it would be good to meet in the city.

The Hyatt is the most famous of all the rock and roll hotels. It cultivates its heritage carefully. A member of Led Zeppelin once drove its motorbike into the lift and there is, I think, a small plaque in there, commemorating the event. The first time we stayed there Graham was evacuated from his room by armed police officers carrying out a raid on the room next door. The famous elevator arrived, the doors opened theatrically to reveal a lift empty apart from Noel Edmonds. Graham said it was the strangest thirty seconds of his life so far and asked me if he was definitely awake.

Anyone wanting to mingle with more inspiring creatures than bikers and Noel Edmonds in the lift needs to go along the road to the Chateau Marmont, a kind of imitation castle. I popped in there once, very late; it was empty apart from Faye Dunaway, sitting at the bar alone. I winked at her but she told me to piss off. It was refreshing to hear someone say what they really meant.

After shopping around a bit, the band settled for Le Parc Suite Hotel. That became our Hollywood home. We all had our own sets of friends in Los Angeles, much as we did in London, but we all liked Le Parc. It's comfy and quiet. In Hollywood, more than anywhere else, it's important to have somewhere to retreat to, away from the unrelenting babble. There is no such thing as a comfortable silence in LA. People just don't ever seem to stop talking. The taxi drivers are exhausting. The only way to shut them up was to say I was planning a trip to Mars.

Inside Le Parc, all is calm. Everything is big and simple. The rooms are big; the beds are big; the phones are big. Everything is so big I felt like a little baby.

Things were going well, I felt, as I opened another bottle of champagne on a lilo in the pool on the roof of Le Parc. Graham was having a nap in the Jacuzzi and we'd just heard that 'Song

2' had been added to super-heavy rotation at MTV, which meant things would soon start going crazy.

In drink I had started to tell people I wanted to go to Mars. Even in the mornings, lately, I'd been talking about it. It was on my mind. People would go very quiet when I started talking about it. Everyone thought it was unreasonable and said 'Why?' rather than 'Why not?', but we're in a golden age of planetary science.

Three hundred years ago it took three months to get to Australia. Now it only takes three months to get to Mars. Soon we will go to other planets. Not because space is a place of infinite resources, but because it's in man's nature to explore. New horizons are exhilarating. Space is the new ocean and spaceships are the new cathedrals.

In Los Angeles fame has long been recognised as the most precious commodity in the universe. Famous people have great influence everywhere, but nowhere is it more obvious than in Hollywood. It's built on fame. The easiest way to sell something is to get a famous person to use it, wear it or stick a picture of their grinning face on it. The big clothes companies are well aware of this and employ celebrity product placement coordinators. Even before our first photograph appeared in the *NME*, we were all wearing free Levis. It's not just the big corporations, either. Even the smallest, most ethical producer of recycled Third World Fairtrade plimsolls would love to supply free plimsolls to recognised persons; it's the most effective form of advertising.

Rather than become another clothes horse, I wondered if I could use my prominence to jump-start a Mars rocket. I called my accountant and told him that I wanted to initiate a space programme. He said he'd see what he could do. He was a very good accountant. I was sure nothing was beyond him.

He called back fifteen minutes later. He said he'd arranged a meeting with someone in Milton Keynes.

Milton Keynes

Milton Keynes is a tidy new town, designed with cars in mind. Whoever designed it was obviously a big fan of roundabouts. It doesn't feel like you've ever arrived. The only way to tell is that there are suddenly a lot more roundabouts than usual. The roads in Milton Keynes do seem to have been laid out with the idea of avoiding the centre of the place. I wonder if it actually has a centre at all. I've got a feeling there is an extra large roundabout in the middle. There is something gently benign about the town. It seems to want to help you, and would like you to stay.

Actually, I was banned from Milton Keynes in 1991. At the peak of the finale of a particularly good show, I threw my guitar into the audience thinking someone would catch it and go home happy. It hit poor Kevin from Newport Pagnell right on the bonce and knocked him senseless. It was very lucky that it wasn't worse. Kevin seemed to be quite thrilled by the whole experience of being bashed by a flying bass, but his poor mother was beside herself. It wasn't good at all and I shrink now, thinking about it. I'd already sneaked back in a couple of times to go to the Marshall amplifier factory, which is either in or near Milton Keynes, it's often hard to say which.

The Open University campus was a microcosm of the larger municipality, more roundabouts and car parks with no definite heart, as neat as Germany and as clean as Japan. I found it to be very quaint, somehow, and serene.

I was with Dave. We were shown into an office and a man with very large sideburns appeared. He fished around for something in his pocket and passed it to me. 'Know what that is?' he asked, smiling. It was a small rock, quite round and pleasing to hold. 'It's a bit of Mars!' he said, as we puzzled over it.

'What? Where did you get it? How did you get it?'

My sense of being alive really kicked in and I realised I was staring at him. I transferred my stare to Dave. He was staring at him, too. He rarely stares, except when he's playing drums. All drummers stare. It wasn't a drumming stare, though. It was more focused and it was fixed on our host, Professor Colin Pillinger, who explained, in a thick West Country accent, that it had been found in Antarctica.

Most of Antarctica is so cold that it never snows. Virtually the whole of the continent is a vast, beautiful frozen desert. Things drop out of the sky and lie there waiting to be discovered. Any rocks found on the ice must have come from space. This can be confirmed by analysing their chemical compositions, which, in the case of this little nugget matched the make-up of Mars.

He talked a lot and we were dumbstruck. Seventy tons of Martian rocks fall out of the sky on to the Earth every year. He thought there was a good chance life started on Mars before it got going on Earth. Mars is a bit further from the sun and would have cooled more quickly to temperatures that would allow life processes to begin. If that was the case then there was a good chance that a bit of Mars with a living cell inside it could have been smashed off the Martian surface by a meteorite impact, landed on Earth and started the ball rolling here. So we could well all be Martians. I loved that feeling of being bamboozled by scientific hypothesising. He saved the best bit until last.

'We need to put a lander on the surface of Mars in 2003. It would be stupid not to. I think I can show there is life there,' he said.

I knew then that I'd found a friend.

We went through a door into a large laboratory. There was a clamour of silent concentration and dexterity. Everyone was wearing white coats. In the middle of the room, which was large, was a small model made from cardboard and wire. It was about the size of a car wheel.

Beagle I

'This is what I want to build. It's going to cost twenty-five million quid. It's a bargain,' he said. I had to agree. Colin was standing proudly beside his model. Even though it was made out of bog rolls, you could tell it was going to be quite complicated.

'It's quite simple!' he said. 'We're going to burrow under the surface with this drill,' and he waved a toothpaste tube attached to a piece of string. I'd already taken an instant liking to him, but this was the best idea I'd ever heard and the best thing I'd ever seen. He was so disarmingly straightforward about the monumental mysteries of the universe. 'In order to find life on Mars, you have to go underground. Mars lost its atmosphere a long time ago, we don't know why, but it's gone and the sun has cooked the soil. You won't find anything unless you get underneath that oxidised layer. NASA build these big bloody rovers, but they're never going to find anything scratching around on the surface. We can beat them to it, but we need to start building this right now. Mars is about to make its closest approach to Earth for twenty thousand years and if we don't start now we'll miss it.'

This was all music to my ears. It was a brilliant idea.

'Are we alone?' is the biggest question we are close to being able to get a definite answer to. It's right up there with 'Where did we come from?' 'Where are we going?' and 'Who are we?' The solutions to those tricky equations still seem to be a matter of opinion, but finding life on Mars would suggest that biology might be commonplace. When you consider the question 'Are we alone?', either of the possible answers is quite devastating. Not to know is just irresponsible.

My impression from meeting scientists is that most of them have an inkling that there almost definitely was, and possibly still is, some kind of primordial ecology happening on Mars.

I was spellbound by scientists. I went to their laboratories and tea parties, to their colleges and museums. Colin was a natural TV star and public support for his Mars mission started to grow. There were a lot of big personalities involved in the project as it gathered momentum. Damien was in, straight away. I was particularly interested in meteorites and was invited with Dave to the bowels of the Natural History Museum to meet Monica Grady, meteorite lady. 'Oh, don't call me that,' she said. Her meteorites were sitting peacefully in glass cases, but there was quite a menace about them. The stony ones had fused, blackened crusts, and the metal ones had been aerodynamically sculpted flashing through the atmosphere. Some of them must have made fairly big dents when they landed. Monica had a few bits of Mars, which she had found herself, in Queen Maud Land in Antarctica. Martian meteorites are among the most valuable, and the most famous meteorite of all is from Mars. It's called ALH84001. ALH stands for Allan Hills, another Antarctic mountain range. It made the front pages when it was first analysed. It's definitely from Mars and it contains what look like fossilised bacteria cells.

This particular meteorite was in the possession of a NASA scientist called Everett Gibson. He was a great friend of Colin's. They'd met when they'd both been working on samples of moon rock brought back to Earth by the Apollo astronauts. He was a kind and enthusiastic genius with an infectious pleasure in meteorite matter. I met Everett at a drinks party at Mansion House, the residence of the Lord Mayor of the City of London. Every conversation I had there I thought about for some time afterwards.

'Of course, if we do find life on Mars, it may turn out that it hasn't evolved around DNA. It might be a completely different story,' said one gentleman. Another man told me the majority of the material in the universe was unseen 'dark matter' and nobody had any idea what it was. Quite a lot of people were talking about the active volcanoes that had recently been discovered on one of Jupiter's moons. Cosmologists studying the cosmic microwave background radiation – the edge of the universe – with radio telescopes discussed football with propulsion specialists working on interplanetary engines. Everett Gibson's prize possession, ALH84001, had recently been stolen from his laboratory but then recovered. Since then he took no chances and carried it around everywhere with him in his pocket. You never knew what these guys were going to pull out of their pockets. A test tube containing an alien life form was the weirdest yet. As he took it out his face cracked into a huge grin. 'It's right here. Someone stole it and was trying to sell it on eBay! ALH84001! Bastard got twelve years! Can you believe it?' It was all quite hard to believe. His prize meteorite was something he liked to share with everybody. That little piece of rock is possibly the most interesting thing ever discovered, and a spring of constant wonder and mystery to him. He was a naturally gregarious character and I could imagine him getting talking to someone in a pub, and producing his test tube. I don't suppose many people believed him.

I went to meet Colin at the Eagle, a pub in Cambridge near his laboratory. It was in that pub that James Crick and Francis Watson, the scientists who first identified DNA, burst through the doors shortly after they'd made that Nobel Prize-winning discovery and pronounced to all present that they had found the secret of life. They too may well have been taken for lunatics. At the best of times it's difficult to tell the difference between madmen and geniuses.

The laboratory where Crick and Watson made their discovery was right next door to Colin's office. By some strange coincidence, the door was at the top of an external spiral staircase. 'Look at that,' said Colin. 'Dead giveaway! I reckon that staircase saved them years of research.' It did seem quite likely that the helical structure of DNA might have sprung to mind on one of countless journeys up and down that staircase. It was the exact shape they were looking for.

If Beagle were to fly, it would be the combined effort of forty university research departments, dozens of businesses and hundreds of engineers. We went to a big hangar in Hertfordshire, where satellites were made. It seemed such an ordinary place, another neat network of roundabouts, grass verges and modern light-industrial units. I'd have thought they might be making lawnmowers or maybe roundabout parts in those mundane-looking factories, but they were making spaceships, quite a lot of them, little cosmic canoes that get fired into near space to float motionless above a fixed point on the Earth's surface as it spins.

There was a high-security research facility in rural Oxfordshire. There was some far-fetched stuff going on in there. There were rows of radio telescopes visible from a distance. It's quite a famous row of radio telescopes. It was at this lab, the Mullard Space Science Laboratory, that a research student called Jocelyn Bell thought she had discovered intelligent alien life while studying for a Ph.D. It was a false alarm, but what she had found was almost as weird – a star as big as an iceberg that weighs as much as the sun. Radio telescopes are dope.

Farnborough

I remember going to the Farnborough Airshow as a small, excited boy. The high point of the day was the British-built supersonic jet, the Lightning. It flew along the runway at head height, its engine screaming as it accelerated to break the sound barrier right in front of the crowd. The turbine noise made my hair stand on end and the sonic boom, loud as a crack of thunder, hit me right in the stomach. It was overwhelming, the speed of the thing, as fast as a bullet, its toy-like beauty and supernatural power, the little red, white and blue decals that said it was one of our things. It spoke a language everyone understood and the spontaneous round of applause and cheering that followed sounded paper-thin after the roaring tsunami sound of a fleeting fighter. It was a true spectacle, something to witness and wonder at.

The next year, by way of upping the ante, the organisers arranged for two Lightnings flying in opposite directions to cross each other at the centre point of the runway, going supersonic as they met. Both aeroplanes pulled straight into vertical climbs and performed an aerobatics display. It didn't seem like anything could ever be better, but at the following show they had six of the things, three flying in each direction in formation. The report as they met was so loud that it broke windows in the town of Farnborough, miles away, and then they weren't allowed to do that kind of thing any more.

There is a thrill of vulnerability at all airshows. There is no way of making everything completely safe. When the machines are being thrashed to capacity and the pilots are flying at their limits to dazzle, things are bound to go wrong sometimes. There have been some historic disasters, but the danger is a part of the attraction.

Farnborough is a big event. It's not just about flying displays. There are dozens of hangars with hundreds of exhibitors from the aerospace industry. They range from companies that make the plastic trays that in-flight meals are served on, to seat-belt specialists, to supersonic engine manufacturers and businesses that will launch anything, from your ashes to your communications satellite, into the Earth's orbit. There are even people who will build you a rocket if you need one. Rockets are pretty much off the shelf these days. If you had the money, you could go to Farnborough and buy everything you need to make a pretty good spaceship, and the expertise to build it.

Although they never did, the first man to fly and the first man to walk on the moon could have met. Things have happened fantastically fast in aerospace and the engine that drives the technology into the future at such a blistering pace is the weapons industry. The advance of mankind and his possible self-destruction dance a strange tango. Weapons manufacture gives momentum to research; it creates a need for precision engineering; it provides the money to develop new technologies. It makes it all necessary. Supersonic jets are, after all, weapons of war.

It was impossible to tell the weapons of mass destruction guys from the academics or the guys who made seat belts.

I'd spent so much time bored on aeroplanes I'd completely forgotten how absolutely brilliant they are. Dave was happier at Farnborough than I'd ever seen him. He had just got his pilot's licence, and asked the exhibitors lots of questions. Colin's stand was attracting a fair bit of interest. He had improved his Beagle model, and it looked quite professional now, although I preferred the one made out of cardboard and Sellotape.

There are so many things to see at Farnborough that, by the time most people arrived, they were numb to further stimulation. After having seen the biggest aeroplane in the world, the Red Arrows, hovering Harrier jets, Stealth bombers and jet packs, a tiny Mars lander seemed quite run of the mill. The science minister, Lord Sainsbury, attended a press conference and gave the Beagle his support. It was looking good, Milton Keynes.

Mercer Street

We'd been travelling non-stop for the best part of nine months, but, as activity around the *Blur* album gradually eased off, I began to spend more time in London. Justine and I gravitated back together and she moved back into the flat in Endell Street. We started looking for somewhere to buy together. The money arrived quite quickly, quicker than the flat did. When we started, we were looking at the cheapest places the estate agents had on their books. A couple of months later, we had more money and were looking at one-bedroom flats. By the time we found somewhere that was right, it was the most expensive property on the agent's books.

We bought a five-storey converted cheese warehouse with a little balcony that backed on to a hidden courtyard. It was bright and opulent with high ceilings and a good showbusiness history. I bought it for cash from an American who wrote musicals. I'd always wanted to live there. It was the nicest house in Covent Garden. Tourists with flapping maps would stop and look up at it. The bedroom overlooked the dressing rooms of the Cambridge Theatre opposite where we could see the hoofers getting their slap on. The back windows looked on to the boutiques and offices of the courtyard.

It had the hallmarks of being one of many homes of its former owner, hotel-like qualities. There was a minibar and a trouser press in the bedroom on the top floor and the whole house was assiduously serviced. It had a staff of two, a private secretary, who the owner took with him, and a housekeeper, who stayed. She wore an apron and everything. She gave me hell about not keeping the place tidy and she didn't like my old piano, either. She kept telling me about the grand piano that the previous owner had, and made it clear that I needed to get one of those. Then she banned me from slopping around smoking in my pants. I wasn't ready for a housekeeper. It was nice having everything in the cupboards and in neat rows, sparkling clean, but when she told Damien it was time for him to go home one morning after we'd been up all night writing poems in the kitchen, I knew she had to go. She went next door to number 25, a house that belonged to a family that had made a fortune from processed cheese triangles.

I was probably the worst person to live next door to in London. Most nights the kitchen would be full of people singing 'California Dreamin'' and dancing to the Bee Gees. Sometimes we brought the piano player back from the Groucho with us, as recommended by management. London was raging. It was about this time that absinthe arrived in the country. That stuff took drunkenness to new levels. It's only alcohol, but it's different from any other drink. It's pure ethanol with green dye and aniseed flavouring. It has twice the alcohol content of whisky, but even when I tried diluting half a shot of absinthe with twice as much water as I would have with a whisky, I still got twice as drunk, or possibly it was four times as drunk. It was hard to say because the ability to do multiplication was beyond anybody drinking absinthe. It took away the maths part of the brain, but it never failed to rouse the wanderlust lobes. I'd had 'the Green Fairy' before in Barcelona. That was the only place it was to be found until then, in the dirty little bars around the Ramblas. It was harder to gauge how drunk I was in foreign countries, though, where nothing was familiar. I woke up on a boat after the first time I drank the stuff in Barcelona and I didn't think twice about it then, but when absinthe arrived in London, I found myself waking up in all kinds of strange places: Dalston, Richmond, Highbury, even Wapping. I would never go to these places normally. They were all quite far away. In fact it's the only time I've been to Richmond.

I left the Groucho at closing time and went to another club, Soho House, with Zodiac Mindwarp, a heavy metal monster with lots of tattoos and scars. He was my new best friend and we sat at a table drinking pints of Guinness. A pretty girl came and joined us and we told her our plans. We'd decided to walk to Rome, and we were just stopping off for a Guinness on the way. That was when Johnny Depp sat down next to me. I don't know why he got so upset, but soon he was very unhappy. He poured a pint of Guinness on my lap. It is hard to know what I might have said in the steam of an absinthe stupor, but things were definitely not going so well to the right. On the left, with the girl, it was looking quite good. She said she lived in Richmond. When I woke up I was in her bedroom. I was emptying my bladder all over her dressing table. People had told me about this kind of thing. It had never happened to me before, though. She woke up and asked what I was doing. I said it looked like I'd made a big mistake. We cleaned it up. We'd only known each other a couple of hours and I don't think anyone could have been any more drunk than I was. Usually being that drunk would make you unconscious, but with absinthe you go on expeditions. I did see her again. Some people you try and make a good impression on and nothing works, others you piss all over their make-up and they've decided they like you and it doesn't seem to matter. Anyway, that was the only time I ever went to Richmond.

9

how I made them sing

Fat Les

Like Damien, Keith Allen is a man of action, a lot of action. He'd been a comedian, he'd been an actor, he'd had his own TV show, he'd been in movies, he'd been in prison and he'd written a number one record for my favourite band. Most of all, he was a great talker and his orations could draw a crowd, anywhere. He was the archetypal fearless Soho wayward genius and his energy reverberated, unassailable, from the dive bars of Dean Street to the cloisters of Le Caprice. He was fifty years old and was in touch with the almighty possibilities of the here and now at all times.

He was nagging me to do a football record. I kept telling him I had a musical to write, which was true, but then on his birthday we went to watch Fulham play an away match. The travelling Fulham supporters are very proud of how much noise they make. They sang, chanted, shouted, clapped their hands and stamped their feet through ninety minutes of drizzle and poor passing and Keith was their conductor. There was someone playing a drum, a lop-sided, clowny rhythm that would stop occasionally and start again, with renewed vigour.

I said maybe we could do something with those drums, but the World Cup was starting in six weeks. We wrote the song 'Vindaloo' around the drums a couple of days later. Once I know what the drums are doing and what it's going to sound like, it's just a question of joining the dots together. I knew it had to sound like the Fulham supporters singing in the rain. It took half an hour to write, words and everything.

I was playing snooker with Andy Ross, from Food, a couple of days later. In the middle of a break he took a call from the EMI chairman. The FA were desperate for a football song and wanted to know if Damon could do anything to help? I overheard and told him I'd just written one. He gave me a 'Don't interrupt when the chairman's on the phone' look, and that was that. I played it to Smithy, but he thought it would struggle to get on the radio.

Keith had started singing the song, and he hadn't really stopped. Damien liked it. He wanted to set up a record label and release it. We christened the band Fat Les, asked everyone we liked to be in it and booked a couple of days at Townhouse Studio.

There were four weeks until the World Cup kicked off when Damien, Keith and I ran into a PR guy called Phill Savidge on Dean Street. I said, 'We need this guy.' Damien had a large amount of cash in a carrier bag, a few tens of thousands in fifties. He pulled a bundle out, gave it to Phill and said, 'Tell me when you need some more.'

I knew when I arrived at the studio at ten-thirty that the record would either be a dismal failure or an improbable triumph. We had a day to record everything and a day to mix. The drummer was arriving at eleven, and we had to do the drums and lay the bass down before lunch. They were the only instruments on the track. Simplicity is often the key. The afternoon was timetabled with various singers, shouters and schoolchildren.

Basslines, my stock-in-trade, are a kind of musical glue; the bassline makes the drums, vocals and guitars stick together and stand. Aside from the music, the role of my character within Blur was similar to that of a bassline in a piece of music. I often acted as a mediator between Damon and Graham. My blasé temperament was a pivot for them both and perhaps it suggested an underlying harmony in an arrangement that might otherwise have collapsed.

Making this record was a different situation. I was the producer. Producing is mainly about getting the best out of everybody. I took a deep breath, plugged the bass in and sang the song to the drummer. The drummer was Roland Rivron. He was famous for being able to ride his bicycle down the main staircase at the Groucho Club. Keith had said we should have him on drums. As it turned out, he was an exceptionally good drummer. By the time the sandwiches arrived the sound engineer and the tea boy were grinning and humming the song. Keith did his vocal in one take and it sounded like a hit. Phill generated quite a bit of press interest, so that with three weeks till kick-off we had sold the master recordings to Telstar in return for an advance on royalties and enough money to make a video. Keith wanted to direct the video. He wanted a hundred people dressed up as Max Wall and as many fat, drunk people as possible. It's not quite what we ended up with, but, with a week to go, his video went straight to number one at The Box and Woolworths ordered half a million copies of the record. It was the biggest week for singles sales since the 'Blur vs. Oasis' pantomime.

Promotion

It all happened so fast. The record didn't get any radio play, but it quickly outsold anything Blur had done. The producer of *Top of the Pops* really liked the song and did a special deal with the producer of *EastEnders*, who, I guess, must have liked it as well and the band were filmed marching around Albert Square.

We were offered a gig at a private party in a warehouse in Islington where the match would be showing on a cinema screen. Keith said we'd do our only song for five grand, cash, and a goat. I think we probably would have gone to the party anyway; it sounded like it was going to be all right. It was good just to be able to assemble the cast. There were a lot of people in the band, particularly after the record took off. It was a happy crowd. Matt Lucas and David Walliams; Paul Kaye; Vivienne Westwood's six-foot mucky muse, Sara Stockbridge; Keith; Lily and Alf, his children; their friends; Joe Strummer; various models and obese men and, sometimes, Bez. The song 'Vindaloo' was so simple that it could be played entirely on the bottom string of a bass guitar with one finger. I had a bass guitar with just one string, so it was quite a weird-looking thing. I'd bought it from a man up a mountain in Japan. It was the obvious choice of guitar. Roland had a square snare drum that he was quite keen on, and Keith had his goat.

It was a marching band, really, and Keith marched in with his goat at the head of the procession. We got on to the stage and the drumming started. The bass comes in on the chorus. I windmilled my arm around histrionically for the first note and, as my finger hit the one and only string, it snapped. I didn't have any spares. It's really unusual to snap a bass string, particularly when it's the only one you've got, and the bass is the only instrument. No one seemed to mind; actually it sounded more like it did on the terraces with just drums and voices. England won, so the party rose out of control to extravagance. Forget the sixties. In the summer of 1998 London was in the grip of a hedonistic fervour not seen since the days of gin houses and the Hellfire Club.

Keith got a taxi home. The taxi was for sale and he had the

five thousand in his pocket, so he bought it. Damien painted spots on it, which made it quite valuable. Damien couldn't paint enough spots. People loved those spots.

There was a homeless man who begged in the doorway of the Groucho. His name was Outside Dave and Keith used to let him have a bath and cook him a hot meal occasionally at his home. They came to an arrangement with the taxi where Outside Dave lived in it, but he had to keep it as close to the Groucho as possible so that if Keith needed to go anywhere he had a driver.

It worked quite well, although it broke down quite often and it could smell a bit ripe. He seemed all right, Dave did. He claimed that there were a couple of women who went to the club who used to take him home for sex occasionally, but he also said he didn't drink, and I think he did sometimes. He was a man of mystery.

I went with Keith and Outside Dave in the taxi to Reading Festival. We didn't have tickets, but Keith was performing with New Order on Saturday night. I was sure that between us we could talk our way in. We didn't have to. The taxi had a Jedi effect on security: all the gates just opened for it and we were waved through the crowds. Dave the tramp drove it right into the backstage area and parked it next to Jay Kay's Ferrari without having to do any talking. Then he disappeared into the hospitality area and was never seen again.

New Order were my favourite band. They wrote modern pop symphonies. I'd learned more about music from listening to their records than I would have done from any amount of music lessons. I had listened to those songs again and again. I studied their compositions without realising what I was doing. I learned the drums, the guitar parts, the keyboard lines. I suppose it was like Patrick Moore looking at the moon through his telescope. The music intrigued me and I scrutinised it and drew my own conclusions.

I went out into the crowd and watched my friend take the

stage with my favourite band for the finale. As they finished, the crowd started to chant for 'Vindaloo'. It felt better than standing on that stage ever had.

Mexico

Blur were supposed to go to Chile, as part of a South American tour. I was reading *The Times*, which I still mainly bought for the crossword, and there was an article with the headline 'Blur To Play Santiago, Despite Warnings'. I hadn't had any warnings. It said the Home Office was advising against travel to Chile in the current political climate. I wondered where Chile was and what politics could be happening there. I'm sure my dad had been; that meant it had to be OK. I called Chris Morrison, our manager, and asked him if he'd be joining us on the Chile leg of the tour. He'd seen the paper, too. He said we'd have to pull the show in Santiago, which was a shame, because, looking at the record sales figures, we were about the most popular band in the country's history. Then he did his big laugh.

It's always surprising how popularity waxes and wanes from place to place on a world tour. Even in Europe. For some reason Blur have never managed to make the slightest impression on the Dutch. They didn't like baggy, weren't interested in Britpop, the 'Woo-hoo' thing passed them by completely and going there to promote the new record had been merely a polite formality. The articulated lorries full of super troupers, mega woofers and special effects would drive right through the Netherlands on a European tour. Most of the convoy would go straight to Denmark to wait at the stadium for us while we performed in the back room of a bar in Amsterdam.

They blew hot and cold in Belgium. At one point we were going to Belgium so often it hardly seemed to make sense and then we didn't go back for years.

Throughout Asia, our popularity rode a similarly random rollercoaster from nation to nation. In Korea, the venue was the same kind of size as most places we played in Europe. In Singapore I wasn't allowed into the venue for being too wayward looking. I had to call the tour manager and tell him I was outside.

The next day, when we landed in Bangkok, we were each appointed four security guards, airside, and bundled through the terminal where there were thousands of massed, hysterical fans. A police escort zipped us to our penthouse suites. It was quite bizarre. A throne was erected at the venue and we were briefed by a member of the royal household on how to conduct ourselves in the presence of the princesses.

By this time we had our own security. Graham and I had particularly random behaviour, and quite often, especially if we all went out together, we were mobbed in the street. There'd be a giggle and I'd turn around to see a couple of girls following me. The next time I'd turn around there'd be a dozen of them. Then one or two would start to run ahead and take photos. It's the flashbulbs popping that makes everyone else take notice. Pretty soon after the cameras started the situation would get out of control and I'd be surrounded by people smiling and asking questions. It was rarely unpleasant or dangerous. It just meant everything took ages.

It can get hairy at night, though. Anyone attracting a lot of attention is always going to annoy someone. It's hard and churlish not to go out at night. The lure of wine, women and song is almost irresistible. Nightclub owners fight each other to get bands to come to their establishments in the big cities. Adventures could end almost anywhere, but they often started in nightclubs. Normally we were made a big fuss of and shown to the best table. Drinks were usually free. Girls appeared and, if there was anything else we needed, someone would take care of it. People did take exception sometimes. It's hardly surprising; it must have been like being invaded by a longboat of drunken Vikings with weapons that there was no defence against. Most of the time, though, the security guys just had to make sure we didn't get run over crossing the road. Graham particularly suffered from getting hit by cars.

None of us had been to South America, but we were told we'd be needing armed security, and that we shouldn't fuck about under any circumstances. On the way to Mexico City at Heathrow was a guy called Rowan, who I'd been running into quite a bit recently. He was part of the glamorous crowd that had put on the goat party where Keith bought the taxi. He said that he was going to Mexico City, too. His brother had a nightclub there and we should all come that evening because there was a big film festival in town and there would be loads of people.

Mexico is one of those places where you sit on a plane for ten hours and when you arrive it's still the same time it was when you left. En route there was quite a lot of speculation about what to expect. Dave said you couldn't have a bath, because things swim up your bottom and lay their eggs. The tour manager warned us about getting kidnapped or arrested, which amounted to the same thing. There was talk of feral children living in sewers and bandits who'd shoot you for your shoes. I thought maybe I'd take it easy in South America.

As soon as we stepped off the plane, it was all instantly and obviously brilliant. It was hot as hell and as green as Eden. It was a kind of a green that was new to me, somewhere between a lime and a lemon. There were about a million people at the airport and there was more bundling going on than queuing. Just getting through immigration and customs was a caper, like an old black and white movie where everything happens too fast. It was a big lovely slap in the face from the unknown. I really thought I knew everything by now and suddenly there was all this as well. Mexico City makes New York look bijou. Miles and miles of jam-packed everything, people living in the central reservations of the carriageways, shanty towns, suburbs, skyscrapers and smog. On and on it went and it was hard to remember anything else existed.

The hotel was of the super-modern business resort variety with ninety-nine floors and glass lifts. There were strange keys for doors that opened automatically like on spaceships. In the suite there was a bottle of Dom Perignon on ice from the record company, an enormous basket of fruit from the promoter and flowers and a thoughtful selection of nibbles to complement the champagne from the hotel manager. The Bang & Olufsen stereo went quite loud. They usually have limiters on them in hotels, but the suite was so enormous it wasn't going to bother anybody. The triple-aspect windows looked out from on high over a roof terrace to the brightly-lit metropolis. I called Graham and told him to bring his champagne.

He was still a bit worried about worms going up his bottom, but you could tell it wasn't that kind of place. The dude from the record company wanted to take us out for dinner. It's important to break free from luxury's subtle suffocation. It would have been easy to stay in the hotel having huge bubble baths and massages, but luxury is more or less the same everywhere and I wanted a big slice of Mexico.

The record company dude said it was all a big load of bollocks about worms, but it was true about getting kidnapped and people living in the sewers. Dinner was ridiculously good. I hadn't quite put Mexico together with Mexican restaurants. There were enchiladas and burritos galore, but dinner mainly involved drinking shots of tequila and slapping each other on the back.

I remembered the nightclub and we went there. It was all happening at once, as usual. After a few tequilas we'd given up on the idea of not having ice in our drinks and started on margaritas. On the plane, someone had said that ice was poisonous.

The ones we were drinking now, caipirinhas, seemed to have some kind of salad in them as well, which was another no-no.

It was at the nightclub that someone started talking about the pyramids. There were huge pyramids, they said, better than the ones in Egypt. All aligned with the bright stars and inexplicably engineered. I wanted to see those pyramids. I ordered a taxi immediately and we were on our way. It was two a.m. and we drove for a couple of hours through the city. It was built up in every direction and the roads were heavy with traffic all through the night. We cruised through the bright lights, skyscrapers and matrices of traffic lights, all new and enticing.

Then the buildings became shacks and we were in a desert. The walled sanctum of the pyramids rose in the distance. It was strangely still and peaceful at the entrance after the constant whizz of the city. We gave the guards fifty dollars to let us in. It was simple. The ancient citadel was built on a biblical scale. It was ginormous. Maybe these people had been giants. As the morning light began to break, the features of the kingdom became more apparent. There were a number of whacking great pyramids dissected by avenues, gateways, temples and stairs. It was more humbling than Mexico City itself, vast, crumbling and beautiful in the breaking twilight. We walked a couple of miles to the foot of the Pyramid of the Sun, the big one. From the bottom you couldn't see the top without craning your neck uncomfortably.

It was just sitting there, the enigmatic remnants of a completely lost civilisation. It was all the more powerful because I had been completely unaware of its existence until a couple of hours before. We grow up knowing about the pyramids in Egypt. Even though they are miraculous, they are familiar to us. That familiarity takes away some of their power to enchant. Suddenly, here I was in a strange desert, which is enough to make anyone come over a bit different at the best of times, but this huge and magical city with its dense aura of mystery sent me spinning. We spend so much of our lives underwhelmed by the ordinary. It is hard to remember that life is a constant miracle in a vast, unexplored universe full of secrets.

It was a long, long way to the top of the Pyramid of the Sun and we wanted to make the summit before the sun rose. The sky was getting bluer and bluer and our faces redder and redder. There were half a dozen of us, the girls in their film festival frocks, the boys doing a tequila relay. Up and up we went, thousands of steps, big steps, perfectly regular. Dizzy, exhausted and freaked out, I collapsed on the top. The sun was coming. The hazy vista was immense, a big long brown turd of pollution sitting on top of Mexico City. That was when the police van arrived. You could tell it was a police van because it had a flashing light. It was very small and it stopped at the foot of the giant staircase. There was no escape, so we sat there trying to enjoy the spectacle of nature on a large scale at dawn as two policemen began to mount the stairs.

It took them a long time to get to us. They were knackered by the time they got to the top and really pissed off. One of them started ranting in Spanish and then spat out a big wad of phlegm with a nod of his head as a full stop. The DJ from the nightclub, a handsome, upmarket American, was able to translate. 'He said we're charged with desecrating a holy relic and that we're in deep shit. Then he spat on the holy relic, just to show he's in charge. We'd better do what he says.' We were marched down the side of the man-made mountain and confronted with their superior, who was standing by the van smoking and spitting. I wondered what would happen. I knew one of our gang was carrying a very large amount of drugs somewhere about his person. He seemed to be the least flustered of all of us. He started to negotiate with the boss man who was demanding we get in the van. They argued for ages. We stole glances at each other but it was impossible to tell what was happening. The DJ kept raising his eyebrows and shaking his head. Then it was settled. We could walk away for five hundred dollars. I'd have given five hundred thousand.

It was a long, long drive back to the hotel through the rush-hour traffic. An endless journey in the thick pollution with a cheap tequila hangover. I've never felt so bad and so good at the same time.

The gig was in a stadium and there were fans at the hotel, fans at the radio stations, fans at the TV studios. They waved, screamed and gave us letters. It was another vast continent, another green world.

Brazil, Argentina

Rio is such an evocative place. It's been mythologised by music to such an extent that it hardly seemed real at all. I walked for miles without ever leaving a song, from Ipanema to Copacabana, along the beaches among the palm trees. It was like Mexico with the contrast turned right up, the strikingly beautiful rubbing shoulders with the grotesque, the diseased, the toothless and the insane. Somehow, the insane seemed to be madder, the further I got from home. There was more of a sense of peril on the streets, but they were all the more enticing for it. We live in a climate of fear, but the world is a safe place as long as you know how to behave like everybody else does. If you stand around holding a map waving a video camera with your shirt tucked into your waist-high trousers, you're in trouble wherever you go. Millions of people live in Rio, after all, and they eat salad and have ice in their drinks and they don't get murdered very often.

We were playing in a bar in Rio. It was a bit of a jolt after the mass adulation of Mexico. I thought there were some fans at the hotel – they kept smiling at me – but they were prostitutes.

I was exhausted from my Mexican antics and kept out of trouble in Rio. My birthday fell on a Sunday, the day of the show in São Paulo. São Paulo is like Rio without the songs or the beach. It's big, bigger than most countries, a city with a population greater than Ireland, New Zealand, Costa Rica and Portugal combined. No wonder Brazil are always winning the football. I'd never heard of this São Paulo and it was fair to say most of São Paulo had never heard of Blur, but it was a bigger gig than in Rio.

On my birthday, most of all I like to play the blues, with Graham. It's a tradition that started at college. Playing the blues involves the thumbs a lot, more than any other kind of guitar music. You strum with the thumb of the right hand and curl the left thumb over the top of the guitar so that it can hold down the bottom string. Then you just need some whisky and you're all set. We'd go on for hours.

It was hard to know how to take things up a notch on my birthday. I was permanently living in the rock and roll fast lane. The year before I'd had a party that all kinds of nice people had shown up at. I did actually throw a television out of the window, just to see what happened, but I had checked that there was no one coming beforehand and it was my television to do what I liked with, which I explained to the police when they arrived. They were very understanding. Overall, it was quite disappointing. It didn't explode, particularly; it just went thud on Shaftesbury Avenue.

Somehow the tour manager managed to find me a Balthazar of champagne. I think a Nebuchadnezzar is bigger – you need a couple of footmen for the Nebuchadnezzar – but the Balthazar is big, the biggest bottle that one person can carry. You really need to put it over your shoulder to pour from it properly and even then it's tricky. There's enough for a party in there, though. It was quite late when I got back to the hotel with my big bottle, but there were quite a few fans there. I invited the five prettiest ones to come up to my rooms. You need five girlfriends when your bottle of champagne is that big. I collapsed on the bed and they jumped on me and covered me in champagne and kisses. It was a good birthday party. I stopped having sex occasionally, but only so that I could have some more drugs. That image of myself soused in champagne being devoured by lusting women in a luxury hotel suite in a vast and unknown city was the pinnacle of my rock and roll excesses.

After the mayhem of Mexico and Brazil, Buenos Aires, Argentina, was a stately and sophisticated city of wide boulevards, grand statuary and chic endroits. It's posher than Paris, in fact, which was all quite surprising. It didn't look like the lettuce would cause any harm in that fair city. More surprising was that the Argentinians adore the English, and more surprising still that I at once felt completely at home there. The other mammoth metropolitan centres of South America had thrilled and tickled. I could never quite get enough of anything, but just to see those places had almost been enough. Here I felt I could live and be happy. I just never knew when I was going to get that feeling. Even though there are an infinite number of ways to live a life and be happy, it didn't actually come out and grab me often that I would instantly and obviously be very at home somewhere.

Justine sent her friend Walter to show me around and keep an eye on me. He was handsome, aristocratic and gay and a fan of the Smiths. Walter took me to gay bars, to lounges, to cafés, to a candle-lit walled garden where they served tea and coffee all night. I met his friends and their friends and it was all benign and agreeable.

Gay bars are the most decadent of all. I found it relaxing to go out and take sex out of the equation. The music is always really good, too, in gay bars.

Trying to Build Jerusalem

'Vindaloo' had made quite a lot of money, so we set up an office. One of the barmen from the Groucho seemed really keen on running a record company, so we let him do it. Then we had to think about our next move. We had a meeting in our office. Where to go next? What should we tackle? I wanted to make gay disco records. Keith wanted to sign his daughter. I was always seeing her out and about, but she was only twelve and twelve's a bit young for showbusiness. Damien said he wanted to do a Christmas record and it seemed like quite a good idea. It seemed the perfect follow-up to a football record and it's the best time to have a hit record as you sell about ten times as many.

I went into a studio with Keith and Roland Rivron, Rod, the piano player from the Groucho, and Joe Strummer, to write something. It was a combination of personalities with a lot of seasonal promise. Christmas had started early that year and it was hard to keep things under control. By the second day there was a gospel choir hanging out as well. By the time it was finished, more or less the whole of the Groucho Club and Browns were in the studio. Lisa from Browns sang the song with Keith, who dressed up as a goblin in the video.

It went top twenty, but we manufactured too many copies of the record, about a quarter of a million too many. It was hard to compete with the major labels at Christmas time. We lost all the money from 'Vindaloo' and a bit more. Keith also lost the taxi, in Rotterdam, which was a shame.

It took a while to recover our pride, and we thought we'd better stick to football records. The singer was, after all, a fifty-year-old baldy man. We were ready by the time the next football tournament came along. I wanted to do something spectacular. The way forward came to me over a martini in Peg's, a member's club I'd just discovered that I lived next door to. It was so exclusive and discreet that it was invisible to passers-by and even livers-next-door-to.

George was usually there. I like George's company. He's an upper-class pixie of some vintage, gay and fabulous. He's from another world that involves things like cufflinks, bone china and ballet. Sometimes it was just George and myself there for lunch, other days there'd be a minor royal or a mega-dega film director, lunching his stars. It was ludicrous. A bar that was empty apart from people who were so famous that they had to hide there between meetings in town. It was a good place to go and have ideas. The barman never spoke. He just made fantastic martinis.

It was behind one of those martinis, my second of the day, that I conceived the most expensive record ever made. Our last football song had been a loutish, one-note wonder. The only way forward now was to go way upmarket. We needed a new national anthem, a song you could take anywhere, that your granny could sing; that would stir the hearts of wayward teenagers; that would scare goalkeepers. It was going to be tricky. I was sucking the olive when I realised the song had already been written by William Blake. We'd do 'Jerusalem', and we'd do it big.

Three weeks later we were in Air Studios with a one-hundred-and-twenty-piece orchestra. Air is the biggest studio in London and that's about the biggest orchestra it can house. Keith wanted to conduct. He didn't know the difference between a French horn and a cor anglais, but he did have winning vivacity and bags of confidence. Confidence is the most important ingredient on the songwriter's shopping list. Nothing else is half so important.

There were harps and percussionists, a long line of double basses. There were violins everywhere you looked. We had cannons. We had five massed choirs: a big gay choir, a children's choir, gospel choir, close-harmony barbershop choir and a chorus. It was immense. There were cameras. There was

Michael Barrymore. George Martin was wandering about the place. We didn't leave anything out. Everyone had learned their parts and I stood in the control room and took a deep breath. The next three minutes were costing a lot of money, more than any other record ever has, and there was a good chance we'd built an aeroplane that wouldn't fly.

I was in tears by halfway through the first chorus. It was immense. I didn't care if it sold five copies. It was a record that needed to be made. It's such a beautiful tune, rousing, but noble, a prayer for the weak and a battle cry for the strong, a poem, a patriotic paean and a perfect pop song. Well, you'd hope so for two hundred grand.

Football was very fashionable. It seemed to be easier to get a table at the Ivy than it did to get tickets for the Arsenal. There was an almighty brouhaha about the tournament, Euro 2000. The song was a news item and I went to Wembley to have my photograph taken with the players. There were about a thousand photographers there. The squad were having a kickaround in the new England strip. Someone blew a whistle somewhere and they all ran to the centre circle and stood in a line with the goalkeepers at one end and the forwards at the other. I could hardly believe it. They were so well drilled. Peep, peep and there they all were in a neat little row. I was asked to stand on the end, next to the goalies. My heart sank as I took my place. I looked along my right shoulder down the line. I was head and shoulders taller than the back four. We didn't stand a chance. Keith and I figured we'd get back the money we'd spent if the team got to the semi-finals. Any further and we'd be in the clover. It was a gamble. Keith said we were going to win. Good football records never go away, though. EMI shareholders should have their money back by the World Cup tournament in 2018, as long as England do well. In the meantime they've got that song.

Decadence

I'd graduated from the Groucho to the Colony Room, a couple of doors down. The Colony was the drinking club that had made Jeffrey Bernard's legs fall off. It has a greasy spoon kind of feel and to enter is to be overwhelmed by an awareness of green. It's like a front room, but it's green, and there is a lot of art on the walls, given by the people who have spent time there over the years. The value of the art is probably worth more than the entire Groucho Club, a roll-call of the great British artists since the Second World War. There was also a piano, which I often played, and Michael, the current heir to the establishment, was always there. Sometimes it was jam-packed and everyone seemed to be mad; sometimes it was peaceful and a supermodel would walk in. I could never tell what was going to happen next there. That was what was good about it.

I was drinking more and more and it took me further into the night.

I liked Trade, a big, gay bonanza in what seemed to be a huge network of underground sewers in Clerkenwell. Parties cost a lot of money and they usually happen to promote someone or something. Trade was different. It was just a party. I started going to Trade because it was open all night and it was mental. It made any party that was ever thrown by a band look like kids' stuff. There was shagging in the bogs, fellatio on the dance floor and people queuing up to buy drugs like it was the end of the world. Somehow it was quite civilised and it never felt as sleazy there as it did in other places that were open after three a.m. People would really lose it in there, though. There was even a kind of casualty ward on site. I know because I woke up there once, covered in blood, being attended to by paramedics.

There was a boat at Blackfriars Bridge, where scary people played cards, basements in Chinatown full of transvestites, stained attics along Berwick Street full of crackheads and prostitutes, mansions in Holland Park full of crackheads and prostitutes. At night the city belonged to all the people who didn't have to get up in the morning – musicians, artists, actors, models, criminals, the aristocracy, the insane, drug dealers, wheelerdealers, comedians, drug addicts, the fabulously rich, writers, a random bag of all ages, creeds and classes. I never knew whether I was going to meet a murderer next or the most beautiful woman in the world. People only stay up all night for three reasons: sex, drugs and rock and roll. It's not the best time for getting things done.

13

I'm not a huge fan of remixes. A pop record is a distilled, definitive work of art, so changing it in any way is unnecessary. Record companies saw remixes as a way of winning over new audiences, but the results were often less than the sum of the parts. Food commissioned some remixes of tracks on the *Blur* album, mainly because we were short on B-sides. The band had a prolific output and there was usually plenty of unused material around, but releasing three or four singles from an album eats up a lot of extra tracks. Each single came out in three formats and each format needed two or three B-sides. The biggest fans buy everything, so if the B-sides were crap, we were ripping off the people who loved the band the most.

Most of the remixes would have only interested people who knew when Graham's birthday was, or which drama college Damon had been to, but William Orbit's adaptations were astonishing. His *Strange Cargo* album had long been a tour-bus favourite and he was on a roll. He'd just helped Madonna make *Ray of Light*, her best record, and he was the most sought-after producer in the world. He was keen to produce Blur's new album and we went to see him. He lived in a huge rented house in St John's Wood with dozens of assistants who worked through the night polishing drum loops, programming digital sequencers and editing guitar parts on computers. It wasn't so much a home studio. It was more a studio that he lived in.

I had a little studio at home, and I'd looked at buying a bigger one with Damien, Keith and Joe Strummer, but big studios are like jumbo jets. In order for it to be worthwhile owning one, it has to be used all the time otherwise it just sits there costing a fortune. I was too happy-go-lucky to want to go to a recording studio every day of my life but my set-up at home was good for songwriting, and when I'd written some tunes I'd take them to a bigger studio and record them.

It pained me a little bit that the band didn't get a studio we could all have shared, but nobody else wanted to. Damon had a studio in a rented building in Ladbroke Grove, west London. It was to studios what the Good Mixer was to pubs. Its beauty was purely in its functionality. At the arse end of a back street, in a slightly rank-smelling building full of shady characters, it was tiny but it worked very well for Damon.

Working in that studio was a bit like making a record in a lift. There was very little space. In the control room there wasn't enough room to turn round with a guitar on without bashing an award-nominated engineer in the face or knocking over a vintage microphone. Having secured the world's most expensive producer, most bands would probably have taken the logical step of going to the world's most expensive studio, but we wrote *13* in one of west London's best-value, rent-by-the-foot industrial units. There was a window, but it looked through a metal grille on to an uninspiring derelict concrete courtyard, which there was no access to. It was high summer and stinking hot. William, fresh from Madonna's record, crouched, I think rather shocked, in a corner. There was no room for chairs. Damon picked up his acoustic guitar and started singing a melody. Graham and I joined in; Dave, who was wearing headphones behind a drumkit in the other room, joined in. I looked up and saw William's jaw drop. He is quite meticulous and contemplative in his approach. He told me much later that the way we were able instantly to conjure an arrangement without talking about it had completely knocked him out. It had taken us a long time to be able to do that. We'd played together nearly every day for ten years and had a keen sense of each other. We could turn it on pretty much instantly. All the recordings were taken to William's laboratory and tweaked and digitally twiddled by his night assistants.

Things did happen very quickly in the studio. After a couple of weeks we moved back into Mayfair, because it had a good drum room. One morning, Graham and Damon were working on a new song called 'Tender'. It occurred to me that what it really needed was a double bass. I went home in a taxi to get mine and came straight back with it, but they'd got bored with working on the song by then and gone for ciabattas. The bass was miked up and I tuned it and told William to play the track back to me. He said, 'I think I've got what I need there.' He just sampled me tuning up and his boffins used their computer technology to turn it into a bassline. It sounded good too, so I was happy. The strange thing was that when we launched the record there were more photos of that double bass than anything else and I hadn't even played it, really. Cameras just love double basses. 'Tender' was a spiritual and we booked the London Community Gospel Choir to sing on the choruses. Gospel choirs come from a different place than rock and roll bands. They are good and godly people. We received a fax requesting that we did not smoke or swear, with particular reference to blasphemies, while they were in the studio.

It was a biggish choir, about thirty strong. They'd learned the backing vocal and harmony parts and rehearsed them beforehand. They arrived en masse and assembled in the live room. We sat behind the window in the control room and William selected the large loudspeakers, turned up the volume and hit play and record. It was shattering. They nailed it first take. As soon as they started singing, it was instantly and obviously a number one record. I'd never been so certain of anything. It was the best thing we'd ever done. The song was a great collaborative effort between Damon and Graham, too, at a time when their relationship was quite edgy. The harmony of those massed voices and the resting consonance of Damon and Graham's solidarity overwhelmed me to tears. William was in a state of shock again. It was the best we'd all felt for a long, long time. As the song ended, William pushed the talkback button so the choir could hear him. 'Jesus H motherfucking Christ!' he said. 'Ooh shit! Sorry!'

William had another studio on the go in a hotel, where he was building a U2 album. Damon was working on a film score in the mornings at his studio and coming to Mayfair in the afternoons. Maybe that was one of the things that was frustrating to Graham. It was to me. They were finding it hard to talk to each other. Damon is very domineering and maybe Graham had just had enough, but I do think Damon went to great lengths to make Graham feel like *13* was his record as well. Damon gave him one of the strongest melodies, which Graham wrote a good lyric for, but Graham wasn't happy and he didn't always turn up. It was frustrating because, when he did, everything he did was brilliant. He never played a bum note. His hearing was the most astute of anybody's and he could pick things up in mixes that would never occur to me, or mixmaster William for that matter.

Madonna came to the studio and said it was all great, but I'd rather Graham had shown up and said it was all shit, or something at least.

The record was as highly acclaimed as it was difficult to make. 'Tender' was released on the same day as a record by a girl doing backflips in school uniform and missed out on the number one spot, but I heard Brad Pitt played it at his wedding.

10

flying!

Up, Up and Away

On drums, David Alexander De Horne Rowntree had quietly become a high achiever. He seemed to have time for all kinds of things. He was learning karate, building computers, improving his bridge play, publishing scientific papers and learning how to fly. I only knew these things because I read them in the newspapers. Apart from spaceships, we didn't have much to say to each other, even though we went all over the place together.

It's the best thing about being in a band, travelling. Travelling is about the best thing there is, at all. I can't think of anything more worthwhile, more enlightening or more full of promise. There is so much to discover, so many encounters to be had, so many sunsets to see, so many ways of cooking eggs.

Travelling is also incredibly tedious. There was so much travelling. It was like spending half my time in the presence of a crucifying bore who didn't give me space to think and wouldn't release me. Every time I got on an aeroplane, there he was. A big invisible companion. Graham was the only person who could make him go away. We were, all four of us, tormented by our travel bores. I loved going on tour more than anything, but we spent so much time in airports, on motorways, on aeroplanes, in cars, trains, boats and buses. Life was one long steeplechase and there was no easy way round it.

At the start of the *13* album campaign we had to go to Manchester to play some songs for a popular radio show on the BBC. It's about as good as it gets. BBC radio is the best in the world. It's the best-run business, has the biggest audiences, the best microphones, and has no advertising agenda or ulterior motives for existing other than to serve the people three-and-a-half-minute slices of heaven all day. I suppose it was all marvellous, but it was starting to feel like I'd done this kind of thing already and that, pleasant as it would be to play some new songs to millions of people, why did it have to be in Manchester and why was Manchester so far away? Couldn't they just play the record? The record always sounds better on the radio anyway. The thought of sitting on the M1 and the M6 for the best part of the day was looming large on my mind like a bad weather forecast at sea. I called Dave.

'Dave! It's Alex.'

'Hello, Alex.'

'Why have they moved this Radio One business to Manchester? It's supposed to be in London.'

'They're promoting the regions. It's part of the director general's new agenda.' Dave always knew things like that.

'Oh, I see. Look, have you really got an aeroplane, Dave?'

'Yes, actually, I've got two.'

'Great. Excellent. Can we fly to Manchester, then?'

'Yeah, definitely.'

Good old Dave. I remembered how much I'd always liked him.

I hadn't been to Dave's house before. We rarely even visited each other's hotel rooms. He likes to have his own space. He was living in the woods in Hampstead with his wife and a large number of cats and he drove us up to Elstree aerodrome in his little sports car. The airfield was an exciting kind of place. There was a tiny runway, a large number of small aircraft parked on the grass, and a café. I had a fry-up while he checked the aeroplane over with a man called Tony. The café was busy. There were little groups of people huddled together conspiratorially; they all seemed to have a lot to say to each other.

Dave and Tony returned and said they were ready. I asked how long it was going to take. Tony said, 'We're taking the Ruschmeyer. It's brand new and it's quick. Shouldn't be more than forty minutes.'

It was autumn and night had fallen completely since we'd arrived at Elstree. The darkness was complementary to the sense of adventure and I was quite excited as we boarded. The aeroplane was the same size inside as a very small car. I sat in the back with Diana. Diana was the band's current keyboard player. She was a scholar of Debussy and she floated around in the stratosphere of a parallel classical universe. Somehow, she had never heard of Blur when she joined the band, just after 'Country House' came out. She was from a deposed Russian royal family background and she also had a lot of cats. Actually, come to think of it, she only had two cats, but it always seemed like there were a lot more. One of them was called Schnibbles, sometimes, I believe.

Dave pushed a button and the engine burst into life. It made the whole aircraft shake and throb. Diana grabbed my hand and held it very tight as we wobbled towards the runway. I grabbed her other hand. I couldn't hear a thing. Tony passed some headsets to us and indicated where to plug them in. That calmed things down a bit. I could hear Dave talking in a strange language, the only words of which I understood were 'Clear Take Off'. He turned and offered us both cigarettes and pulled on to the runway. He pushed the big lever forward. The engine screamed. Diana's eyes were very large in the light of the burning match as I lit her cigarette. 'Let's rock, motherfuckers!' said Dave and took his feet off the brakes.

We were thrown back into our seats. The runway lights rushed by and the rattling aeroplane swept right into the sky. There was nothing to compare to it. The ground, the world and all of its trivial concerns fell away beneath us in strange accelerations and suddenly all was calm and we were apparently still again. Towns floated by beneath us like magical sets of fairy lights, Watford, Milton Keynes, Birmingham. Birmingham already! It all looked so benign and magical. I was enchanted, rapt with a new perspective of a wonderful world.

We landed behind a 737. I didn't want to go anywhere by car any more. The next day I bought Dave's spare aeroplane.

Oxford Union

I had just set my hair on fire, somehow, at the *Q* Awards. Then I had my photo taken with New Order. Then the phone rang and it was someone asking me if I would address the Oxford Union the next day. I said definitely. I was still a bit miffed about not getting into Oxford. I knew they would need me one day, and that day was tomorrow. Keith was at the *Q* Awards, too. He was at everything. I asked him what the Oxford University Union was. He explained in so many words that it was a debating chamber where the future leaders of the country sharpen their claws by arguing the toss about any old bollocks. Then his phone rang, just like that, and it was someone asking him if he wanted to address the Oxford Union the next day. He said he'd do it, for five hundred quid, cash, and some cake.

The party moved to the Groucho and Magnea was there. She'd moved to London, she said. I went home with her and woke up in the wrong bed at midday. I called Justine and said I'd be home in a minute, but she'd had it. Then I remembered I had to go to Oxford and called her back but she didn't answer. The thought of going to Oxford tomorrow had been quite a nice thought yesterday. The idea of going to Oxford today, in the clothes I'd slept in, was nowhere near as appealing.

I called Keith. I don't think he'd been to bed, which made me feel better. He said we had to pick up Mariella Frostrup on our way to Oxford as she was opposing the motion. I liked Mariella. To describe her as a writer and broadcaster, which is what she is known for, would be selling her short. She is a linchpin of London high society. She knew absolutely everybody, from company directors and executives to broadsheet, tabloid and magazine editors, film stars, rock stars, photographers, writers, artists, moguls and billionaires and they all seemed to have a special affection for her. I certainly did. She seemed to be able to call anyone, anytime.

She had about a hundred pages of notes and her speech all prepared. It had even been neatly typed out by her PA. I had a PA by this time, but she couldn't read my writing.

Keith and I were both the worse for wear and we didn't know what we were supposed to be talking about; Mariella was looking fabulous and she'd done her homework. The title of the motion was 'This house believes that music is the highest form of art'. I didn't need notes to talk about that. I believe it and breathe it.

We dined with the president of the Union in an oak-panelled dining room. The cream of the student body of all the combined colleges of the university was assembled in that room. You could have blasted the whole thing to another planet and there would have been enough knowledge to start a new civilisation from scratch, with no outside assistance.

It was very formal, with prayers, a loyal toast and port that passed to the left. Fair to say, there was definitely a better chance of forming a decent band at Goldsmiths than there, but it was fantastic. We'd lived on pasta sandwiches at Goldsmiths and we rarely bothered with glasses, let alone decanters or grace.

The debating chamber looked just like the House of Commons does on the television. It was a hallowed hall and many great minds had spoken their sensible thoughts there. I had the benefit of speaking last. So far, Keith had stripped to get everyone on our side. Mariella had countered with a suggestion that it was nonsense to compare art forms; a saucy writer of bestselling romantic fiction had told her to get stuffed; a boring DJ type said that music only existed to make money. Then I had the floor. The chairman whispered that he would wave at me once I'd been talking for fifteen minutes and that suddenly seemed like a very long time.

It was silent. All eyes were on me. I hadn't done my homework, again, a familiar stumbling block with this institution.

I do believe music is the highest form of art. It's the ultimate condition and the highest form of anything. Music is an absolutely fundamental quality of the universe. Films are not fundamental entities, nor are paintings, or sculptures. They represent things and have functions. Music actually is something. Music is omniscient, a quality that echoes across space and time: from the concord and balance of galactic superclusters down to the vibrating ten dimensional filaments of superstring theory. The entire cosmos is a musical situation and all artistic and scientific endeavours tend towards music. All life aspires to the state of music. Music is a mystery, pure abstraction, calling from deep to deep. Voices raised in song are louder when you're in love, when you're happy, when you're sad. Music can make hearts beat faster and cause tears to flow. Melody is a universal language. Harmony is the resting place of consciousness. Rhythm hammers the mind into the right shape. Rock stars are the only real deities. We are the music makers. We are the dreamers of dreams.

I said. We lost, but only just. There were drinks and commiserations. The president of the Union joined Fat Les and it was time to go back to London.

Le Touquet

It wasn't obvious whether the Colony Room was one step further towards the gutter or the stars. I was being pulled in two directions. The straight and narrow and the highway to hell were both calling. The spaceship was being built in Milton Keynes and we'd made our best record yet, but I was drinking a lot. I'd take a few weeks off to sort myself out, and then I'd be back with renewed vigour, nailing my pants to the wall of the Groucho between a Damien Hirst and a Peter Blake and climbing into the Colony through the window.

Learning how to fly was exactly what I needed. Playing the bass isn't a position of high responsibility. Lives are not at risk when you plug in a Fender Precision. There are no huge mistakes to be made, or tragic consequences of irresponsible basslines. It suited me. I'm light-hearted, I was young and I didn't want to be weighed down by anything remotely realistic.

I needed a challenge. A pilot is taking his own life, and the lives of his passengers, into his hands. It's the same when you're driving a car, I suppose. There is no one thing about flying an aeroplane that is any more difficult than reversing a car round a corner. Flying is a lot of simple things happening at the same time, often quite fast. It's like reversing round an uphill corner while talking on the telephone, reading a map and looking at the rev counter. At two hundred miles an hour. It's crucial never to run out of petrol either. There's the radio, the navigation systems, the weather, the handling of the aircraft, the emergency procedures to master. I loved every minute of it.

To begin with, I wanted to fly because I thought it was a

good way to get around, but I soon realised that it was flying I loved.

Tony, who had flown with us to Manchester, was my teacher. He was fanatical about flying. He considered time spent on the ground as time wasted. He had the keys to nearly every aeroplane at Elstree and in his day job he was a British Airways pilot. We'd go to Leicester for lunch and practise taking off and landing. Then we'd fly to Wales for tea. They had really good cake in Cardiff. Then we'd come back to London, low level over the Cotswolds, practising engine failures, stalls and steep turns. Nothing looks ugly from the sky, but the Cotswolds surprised me. I'd never been there, but that part of the country looked the most beautiful from above. The grass was the greenest. The gently rolling landscape with its neat farms, honey-coloured villages and grand piles nestling secretly in their formal gardens was as beautiful and otherworldly as an underwater tableau.

Once I had my licence I went to France most weekends. The 'glamour run', from Elstree to Le Touquet, took about forty minutes in my new aeroplane, a Beechcraft Bonanza. It was like a flying Bentley with big ashtrays for fat cigars. It was the same kind of aeroplane that Buddy Holly had died in. I never told anyone that until we got home safely, though.

Le Touquet is a seaside resort about ten minutes' flying time west of Calais. After takeoff at Elstree it was usually possible to get clearance from air traffic control to fly over London beneath the airliners. I'd fly low down the Lee Valley to Canary Wharf, with Tower Bridge and the West End to the right and Greenwich on the nose. London is miraculous and passengers were always still reeling from it all as we turned right at the Thames Barrier to cross the Kent marshes for Dover. As the white cliffs slid behind, France looked like you could reach out and touch it. The Dover Strait is surprisingly narrow. Coasting in at France, Le Touquet, Paris Plage, is the second town on the right. In days gone by it was the exclusive playground of the rich and famous. More recently they huddle together at the southern end of France on its grisly private beaches and within its gated communities. It's all the same people you see in New York and London down there. Northern France, and particularly Le Touquet, are a well-kept secret. The expansive beaches are deserted and the whole place has a natural glamour. The French are a sophisticated race. Whereas Bournemouth tends to die at the end of summer, Le Touquet becomes cosier and more romantic.

It's just a ten-minute walk through the pine forests from the airport into town, or you can rent bicycles. There are chocolate shops, a casino and silly things to rent and do. There are restaurants galore and hotels from the grand to the grounded. After a while, I began to like the cheap hotels. They had the most character. Luxury looks the same in Le Touquet as it does in Leeds. You lose all sense of luxury if you never step outside of it. We all need a bit of rough with our smooth.

Airborne Cruising

Flying turned everything around. Where I had dreaded the daily schlep to the next place, now it was the thing that I looked forward to the most. Dave had graduated to a multi-engine, six-seater Cessna. It was a real heap, but it got us around. We took a pilot with us on tour. His name was Bob. He prepared the aeroplane, fuelled it, filed flight plans, checked the weather and paid the landing fees so that Dave and I just had to jump in and take off. Bob was a test pilot for Lockheed Martin. Previously he had made many millions from running a successful aerobatic display team, but he had spent all his money on jet fighters and helicopters. They are the aviation equivalent of crack cocaine and heroin. He told me never to get into jets. He was on top of it now, he said; he still had one jet trainer but he only used it at weekends. Then he said I had to try it. It did Mach 0.8, was fully aerobatic, and he'd just bought new ejector seats for it.

Damon said there was no way he was ever going to get into an aeroplane with me, or Dave, let alone both of us. Then we were in Germany on a Monday. We left the stage and I told the tour manager to call a taxi. Damon asked where I was going and I said I was going home and toodle-oo. There was no scheduled flight until the morning and by the time we'd done the encore Damon had completely changed his mind about which people he got into aeroplanes with. He was quite nervous and drank a lot of vodka on the way to the airport. It was a large international airport, all the runway and taxi lights were on, but there was very little traffic as it was so late at night. The terminal buildings were empty. We had the place to ourselves. It was ethereal. There was a café for the freight pilots and we ate chips and mayonnaise with a cosmopolitan assembly of flight crews while Bob activated the flight plan and made a final check of the weather.

The weather outlook was quite bad with thunderstorms over Belgium, said Bob. Hopefully we would be able to avoid them or it would be very bumpy. Then he and Dave got into a conversation about de-icing equipment that I couldn't follow. Dave was some way ahead of me as a pilot. He had an instrument rating, the very top flying qualification. In theory it meant that he had the skills to land at Heathrow, in a thick foggy thunderstorm in the middle of the night while simultaneously handling an engine failure. It was no use telling Damon that. He was looking worried and he'd opened another bottle of vodka at the mention of thunderstorms.

The airport was massive and we spent a good ten minutes navigating the brightly lit taxiways. The moon was up in a cloudless sky and we were cleared to enter controlled airspace at our cruising altitude, as we'd hoped. There was a good tailwind. Then the moon disappeared and it started to get bumpy. Bob was asking air traffic for 'radar vectors' around the bad weather.

Dave was writing things down. Damon was drinking vodka. I lit a cigarette. Bob screamed, 'PUT IT OUT! If we get a lightning strike and you're smoking, we're toast.' Poor Damon. The aircraft, which must have weighed five tonnes, was getting tossed around like a feather. I'd never known turbulence like that. I had to tighten my seat belt to stop my head banging the ceiling as hailstones crashed around us. The darkness was complete apart from the warm and comforting glow of the instrument panel. My head was thrown back and I could hardly support it, then I would feel weightless. It was a runaway rollercoaster. The Cessna 310 was being put through its paces. Bob was enjoying himself at last. Our manager had insisted that at no time should the four of us ever fly together in a light aircraft, as it would invalidate our insurance. There were risks, but in less than three minutes we popped out of the storm cell into clear skies as if nothing had happened.

Then Damon needed to go to the toilet. We had a hot-water bottle for that, but it had never been put to the test. The flying magazines all recommended hot-water bottles as being the best receptacles. They don't work. They're too floppy, that was clear very quickly, and it was a while before Damon flew with us again.

The Fat Les brigade were all too happy to jump into an aeroplane when we were given some tickets for England vs. Germany in the European Championships. I hired an enormous Piper Navajo from a geezer at Elstree. It was a real old banger, a musty twelve-seater with a loo. The match was in Belgium, but the weather was clement. Michael Barrymore was in the band by that time. I'm not sure exactly what he did in the band, but he was good to have around. He was extravagant, funny, highly intelligent and incredibly famous. I was used to walking around with Damon and seeing heads spin and jaws drop. I got a bit of it myself, but Barrymore was in a different league. Absolutely everybody recognised him and loved him too, from kids in pushchairs to grannies on Zimmer frames. Whenever he came to my house, by the time he left, which sometimes was days later, there was always a crowd of paparazzi outside. I was a bit nervous about taking a high-profile homo into the lions' den of an England/Germany clash. He was wearing a baseball cap, in an attempt at anonymity, but he just looked like Michael Barrymore in a baseball cap. The Navajo has turbocharged engines and goes like stink, but somehow the passengers all managed to get completely shit-faced in the back of the aircraft in the twenty-five minutes it took to get to Charleroi. They sang all the way.

The city was a war zone. You could taste the testosterone on the breeze. There were no women or children in the town, or any Belgians. The shops were shut and marauding gangs roamed the streets looking for trouble. It wasn't Jerusalem. It was horrible. I haven't been to a football match since. Fortunately, Barrymore was a big hit with the apes, whose mums were all fans, without exception. We saw the tender side of many a football toughie as they politely asked Michael for autographs for their old dears. Inside the stadium it was chaos. The seats were jammed close together like a fairground ride, and all right on top of each other so that if anyone in the top row fell over, everyone would go down like dominoes. There were mountain rescue teams in place in case that happened. People were vomiting, screaming and throwing things. The man I was squashed next to had got so drunk that he'd messed his trousers. He really hummed. He hugged me when England scored and after that I hoped they wouldn't score again. I just wanted to get back into the aeroplane.

Mick Jagger was at the airport, getting into his Learjet. I heard someone say, 'Hey, Michael!' and Mick turned around. Somebody was running towards Michael Barrymore waving a pen and paper.

More Beautiful Women

Robert, the magnet guy, the artist I'd met in New York, came to stay at Mercer Street. One of his flying lawnmowers was on show at a new high-tech gallery in the East End. An American art dealer had converted an old warehouse into a church of contemporary art. This dealer was new in town. He explained to me that he liked the East End because it was still 'kinda edgy'. It certainly was. On the morning after the gala opening three men walked into the gallery, locked him in the cellar and stole all the equipment: the computers, monitors, projectors and lights. They didn't bother with any of the art and some of the artists were offended by the snub.

It was great having Robert around. He knew how everything worked. He enjoyed dismantling mechanical household appliances and putting them back together again so that they worked perfectly. He had already tuned up the dishwasher, given the washing machines a service, and when I got back from the studio he was stripping down the boiler. He felt it was a bit noisy, and that its performance could be improved.

I thought it would be good for business to take him to the Serpentine Gallery summer party and he squeezed into one of my suits. The Serpentine is in the middle of Hyde Park. Every summer a leading art figure is commissioned to create an experimental piece of architecture in the park next to the gallery and the good and the great all come and drink champagne within it. At the end of August a wealthy patron of the arts buys the 'Summer Pavilion' and puts it in one of his gardens, next to his tree collection, where it increases in value for ever more.

It was a sit down dickie-bow dinner. I was trying to listen to the football on a transistor radio. England went out and we hadn't sold anywhere near enough copies of 'Jerusalem' to pay for all those violins. Then there was an auction. Charles Saatchi, the Saviour of British Art, bought a Mini covered in spots by

Groucho Club, 9.30 a.m.
with Damien and Keith

With Sam Taylor-Wood and
Kate Moss at Claridge's,
2001. Where else?

Barrymore joins Fat Les

Ready for departure at Elstree

Oxford Union

Beagle, 2002

Right: Claridge's again, 2002

Bottom left: Claire

Bottom right: Where's Gra?

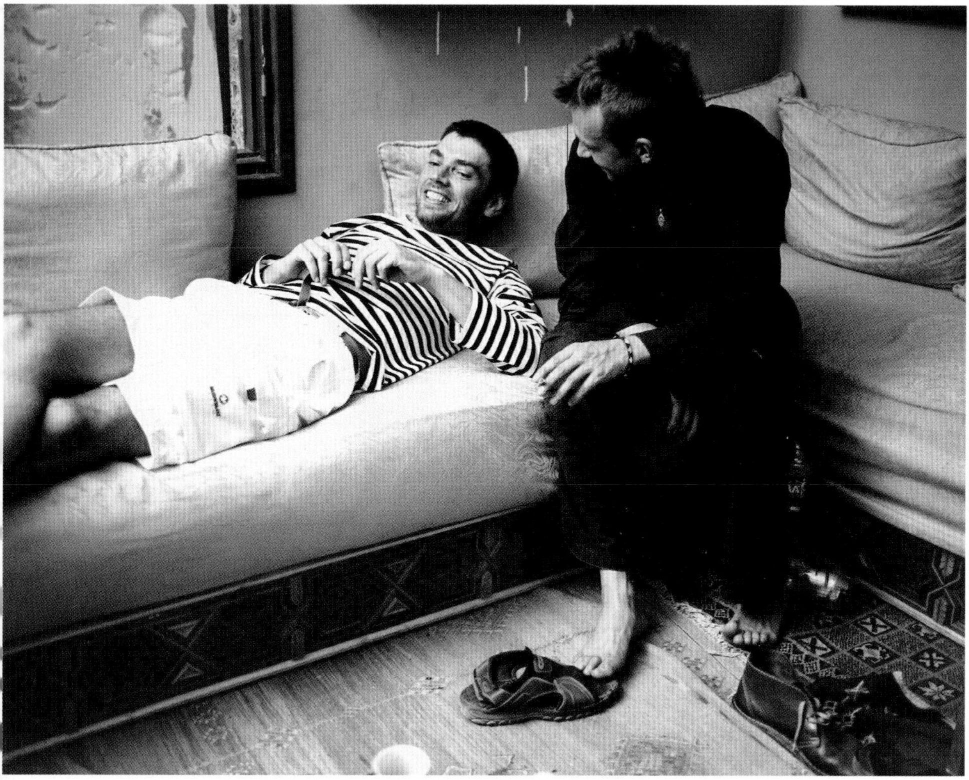

Morocco, recording *Think Tank*, 2002

Swimming in Devon in December 2002 with Mike Smith. Dave (on the left) didn't fancy it

Mr and Mrs Neate
James, April 2003

The band reunited at the wedding

About to go to Nice in the Bonanza

Above & below: Premature babies, 2006

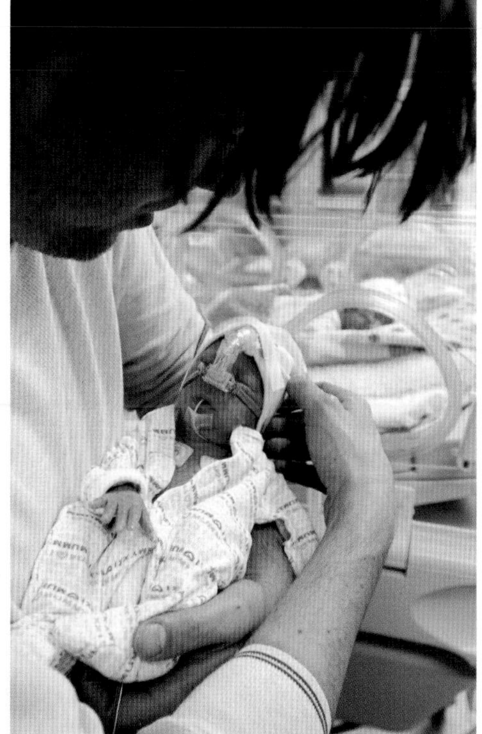

Flying baby

The New Forest, 2006

Patagonia, 2005

In the country, 2007

Damien, similar to the taxi Keith had left in Rotterdam, but not as good. He paid half a million pounds for it. It was not my night, I figured. Then a man at the next table said, 'Hey, this girl wants to meet you!'

I couldn't recall ever seeing anyone so beautiful. I couldn't recall anything for the moment. She was long, willowy and delicate and she held her infinite gaze on me with perfect poise and immaculate balance. It was like being killed. I was consumed in her gaze. I noticed then that I was laughing and I asked her if she wanted to come to Rotterdam, but we went dancing instead. Robert was having a good evening, he had sold a flying lawnmower to a lonely countess and although he'd split his trousers he was in the mood and, suddenly, strange things were happening again. We were escorted by discreetly armed SAS men to a cavalcade of Daimlers. The men kept looking around and talking into their sleeves. I got into the first one with Robert and the girl. The Duchess of York and Prince Andrew – or maybe it was Edward, whichever one she had been married to – got into the one behind. The remaining cars were for security. The procession glided into Berkeley Square and we hit the dance floor at a club called Annabel's. I remember doing the Macarena with the duchess and ordering a magnum of Cristal, and I remember leaving with Robert. Then we walked back to the Colony where we belonged.

She called me, that girl, but I didn't know what to do. I was already infatuated and I knew if I started seeing her I'd be in love, just like that. I was already in love, with Justine, and having sex with people was one thing, but falling in love was much more complicated.

I was with Colin Pillinger at the Groucho and we'd drunk too much absinthe. I was running to the toilet to be sick, but I didn't make it and I lost my lunch on the floor of the upstairs bar. I felt much better and insisted on clearing it up myself. I was still mopping when Courtney Love arrived. She liked my shirt and she lifted my mop and gave me her phone number. I thought about it and I liked it and I called her. I wondered what booze to take to her house. I settled on a magnum of rosé champagne. Rosé champagne is never, ever wrong. You could take it to your granny's. You could take it to Buckingham Palace. It was fine for Courtney too.

She was wearing a dressing gown when I arrived. We drank the champagne quite quickly, from the bottle, mainly. She's had so many songs written about her, probably more than any other living person, and now I know why. She is a beguiling woman. I really liked her, we were having a great time, but I had to go to New York. Damien had another show, and, being banned from the Mercer, had taken the top floor of the SoHo Grand for his stay. It had a large roof terrace.

Things were really spiralling out of control. As the sun came up Keith, Damien and I burnt the backs of our wrists with hot lumps of charcoal from the barbecue on the roof. The circular scar was the sign of The Embers, a select brotherhood about which I can say no more here, as it is highly secret. Damien's girlfriend Maia wasn't allowed to join The Embers, but she wanted to join in so she burnt the back of her heel. Our friend Charles, the chef, was eligible for Embership but he didn't want to go through the ritual. Later he got drunk and used a cigarette.

The burn gave me gyp the whole weekend. By the time the show opened, I'd been up for three days and I had pus dripping down my left hand. The gallery was rammed with gruesome New York high society at a high frenzy. It was like Harrods on the first day of the sales. They pushed and shoved and were every bit as grotesque as the people at the football match in Belgium. There was a girl called Fanny. She'd written a novel. We left right away. We went back to my room at the Mercer and danced to the Bee Gees. So many of the great episodes of my life have been interspersed with the music of the Gibb brothers. We went out for breakfast and I put her on a train to Brooklyn. I had a bad case of the horrors and went back to my room to die. To my surprise Keith was sitting on the bed tucking into a room-service breakfast. He was wearing a pink suit. I wanted to know how he'd got into the room and he said he'd told reception that he was my boyfriend. He had some vodka with him and that took the edge off everything. Keith did too. He never felt any shame. He was never horrified about anything he'd done. He had absolute faith in his every action. His company was just what my screaming superego needed. We walked round to the SoHo Grand in the sunshine, comparing burns.

The roof terrace was a battle scene. The best suite at New York's second-best hotel was littered with the unconscious, the unsavoury and the undressed. I felt much better, drank some vodka and took all my clothes off.

That was when Damien threw the watermelon. It was the size of a beach ball. He picked it up and hurled it backwards over his head with both hands. It sailed clean over the parapet. I do wonder why he did it. He never got drunk enough to lose his charm. He must have known what he was doing. The street fifty storeys below was a busy one. A direct hit by an apple from that height would have been touch and go. A watermelon travelling at terminal velocity would have taken out a car. Way down below, there was watermelon everywhere. No one had taken a direct hit, but only by chance, and a fair number of people had been completely slimed. The police arrived quickly. There were a lot of them. They arrested everybody, especially the naked ones. I said I had to go inside to get my clothes. The door of the suite was open and I darted through it, unnoticed, scrambling into my trousers and leaping into the lift half dressed when it arrived. I only just escaped from New York that time. My arm was swelling up. Justine took me to the doctor, who wanted to know how it had happened. The doctor asked a lot of questions, to see if I was mad, but I managed to convince her that I was just stupid. Courtney had somehow found and called the home number while I was away. Justine was really good at handling those calls. Stella McCartney called a couple of times, just on friendly business. There was nothing going on there, but Jus was fed up with the girls she didn't know calling the house and she made them all suffer.

'Hello, can I speak to Alex?'

'Who's calling?'

'Stella.'

'Who?'

'It's Stella McCartney.'

'Could you spell that please?'

'M-C-C-A-R-T-N-E-Y.'

'Yeah, I'm sorry, er, Sheila, but he's watching telly. I'll tell him you called.'

Grand Prix

The temperature was still rising. The tempo was increasing. It was the final spin cycle and things were getting still more far-fetched. I returned from Greenland after crossing the Atlantic four times in seven days, once on Concorde. I can't remember a thing about Concorde apart from the noise. I was invited to the Grand Prix in Monte Carlo, to write a story for *Harper's Bazaar*. I couldn't see a downside. They'd put me in the blah-blah five star this, give me dinner at the blah-blah Michelin star that, and I'd have a driver and a pit pass and everyone would be there and it was all going to be super-duper. Damien said that he was going and that I should come and stay with Anne and Mungo at their places. They had an apartment overlooking the grid and a villa in the hills.

Anne is an art dealer from an old Monaco dynasty and Mungo is an expert Perudo player. I guess he must have made a stack of money somehow or other. I kept meaning to ask him what he did, but there was always something else going on. They led a life of exquisite tastefulness and elegance. I liked them both a lot.

'They were going to put you in a hotel, darling, how horrible! What? A driver from Jaguar? Sweetheart, you can't drive anywhere in town without Monaco plates this weekend. Take my car. *Le quoi? Mais c'est terrible!* You can't possibly eat there. Everybody will be at Rocamadour tonight. You must come. Will you? Mungo, get this boy a drink!'

Largely thanks to Anne and Mungo, it was a weekend of great delights. How dull the weekend would have been without them, it's hard to say. I would probably have thought I was having a good time. It's funny how 'very good indeed' is no substitute for 'the best', once you know that 'best' exists. This was well illustrated in the harbour. Jemma, who was on/off dating one of the drivers, had told us to meet her on the big boat. Which big boat? we wondered; they were all big. It was a monstrous parade of obscene ostentation. It was tacky. The further we walked along the pontoon, the larger the boats became. Soon we were looking at ships. Then we saw the big boat. It was definitely the right one. On one end there was a helicopter pad with a shiny Augusta 109 sitting on it. The Augusta 109 is the fastest, fanciest, most expensive helicopter on the market. At the other end, an ocean-going yacht was suspended above the deck, in case anyone fancied a sail. It was dwarfed by the magnitude of the mother ship. The whole caboodle gleamed with mint newness and bespoke magnificence. The boats on either side were the second and third nicest things I'd ever seen in my life, both floating fortresses of far-fetched fabulousness. But they were deserted. Absolutely nobody was in the slightest bit interested in second and third. The whole world was aboard *Le Grand Bleu*. And that's the way it is in Monaco. The big guy gets everything. I'm not sure if the owner was even there, but everybody else was.

Social standing in the world of high glamour is precarious. The previous time I'd been in the South of France was with the band for the Cannes Film Festival. We'd flown into Nice by private jet and transferred to the festival by helicopter. We were staying at a hotel with massed crowds outside. My room was the only one with a roof terrace. It overlooked the cordoned-off red carpet that led to the hotel entrance. We'd come in through the back doors, but there was a constant flow of celebrity traffic along the carpet, taking bows and signing autographs. I suppose film stars only encounter multitudes at premieres and they wanted to make the most of it. It is a unique and addictive feeling to be confronted with a crowd that loves you and is willing you to surprise or enthral it. Bands encounter thronged humanity every day. It's normal. Surprisingly the bigger the horde, the easier it is to take command. It's a thousand times easier to whip a swarm into a whirl than it is to get one person agitated. Crowd behaviour is surprisingly easy to control, as long as you have the right kind of spanner; the police use horses; we used guitars; the film stars had to do it all with their teeth, flashing their flimsy smiles.

The stage was on the beach, and the only way to get to it without going through the crowds was by speedboat. We played a couple of songs and we were done. The record company had hired the speedboat for the whole day, so that was at my disposal. Things were looking good. Roof terrace, private jet, speedboat, new friends – I was on the Soho House boat, with Ewan MacGregor, when the tour manager called and said it was time to go home. I told him I'd decided to spend the rest of my life here. He said that was all fine, and he'd leave an open return ticket at the hotel.

Then Mariella was there and she asked me how the hell I was going to get to the Hôtel du Cap by speedboat. I did not know this hotel. She said we had to go there right now, because it was where 'it' was. There is a lot of dashing around trying to find 'it' at Cannes. 'It' never stops moving. 'Come on,' she said, 'I've got a moped.'

It was indeed all happening at the Hôtel du Cap. Security was draconian. From nowhere, Mariella produced sheaves of paperwork, badges and accreditation, and we were in. It seemed to be more of a magazine than a hotel. There was a different story going on in every room. Apart from the bar, which was buzzing nicely, it was peaceful. The management had gone to great lengths to preserve the refined calm of the establishment. In town it was a bunfight; up in the hills it was all about candles and whispers. It was a wonderful atmosphere. I struck up an instant intimacy with a billionaire who invited me to come and stay on his boat in the south seas.

We were drinking Bellinis – champagne and peach juice. Pretty soon everyone was. At the exact point when things could never get any better, I left, taking two beautiful women with me.

It was late and all was calm on the Promenade des Anglais. We sat on the terrace looking out to sea and singing.

Then two men were pulling me out of bed by my feet. I was naked. God, I felt awful. What was happening? I kicked but they kept pulling and they were shouting now.

'*Messieurs, s'il vous plaît!?*'

'Room is finish!' said one.

'Fine. I'll take it for another night.'

'Is finish!'

'*Moi, je n'ai pas fini. Moi! Je payerai.*'

'Is all full.'

'You're telling me it's awful, it's a disgrace, mate.'

'*Non, monsieur*. All. Full. Full.'

That was it: boom to bust in twenty-four hours. Dragged out into the corridor by my feet. One of them went back to get my stuff while the other one stared at me. The girls had gone. The speedboat was making someone else's day today. I was wrecked, knackered and homeless. There wasn't a vacant room within a hundred miles. How are the mighty fallen. I didn't call anybody. I went back to live in England immediately. Nobody loves you when you're down and out, baby.

In Monaco this time, things were on more of an even keel as I was with friends. There was something vaguely familiar about those cars flashing round and round in circles at high speed and volume. When they'd finished they threw champagne everywhere. As soon as the race was over, the sky filled with helicopters. It was gridlock up there.

We all walked to the beach. Anne said the gaffer, Prince Albert, was going to be there. I asked Mungo what I should be doing if I had a royal encounter. Mungo knew all about etiquette. He had shown me four different ways to tie a tie the previous evening. Then he had explained who made the best ties in the world and why they were great and where to get them. Then he'd kicked my ass at Perudo again. I felt like a small but favoured boy. With regards to any Albert activity, he said that it was an informal occasion so it would be quite relaxed, but it would be good manners to stand if we were introduced, not to shake his hand until offered, to let him lead the conversation and to refer to him as 'sir'. It all sounded sensible.

Monte Carlo's one small beach is reserved for its senior players. It is fastidiously maintained. It's more of an open-air restaurant where you eat lying down. Anne and Mungo's pitch, with its loungers and parasols, was permanently reserved and it neighboured the royal enclosure. Sure enough, Good Prince Albert was there and he and Anne were deep in conversation. I was introduced and I stood up and it all went very well. Then Damien's brother Bradley arrived. Part of Damien's charm is that he is not from a privileged background. He's more of a home-grown king, a triumph of merit and charisma, which have their own nobility. I love Damien's family. Bradley is a Formula One fanatic and he was having the best day of his life. He was very drunk and excited and he was dripping from the sea. 'Foookinell, did you see them bazongers? Them were beauty.'

'Ah, Bradley, this is Prince Albert of Monaco.'

'Fokinell, alright mate. Did you see them tits?'

Prince Albert of Monaco was smiling.

Several Sorties

August was a holiday. I spent the first week in the Colony and then I flew down to Land's End to see Fanny. She'd come back from New York to stay with her parents. I terrified her poor mother. I drank all the brandy and knocked all the delicate things over. I had trouble on the way back, getting caught out by bad weather. I'd checked the forecast thoroughly, but the forecast got it wrong. I wasn't qualified to fly in cloud. There was fog behind me and the cloud ahead was lower than the hill-tops. I was in a blind panic and considering putting out a Mayday. I knew very well that the average time an untrained pilot retains control of the aircraft in cloud is less than three minutes before spiralling into the ground. I heard someone say on the radio that he was above the cloud at fifteen hundred feet. There was no way forward or back. The only way was up. I was flying at five hundred feet and at a normal cruise climb I figured I'd be in cloud for two minutes. I just had to keep the nose up and the wings level and watch the airspeed. Sounds easy, but I've never been so scared, not even being chased down an icy road by a hundred of Magnea's boyfriends. Not even close. Time stood still in the greyness. You can't trust your sense of balance in cloud. Only the instruments can tell you what's happening. I tried to do everything slowly but my mind was racing, my heart was whirring and sweat was teeming from every pore. Suddenly, as if someone had turned the lights on, there was brilliant sunshine everywhere. It was like being born again. I swore to do an instrument rating. I landed at Bournemouth and stayed with my mum and dad for a couple of days. My dad said he was concerned about how much I was drinking. Still, we went to the pub and the landlord wouldn't let us pay for anything and kept bringing new whiskies for us to try. He didn't want us to go home at closing time and kept bringing forth older and grander whiskies. By the time we sailed out at two a.m. my dad was singing 'Roll Out the Barrel' and agreeing that it wasn't easy to stay out of trouble.

The weather cleared, eventually, and the hangovers, and I said I'd take my parents to the Isle of Wight for lunch. My mum is quite a nervous flyer and it was the first time I'd been able to persuade her to come on the aeroplane. At the airport, as I went to complete the pre-flight checks on the Bonanza, I noticed the Red Arrows parked in formation on the apron. When I was happy with the aircraft, I signalled to Kelly and Jason in the terminal to make their way over. As they were getting in I noticed the Red Arrows starting to taxi. It was a stirring sight. They all moved as one. I called the tower.

'Golf Sierra Tango request taxi.'

'Golf Sierra Tango, roger. Follow the Red Arrows, please.'

Kelly was sitting next to me and her mouth was gaping wide open as they flowed past and we pulled out behind them. She kept looking from me to Jason and back again. She grabbed my hand and it was pretty spectacular as they reached the runway and rocketed off as one. If you ever meet my mother, you will know her because she is the one telling that story. She tells everyone about that.

I went back to Cannes with Mariella. It took four hours in the Bonanza, due south all the way and not a cloud in the sky. We stayed at the Hôtel du Cap. The film festival had popped like a bubble and disappeared. In high season the clientele comprised bored billionaires' wives, presidents and royalty. It is said to be the finest hotel in the world. They only accept cash as payment, and there are stories of people taking suites for the entire summer and settling up with briefcases full of bundles. You couldn't make anything more luxurious. It was so luxurious it had a tranquillising effect. Everyone was in bed by ten, exhausted by the utter tedium of complete perfection. We got drunk on Bellinis and went for a swim in the pools at midnight and it felt like we'd done everything there was to do there.

We left in the morning to find Damien in Provence. He was playing volleyball. His host was slaughtering a lamb. We went for dinner in the world's most expensive restaurant. From the moment the junior waiter unfolded your napkin for you until the nice lady lit your cigar, things could not have been more tippety-top. Leaving the best hotel with my exalted consort, to arrive at the most expensive restaurant in my own aeroplane, to meet the world's richest living artist. The next day we flew to Mick Jagger's chateau in the Loire.

It was going to be downhill all the way from here, surely? This was the top of the hill. What else could life hold? It's funny, but when I look back I think that period of my life was the bottom of a pit, rather than the summit of Mount Fantasticus. I was a morally bankrupt, pissed fatso with a stupid grin and a girlfriend with a murdered heart.

11

rounded and grounded

Keep Fit

Will Ricker had a knack with restaurants. He knew where to put them and what fashionable people would want to eat next. He's nothing like the gentlemen behind the Ivy and Le Caprice who always suggest a saintly otherworldliness, as if they've astrally projected down from heaven to keep an eye on how things are going here on earth. Those fellows glide around the tables of their establishments, slightly beyond and above the hubble-bubble of lunch and dinner. Will, though, was one of the boys, and gave the impression more of being en route to or from an unmade bed; but every time he opened a new restaurant it filled up with the famous and the fabulous. People tend to get much more excited about seeing Johnny Depp than they do about food, even dessert. The kind of women who get excited about sticky toffee pudding go completely la-la when confronted with a munching movie star. It's a different order of excitement. Will had some kind of celebrity-invoking juju powers and everybody wanted to be his friend.

'Alex, buddy.' He said, he's Australian, as you can see. 'Alex, I was watchin' one of your Blur videos yistidy. Mate, it's a cryin' shame. You've gotta lose some weight, mate. I'm sindin' my man round.'

Resistance was futile. A spritely Australian appeared on the doorstep the very next day and brought in dumb-bells, boxing gloves, a bicycle, chest expanders and other instruments of torture. Then he told me to put my running shoes on. I didn't have any running shoes. I had quite an anti-exercise outlook. I believed that people in bands should concentrate on other, less realistic things, like being decadent and fantastic. But here he was, and it was true that I was starting to look rather frog-like, bulging at the eyes and the neck and the belly. Girls didn't seem to mind, so I'd been ignoring it. I'd rather been hoping things would sort themselves out, which was the strategy I applied to most crises.

Fortunately, the press office darlings of Adidas, Puma, Gola, Lacoste, Converse, Reebok and Nike had been bombarding me with trainers and I grabbed a pair from a big stack of unopened boxes, put my cigarette out and took a deep breath. By the time we'd run as far as Trafalgar Square, I was taking much deeper ones. I was in a different world of pain from my accustomed hungover malaise. Chest on fire; heart beating like a machine gun; legs, arms, back aching and needling me with intense agonies. I stumped around the pond in St James's Park and traipsed back up St Martin's Lane groaning and bellowing so loudly that heads turned. Jason, my tormentor, didn't break into a sweat. I was wearing a heart rate monitor. He said he'd never seen it go that high, which seemed to please him immensely. Then he said, cheerfully, 'Roight, boxin' toime.' The gloves that he gave me had seen plenty of active service and gave forth an unforgettable series of stinks as they warmed up. Having destroyed my legs, he set to work on my arms, teasing me exquisitely with phantom punches if I let my guard drop.

After a couple of minutes I decided to try and kill him, but I couldn't get near him. He finished me off with some sit-ups and said he'd see me next week. Next week sounded awfully soon. I asked him if it was really necessary to go through all that every week and he said that, to start with, daily would be the best way to make a difference.

I phoned Will and told him he was a bastard, took a cool shower and sipped some orange juice. Then, quite slowly, I started to feel excellent. My hangover had evaporated. I felt energetic and nimble. I felt weightless, fearless and calm. I was in a genuine altered state, but it was the exact opposite of drinking, which feels great while you're doing it and horrendous afterwards. I felt so good that I went to the café and had a fry-up.

Jason's visits became regular. His clientele were the chieftains and queen bees of the city jungle. He knew more famous people than me and he had them all grunting and groaning. Most of them had swimming pools as well, poor souls. He came to me early in the morning, at six-thirty, having already given a fashion magazine editor the works. She followed her fitness training with an hour of yoga, five days a week. I couldn't tell if that was right or wrong. Directly after me he went to Chelsea and bossed Bryan Adams up and down his swimming pool for a bit, before going to fight with Will Ricker. Will was getting quite fanatical about boxing. I was starting to enjoy the excursions around the park in the peace of the early morning sun. Gradually, we extended the run around Buckingham Palace and Green Park. There were times when I hadn't slept, but I knew my hangover wouldn't be as bad if I ran around the parks. That still wasn't sufficient motivation to get me out of bed, but Jason saw to that. Pretty soon, I started to run on my own as well.

I'd spent about a million pounds on champagne and cocaine. It sounds ridiculous but, looking back, I don't regret it. It was definitely the right thing to do. It was completely decadent, but I was a rock star, after all, a proper one, with a public duty to perform. The smorgasbord of life's exquisite delights was my *raison d'être*. I wanted to live life in the moment as fully as possible, and stocks and shares weren't the ticket. I don't think I could have enjoyed the full twelve courses of the menu gastronomique with any less of a capital investment. Oddly, if I'd been more conservative, and spent the odd hundred grand, which was probably about par for a successful musician, the rest probably would have just disappeared, but my excesses were so well documented, and 'key to the image value of the Blur brand', that the cash I spent formed a kind of advertising campaign and I'm pretty sure I recouped the whole lot, one way or another. Certainly, the accountants managed to claim back the VAT on most of the champagne. If you spend enough money on something, it starts coming back eventually.

Still, I was at a watershed. There is a natural elegance in youthful excess, which gradually turns uglier as one gets older. Uglier and uglier and uglier. Did I want to be chasing women when I was sixty-five, or, worse still, drunk, legless and lonely like Jeffrey Bernard?

No.

The Road of Excess leads to the Palace of Wisdom.

Instrument Rating

Nothing terribly bad happened when I wasn't drinking, but the worry was that nothing terribly fantastic happened either. I'd always adhered to Storm Thorgerson's advice to take a rest from drinking for one day every week. It wasn't ever easy, but it served me well. Sometimes I'd take a week off, and I'd even gone sober for a whole month here and there. By now, hangovers were unsupportable five-day epics with special effects and I thought I might try to abstain for a whole year. It was quite a big step to take. Being elegantly wasted was kind of my job, and my social life, too, revolved around hedonistic abandon. When I'd stopped drinking in the past, it had been a matter of just hanging on until the time was up, but to spend a whole year in temperance meant that my life would have to change.

For any drinker the entire pattern of existence changes when alcohol is off the menu. New routines emerge, things get done and good things do inevitably develop, although at a slower pace than the whizz, bang, wallop, wa-hey, whoops-a-daisy of the boozy escapade. Eventually, I started to feel I might be starring in a different kind of film altogether.

Pro Flight Aviation, the flying school at Bournemouth airport, was one of only three in the country that offered airborne training for the instrument rating. I'd already completed a correspondence course that involved many weeks of fiddling around with a slide rule and memorising acronyms, followed by a week of intensive residential study and three days of exams at Gatwick airport. An instrument rating is the ultimate pilot's licence. An instrument-rated pilot is licensed to fly not just in cloud, but also in controlled airspace, with the airliners.

Airliners never fly direct to their destination. Air traffic would be unmanageable if that were the case. To keep things organised, there is a global network of airways, which are like motorways. The jets join the airways system after the takeoff procedure, and leave the network only to descend at the destination aerodrome. This means that all the world's serious air traffic is funnelled very close together. The separation margin between me on the way home in my Bonanza and you eating nuts on a 747 coming in the opposite direction at a relative speed greater than a Kalashnikov bullet might be as little as five hundred feet. That's just a bit longer than a football pitch. It's not much when you consider a 747 is just a bit wider than a football pitch and we might both be in cloud. This is why the instrument rating is so difficult. The CAA, the governing body, make it difficult on purpose. Fifty feet is the tolerated margin of error. No autopilot, no GPS, and screens over the windows so you can't see out.

The flying school was in a different time zone from everywhere else in Bournemouth. I called them and a voice told me to report for training at 'zair-o nine-ah hundred ars Zulu'. I knew what Zulu meant; it's Greenwich Mean Time, but I can never remember if it's an hour ahead or an hour behind the normal kind of time. Sometimes it's the same, particularly in France. I asked, 'Eight a.m?' The voice said, 'Affirmative. Eight local currency', but from his tone I gathered the local currency wasn't accepted.

Zulu time is the only one that counts for pilots. Instrument clocks in aeroplanes are all set to Zulu. A pilot departing Kuala Lumpur has to say what time it will be in Greenwich when he wants to take off, rather than what time it will be in Kuala Lumpur.

To climb into one of the flying school aircraft was to step out of local time and out of recognisable space into a new scheme of references. The outside world was obscured by screens and represented solely by six wobbling needles. To start with it was terrifying, but after a few weeks I could take off without looking out of the window, fly to Southampton, make an approach, get within fifty feet of the runway, have an engine failure, execute a missed approach on the remaining engine, fly back to Bournemouth, wait in the hold, descend and cross the runway threshold without taking my eyes off those six needles.

It was the most difficult thing I'd ever done. Every waking moment I was consumed by it. I couldn't concentrate on anything else. There wasn't room. Towards the end of the training, taking a day off would be enough to take the edge off my flying skills and set me back two or three days. Not everyone was up to it. The pressure reduced grown men to tears daily, as their dreams of becoming commercial pilots proved to be beyond them. There was a handsome RAF Tornado pilot, on leave from active duty in a war zone; he briefly became my hero, but he just couldn't get the hang of flying holds. He'd definitely get there, though. There was a cheeky kid who'd been left some money by his granny. He was never going to make it. A flying instructor who had more knowledge than most of us to start with, and been a little bit of a know-all, steadily and surely became overwhelmed and ran out of money. He'd taken out a bank loan to finance his training and over the weeks he changed beyond recognition. It broke him completely. I was changing, too. I wasn't thinking about drinking or shagging or anything except instruments.

Claire

I got my stripes and returned to London in April, on the day that spring arrived. It was a Thursday. I went to the Groucho to meet Bernard Sumner from New Order and, to quote Bernard, it was as if the whole city was feeling 'a sudden sense of liberty'. The calm sunny evening had drawn people into it and as I strolled from Covent Garden into Soho, crowds were lingering outside pubs, suddenly able to dream and do nothing in particular again. When I arrived at the Groucho, the whole world was there. In the upstairs bar, Moby was playing 'London Calling' on the piano, Joe Strummer was singing and Wayne Sleep, the ballet dancer, was turning pirouettes on the bar. Keith was in full swing as impromptu ringmaster, leading the jolly gathering to join in with the 'and I . . . live by the river-uuh' bits.

It wasn't torturous being sober in the Groucho. I'd been absolutely rigorous about not drinking for one day every week, so it wasn't like it was the first time. I still liked it there, with the right company.

I was introduced to the bass player from Coldplay, who was at the bar. He was a very serious young man. He was observing the chaos with some hauteur. He explained carefully that his band's reinvigorated North American promotional strategies would boost sales in key secondary markets, coast to coast, album on album. Fair to say it did.

I went and sat with Bernard. He said he didn't care how long I stopped drinking for; there was still no way he was ever going to get into an aeroplane with me driving. We were talking about boats when Dan Macmillan arrived. He said he was going to Cabaret and asked if I wanted to come with him. A girl had been winking at me and, if I'd have had a few drinks, I would probably have stayed in the Groucho and surrendered. I didn't and the random caprice of Dan's soaring wanderlust led me unwittingly to an almighty turning point.

It took ages to get to Cabaret, even though it was only round the corner. Dan wanted to fight the parked cars. Then we had some trouble getting past the doormen. As we dawdled on the threshold, two girls pushed past us. One was laughing and beautiful, and the other one I vaguely recognised. The lady in charge arrived and started kissing Dan. All his friends were there and we danced. The beautiful laughing girl was dancing, too. I didn't get her name until we were in the taxi.

It was Claire, she told me on the Edgware Road. We were nearly at her house when she asked if I had a girlfriend. I said of course I had a girlfriend. I had loads of girlfriends. Girlfriends everywhere. I was a fucking rock star, for Christ's sake. She made the taxi stop and told me to get out. We were in Kilburn and it was barren of taxis, so I said I'd drop her off and take the one that we were in back to my house. And then we were kissing again.

She had very long legs and a business card, which said that she was an executive producer. I didn't know what that was, or who she was. I just had lots of scratches down my back and a big smile on my face.

Think Tank

We'd started recording a new Blur record before I went to Bournemouth. Graham hadn't turned up. Maybe we should have waited, but we started it without him, hoping he'd come back. We'd all developed as musicians and songwriters. Since we'd last made a record, Damon's *Gorillaz* album had outsold any of Blur's albums and 'Vindaloo' had outsold any of Blur's singles. Still, it's a delicate equilibrium that makes a band really thrive and it wasn't clear how it would work without Graham.

A good simple melody is an unfathomable work of genius, and an acute sense of melody was Damon's gift. Melodies are probably the trickiest thing of all. Having said that, Graham is definitely the best guitar player in the world. It's absolutely true. Graham can also write good melodies, but I think his greatest capacity is for harmony. His mind thrives in the expressiveness of harmonic forms. He added sixths, he diminished sevenths and he adjusted fifths with a natural flair, adding exquisite depth and colour to Damon's effortless top lines.

Damon was keen to work at his studio in Ladbroke Grove. I was a bit dubious. When you get down to the nitty-gritty chemistry that drives great bands, it's really just a power struggle. I thought working in Damon's studio might be giving him too much ground. It was soon obvious that it was the best place to work, though. Damon was always going to be in charge, but it wasn't really my job to agree with him about anything. I think we all always thought we knew best.

The studio was very near to Claire's house, and agreeing to work there turned out to be another monumental decision I had no idea I was making. I saw her again at a party that Dan Macmillan threw to launch his lifestyle emporium. Sometimes, when I'm in a contemplative mood, I still ponder over how we might never have met. For years we'd been missing each other. She knew people that I knew and we went to the same places. I would have been as likely to meet Claire in New York as London. The affair got serious when she fell off her horse and mangled her arm. She had a month off work then, and as her house was next to the studio I'd pop in and see her in the mornings. Soon I was going round after the studio as well.

I loved Justine. We'd shared so much, but it was all over by then. We clung on to each other, trying to make it work. She was uniquely beautiful and still more important to me than anything else that had happened in my life. I wanted her to be happy, but I was making her sad. We'd become flatmates, best friends rather than husband and wife. She was practically the only woman I knew who I wasn't having sex with. I told her I was going and she cried and I cried and we held each other for the last time. I hope I never have to do anything that difficult again. It's the benchmark that I measure all other pain against.

I moved into Claridge's. Claridge's is regal. When Buckingham Palace is full, the Queen sends her spare guests to stay there. It's the Brook Street annexe of the royal household and it's quite simply the best hotel in the world. I'd been making a careful, close and continuous study of luxury. It was a kind of hobby. For Mr Claridge it was evidently more of a mission. I can't think of anything about the whole of Claridge's that could be any better. It takes thirty seconds to run a bath and an hour to have breakfast. Everything about the place, from its Mayfair location to its pastry chefs, is the stuff of special occasions. I'm pretty sure that if, as an experiment, somebody was made to stay there and given nothing in particular to do, pretty soon they'd have made a huge success of themselves. The whole place is brimming with infectious achievement and to wake up there is to wake up invincible.

I swooned for Claire. I hung on her half-finished sentences, reading meanings into pauses and glances, searching for signs that she was feeling what I was feeling. I mooned around while she was at work. It was bugging the hell out of Damon and Dave. Damien became quite distant, too. A few months earlier my distraught mother had said that if I didn't stop drinking, pretty soon I'd have no friends at all. It was well meant, but in fact the opposite thing happened. I had far fewer friends now that I'd been sober for six months.

You can know a lot of people, be very popular, enjoy yourself with a host of chums and buddies, but you can't ever have a lot of really close friends. Intimacy doesn't spread thinly. My closest friends were fine about me being sober, but the ones who love you the most and know you the best are the ones who find it hardest to cope with you falling in love.

Morocco

It's probably possible to make good records without ever leaving a recording studio. Some bands do it like that. They lock themselves away from the world to craft their gypsy trick masterpieces. We flourished only with stimulation. The stimulants changed as we grew up and changed as people. Drink had been reliable to start with. Drugs are always good for one album, but no more than one. Love is always there to fall back on, love lost or love won. We thought we might feel more alive if we took ourselves out of our usual situation and went somewhere we'd never been before. That's why we went to North Africa to finish *Think Tank*. The plan was to rent a riad, a Moroccan house, near Marrakesh, build a makeshift studio and see what happened.

Three lorries full of gear trundled across Europe towards the Strait of Gibraltar. One of the lorries just had leads in it: bantam leads, jack leads, balanced XLR leads, MIDI leads, looms, speaker cables, computer cables, optical connectors, power lines, strings, wires and rope, that kind of thing.

While we were in Africa, Dave and I were planning to fly down to Timbuktu. When you tell people that you're a pilot, they usually want to know where's the furthest you've been.

Timbuktu, we both agreed, was the best possible answer to that question and a good enough reason to go there. Even taking the Bonanza to North Africa was quite a serious undertaking. We'd bought a lot of charts, a desert survival kit and a life raft. If the plane had any technical problems, we'd probably be best fixing it ourselves, so we also took spare tyres, engine parts and a tool kit. We had the aeroplane serviced before we left and when we arrived at the airfield it was sitting on the tarmac next to the Queen's helicopter. There had been big problems with Dave's Cessna. We'd been merrily flying around in a machine that had such bad corrosion that the wings could have fallen off at any time. That's got to be one of worst things that can happen to an aeroplane. When we found out, we decided that in future we'd have the best engineers we could find to keep an eye on things under the cowlings. It was reassuring to see the royal chopper as we set out on our maiden inter-continental voyage.

We wanted to have lunch and refuel at La Rochelle. We didn't really need to land and pick up more avgas until we reached the southern coast of France, but were in agreement that the *baguettes fromages* at that airport were the best cheese sandwiches we'd ever tasted, and it was worth a detour. Those sandwiches are a sensational case study in beautiful simplicity. Just French bread and Camembert, no butter, no nothing. We almost always had cheese sandwiches for lunch when we were working, and the La Rochelle special was the benchmark standard that all were compared to. The Primrose Hill delicatessen offered notably good high-end, custom-built ciabattas, but the proprietor inclined towards the over-elaborate. It's the way things are going. In order to compete with each other to give people what they want, the sandwich makers of the world feel they have to create more and more fanciful-sounding fillings, trying to cram three courses of contemporary fusion cuisine between ever-increasing varieties of bread. The marketing gurus would tell us we're not just buying lunch any more, but that we're making a statement about who we are. If you can swallow that, you can probably swallow one of their cold cling-filmed sandwiches.

I became suspicious of marketing when I was working on a feature film score. The film was all finished and there was a screening at a shopping centre in Essex – composing film scores is plainly not as glamorous as being a rock star. The film was being shown to a special audience, who'd been recruited from outside McDonald's, from park benches and street corners. It was being targeted at a young audience and the financiers had tried to assemble a representative crowd. In return for seeing the film for nothing the group had to answer some questions about it afterwards. They were all having a lovely day, but the director, the man who'd spent the last six months ordering Ray Winstone around, was terrified.

Every time the audience laughed, a lot of clipboards rustled. If they chattered or showed signs of confusion, there was more rustling. At the end a nice jolly man stood at the front and went through gruelling lists of questions about how everyone had enjoyed all aspects of the film; the characters in turn, the music, the plot, the sub-plots, the whole picture. By this time, the director and the producers were on the edge of their seats with their feet in their mouths. A particularly smart-arsed twelve-year-old boy didn't like the way the story ended. He was encouraged to say why. An involuntary moan escaped from somewhere deep inside the director as the child rallied his allies and led a revolt against the film's denouement. Would it be better if the film ended, completely differently, maybe like this, with the old lady dying, said the nice jolly man.

'Dass miles maw betta,' said the boy, and his friends agreed. Then a little girl piped up, said that she liked the old lady and she was pleased it had all worked for her in the end. The director and producer were exchanging open-mouthed glances. The finale of the film that they had spent the last three years of their lives living and breathing – its whole meaning and purpose, all their expertise – was in the hands of two gobby twelve-year-olds. It went back and forth for some while and in the end the old lady was granted a stay of execution by the jury. If the focus group doesn't like the ending, the studio will reshoot it. No question at all. There's too much money at stake. It was harrowing. The ending survived intact. It put me right off films, though.

Focus groups, wielding the almighty authority of the witless pleb, rule the world, but there in La Rochelle, like a beacon in the void, was a grumpy old lady with the best cheese sandwiches in the world.

It was a clear day in early October and we tootled on, flying south with the birds and the butterflies, zooming low over the rising backbone of continental Europe and landing in the dark at Avignon. That was when I really realised I'd left Claire behind. I called her and she was out with a group of film directors. Film directors think they're cooler than rock stars, but I knew the truth about them, and their run-ins with twelve-year-olds in Essex precincts. I wondered if she did, too. We were going to Morocco for six weeks and it suddenly felt like a long time.

Down the rocky coast of Spain, the sea far below: mountains large and close in the right-hand windows. We passed over miles and miles of polytunnels, endless ugly greenhouses in appalling contrast to the green fields of home. When Africa came it was like a surprise snog from a superstar. It loomed unexpectedly green and soft beyond the harsh desert of southern Spain, dissolving into distant mist. We stopped for fuel at Tangier and followed the gently meandering beach towards the distant and fabled city of Marrakesh. It was an untouched, subtle and wonderful wilderness. There was nothing except nature and nothing was ever so beautiful.

'*Vous avez fait un infraction, monsieur. Il faut payer*,' said the man in uniform. He was saying we had committed an aviation crime and that we were in big trouble and we would have to give him some money. It was dusky, we'd made Marrakesh and we were unloading the aeroplane and stretching our legs. 'Tell him to piss off,' said Dave. Dave knows his rights.

'I'm terribly sorry, I don't speak Moroccan,' I said, and smiled and nodded. The man flapped his arms around and kept on about '*infractions*'. He followed us to the tower where we paid the landing fee, but he'd scuttled off wagging his finger by the time we'd got to the terminal. Corruption was rife. A lot of the equipment was bound over in customs, said Damon, who'd come to pick us up from the airport in an ancient, knackered, tiny Peugeot. It wouldn't have passed an MOT in Europe, but here it was a status symbol.

The traffic was very scary. There were pedestrians, fully loaded donkeys, bicycles carrying passengers, whole families wobbling along on phut-phuts, cars with no lights, impatient taxis, crank buses and very big lorries all competing for not very much road. It was a swarming, smoky, brightly lit circus. Unusual smells and strange musics assaulted us as we crawled around the colossal biblical scene in the main square. There was a man with a snake; a man selling teeth: individual human teeth; two men were bare-knuckle fighting and a crowd was watching; there were people eating goats' heads with spoons; there were bonfires, and everybody was very smartly dressed.

The riad, ten miles outside the city, sat among olive groves roamed at night by packs of wild dogs. There were strange creatures everywhere. Jason, the sound engineer, was the finder and keeper of a particularly menacing translucent insect as big as a hen's egg that curled its tail and spat goo when he poked it, which he did for the benefit of all new arrivals.

It was a vast, sprawling kasbah and everything about it had either just been patched up or was just about to break. The gear was set up in a derelict annexe; a young man lived there with no running water or worldly goods apart from the clothes he stood up in. He was always smartly dressed and eager to help.

There was a place where mobiles worked, high on one of the roofs, and a freezing swimming pool. The mosaic-tiled interior had once been magnificent and the bedrooms formed an open courtyard around a fountain. I took over the west wing, sprinkling rose petals and lavender from the market everywhere and lighting it with candles. There was a flat roof, which looked beyond the orchards towards an uncultivated lunar landscape with splashes of green oases and the Atlas Mountains towering in the distance.

Everyone developed body-rocking diarrhoea immediately. There was no escape. Dave's bicycle was kept in the control room and at any time without warning one of the party might suddenly take flight towards the nearest loo in the house a couple of hundred yards away. We shaved our heads and plugged in our guitars. The illnesses ebbed and flowed, the food was awful, the place was practically a ruin, but the music sounded better than anything we'd ever done. I was the happiest man in the world. Claire was coming.

Into the Light

I picked her up from the airport in the Peugeot and took her straight for hammam. Hammam is the most intense spa-type experience in the world. It eclipses the shiatsu beatings of the Japanese, sees off the Icelandic birch-whipping ceremonies, casts Swedish super-muscle mashings into the shade and even outshines the Russian baths on Avenue A in New York City – and they're something special.

We were sprayed all over with scalding water, as we lay naked, prone and side-by-side on the hot stone floor of a tiled room full of steam. It wasn't a steam room, though. Steam rooms are chilly by comparison. This was more like the inside of a pressure cooker. Girls dressed in light towelling shorts and bikini tops got busy with loofahs and scrubbed us pink. Then there was a bone-creaking kneading involving knee-in-the-back half-nelsons and leg-bending body presses. We floated all the way home to Riad Nadjma.

I didn't lose the floating sensation. I was feeling the sway of the secret and limitless feminine. When you start feeling like that, it's time to say, 'I love you', so I took Claire into the desert.

There are different kinds of desert. Some are rocky; some are made out of gravel, like massive untidy car parks. You have to get your wildernesses in perspective. They're no good those ones, they're a waste of gravity. All rocky planets have them. We were heading for the dunes. Ahmed, the local fixer, sorted us out with a 4×4 and driver, we loaded up with water and set off for the Sahara.

Through the snow-capped Atlas Mountains with their precipices and nestling fortresses, we trundled, on and on through night and day, through new geography. We saw goats up trees, the ruins of crumbling palaces, the magic trails of rivers and the mud houses that populated them. When we stopped, people invited us to stay with them, people with no shoes, people with no teeth. It was a benign kingdom. I never felt any apprehension of violence or danger.

And the dunes rose in the distance, cartoon-like, surreal, fantastic.

A 4×4 is no good in the sandbanks. The only thing that will do for the dunes is a camel. There was a Berber, immaculately turned out in an electric-blue kaftan, who had some camels and agreed to be our guide. He was highly intelligent, a comedian with a quiet smile and an acute sense of comic timing. Things are never like you expect. Deserts, I'd imagined, were populated by more serious types full of wistful melancholy. He packed up the camels with blankets and provisions, nimbly lashing a cooking pot here, a lantern there, having a conversation with himself that consisted only of the words, '*Comme ça*'. He was able to express a wide range of emotions, and extract a good deal of comedy from those two words. He flipped ropes into elaborate knots, muttering '*Comme ça, comme ça, comme ça*', every time the ends crossed, with a final definitive '*Comme ça*' as he yanked them tight. As he moved around to the other side, I could hear him quietly musically murmuring '*ça-ça-ça*', and the final triumphant '*ça*'. Then the '*ça*'s became interspersed with the odd 'Ah!?' followed by a pause, when things went awry. It was a brilliant routine. He knew he was making me laugh. 'Camel are smelly,' he said and smiled.

We rode into the sands, perched high on camel humps. There were no discernible landmarks, just undulating dunes that rose to great heights like a calcified stormy sea. The most complete silence fell. There was no birdsong or rustle of leaves. The sand soaked up the sounds of our voices as if to suggest not to compete with the hush. The abstract peaks and troughs rose and fell with cartoon-like simplicity and everything suggested infinity: the endless blue sky, the evenness and constancy of the sand, the celestial silence. And Claire.

We'd been trekking for many hours, but our guide didn't have a map or a compass. There are no maps of these shifting seas.

'How do you know where we are?' I asked him.

'I came here yesterday,' he said.

Then an unusual thing happened. The sky went grey and then black and it started to rain; heavy rain in heavy drops. It hadn't rained for five years. The camels bellowed as it lashed down. Maybe it was all as new to them as it was to me.

After an hour it stopped and, an hour after that, it might never have happened. There was no trace of moisture or a cloud.

The oasis, too, when we arrived at dusk, was still dry on the surface. The only clue to its existence was a cluster of Bedouin tents. There was a tent for Claire and me, and nothing was ever cosier. It was dressed with soft rugs and blankets. Candles flickered and incense burned. Mohammed, our guide, set about making dinner. He unwrapped packets of provisions, unscrewed flasks and made gunpowder tea. 'Berber whisky!' he said. It's powerful stuff, loaded with caffeine, sugar and scented herbs. Somewhere someone was banging a drum and having a wail.

Moroccan food is not my absolute favourite. I was finding the endless casseroles a bit wearisome, but the simple stew that Mohammed prepared was the perfect accompaniment to the Saharan night, and I think the best meal I've ever had. We were naked in the desert. It's another world and our senses were roving in the alien surroundings and our minds wandering into new speculations. We were snapped right back inside ourselves by the nourishing, warm, essential familiarity of food.

I've not had that feeling in the Ivy, not even when Posh and Becks walked in.

The desert is the best place to put telescopes. The air is dry and the darkness is absolute. The dazzling stars, a hundred thousand million billion of them, sparkled through the roof of the tent as we lay in each other's arms. I said, 'Will you marry me?' and she said, 'OK.'

Home and Dry

Dave had to return to England a couple of days early. I flew home from Marrakesh with my dad. He loved the aeroplane. We flew back up the African coast with the transponder unplugged. The transponder is the piece of equipment that sends regular messages to air traffic control telling them your altitude. Unless you're taking off or landing, the altitude should never be less than five hundred feet. It's all clearly explained in Rule V in the CAP 53 of the ANO, as any pilot will tell you. I estimate our height above sea level along the North African coast was an average of about thirty feet. It's pretty dangerous, but on the outbound journey I hadn't seen so much as a house or a person for a couple of hundred miles and if there was ever a time to mess with Rule V, this was it. We rocketed along the deserted beaches at head height, the cliffs above us on our right, flamingos scattering in our path. We made steep banking turns around headlands, sometimes pulling more than twice our body weights, sometimes floating out of our seats as we zoomed and dived towards home in our incredible flying machine.

Winter was drawing in at home. In Marrakesh we'd recorded an orchestra and a couple of new songs and a lot of vocals, but the record wasn't finished or mixed. The lorries took all the gear direct to another barn in Devon, where we added the finishing touches. I dashed between Devon, London and the Cotswolds in a rental car. Claire and I were renting a cottage on an estate in Gloucestershire. There was a river running through the garden, and chickens and peacocks pecked around. The Cotswolds was every bit as pretty as it promised from the air. The vast walled domains, the fossilised remains of astronomical wealth and power still dominate the rural landscape. The industrial revolution passed the area by almost completely.

Claire was worried about me starting my new drinking campaign in January. She'd only known me sober. I assured her that I was very good at it.

It was February and a nice man called Bill was saying, 'And tell me what you remember about the party.'

'Well, I remember swapping shirts with the principal dancer of the Royal Ballet Company.'

'OK. Good. What next?'

'I think I snogged the dog.'

'Right. OK. Then what happened?'

'Well, I had a row with Claire and went home. I locked her

out, and when she was banging on the door, I pissed on her head from the fourth-storey window.'

'Why did you do that?'

'Well, that's what she wants to know.'

'Anything else happen?'

'No, not that night, anyway.'

Bill was kind and he listened and he helped me and I stopped drinking altogether after that and tried yoga.

The thing that irritated me most about yoga was how expensive it was. It was sixty quid for an hour. Will Ricker was only paying thirty quid an hour to punch the crap out of Ozzie Jason. The advanced flying instructors were on much less than that. Apart from yoga, for between twenty and thirty quid you can get someone to come to your house and teach you just about anything you can think of. I'd tried an hour of 'Japanese for Beginner'. That was twenty quid well spent. A Japanese lady came to the house, made some green tea and taught me how to say, 'Hello, I like cheese, cheers.' That got me by in Japan for years.

Learning is a bargain, but I'd always shied away from music lessons. I seemed to know how to speak fluent bass guitar; it was second nature, but I had absolutely no idea what it was I was doing.

I wanted to know more, but I was apprehensive about my bubble bursting. I'd had a bad spell cast on me by *The Times Guide to Better Writing*. At the time, I was writing a weekly column for *Time Out*, about staying in. I'd done one about my enthusiasm for jigsaw puzzles, one about bubble baths, that kind of thing. It was going well. That was when I read the book about how to write stuff even better. The features editor was waiting for a treatise on the baked potato, but once I'd crossed out all the bits that the man in the book wouldn't have liked, there was nothing left. I couldn't write anything for weeks. The book was very strict and authoritative and it completely undermined my confidence.

Confidence is the most important attribute for any kind of creative activity, a dumb self-assurance that you know better than anybody. This is something that can't really be taught, but if you can think you're brilliant and you can turn up on time, you can do whatever you want.

Self-confidence is easily shattered and I was worried that analysis of my musical style would have bad consequences. Blur were playing in Bournemouth and I offered to go back to school and talk to the boys about rock and roll. I'm really glad I did. It seemed a wonderful place. I sat in on a third-year music lesson and tried to explain myself. Then they asked questions.

'How does the bass affect the harmony of a piece of music?' asked the teacher. I thought that was a very good question. I looked up to see who would answer, but everyone was looking at me. I wanted, more than anything, to say, 'Don't know, Sir', but it clearly wasn't appropriate. I said the thing about the bass, really, was that it never sounds wrong. If the bass isn't right, everything else sounds wrong, but the bass always sounds right, even if you make a mistake. That was why bass players always looked the coolest.

I had some piano lessons after that episode. The bass guides the harmony. That's what it does. It guides the harmony and supports the upper voices. It was good to know, in writing.

In Devon, horse-riding lessons were only twelve pounds and they threw in a horse as well. The Cotswolds is very horsey. Claire had been having lessons and riding quite a lot. While Damon, Dave and I were finishing the album in Devon I got up early in the mornings and drove to the local stables to try and get the hang of it. After galloping along streams in Iceland in the middle of the night, I didn't really have any apprehension about trotting round a riding school with a hard hat on. By the end of the first week I was jumping over fences and that, I felt, was that. I could ride a horse. I really wanted to go riding with Claire. It's definitely more dangerous than flying, and the thrill is intense.

It's an earthy, overtly sexual business, especially for women, as they thrust their pelvises around and get sweaty and start panting. The danger is a part of it, too, for sure. You can never be sure what a horse is going to do.

Pilots want everyone to be pilots. They love taking people flying who've never been before. They universally encourage the novice to join the brotherhood. Horse people in Gloucestershire weren't like that. It was the opposite kind of thing.

I went to the local stables back at the cottage and said I wanted to go for a hack. I spent weeks going round in circles, arching my back, tucking my heels in, thrusting my pelvis. I would never have known I could jump if I hadn't gone to Devon first. They said I was brilliant in Devon. In Gloucestershire I never made it out of the yard.

Given a choice of not being particularly great at something, but believing I was a natural, and actually genuinely being good at something and being reserved about it, I would take the conceited option every time. It's much more fun.

Farmers for Fifteen Minutes

Claire and I were married within a year of meeting each other and we set about looking for a house in the Cotswolds. I wasn't sure if I wanted a big one or a little one, which really confused the estate agents, who were thrown by the car, too, Claire's old drug dealer-style BMW. It had been broken into in London, and had a cardboard passenger window as a result. It had also recently caught fire, and smelt a bit on the funny side. It always seemed to be very muddy, inside and out, and most people thought we were time-wasters when we rolled up their carriage drives in that heap. It's just hard to care very much about cars when you have an aeroplane.

We looked at some tarted-up, overpriced cottages. Then we

started looking at houses. It was quite depressing. The figures involved were astronomical. Prices were similar to those in London. The whole world had gone mad. Houses were a million pounds. For a cool million, a price that was fairly ridiculous, all you seemed to get was a fairly nice house with a fairly big garden, nothing fit for a rock star. It didn't make any sense at all. Surely a million pounds was enough for anything? I can clearly remember wanting to have a hundred pounds when I was young. It seemed like a good amount to be aiming for. I never dreamed I'd have a million pounds, let alone that it wouldn't be enough.

We went to look at a farm that was for sale for a million and a half. The numbers were scary, but for half as much money again you got about twenty times as much. The rambling farmhouse sat in two hundred acres. It came with half a mile of the river Evenlode and three woods. It had a little lake with an island in the middle. The title included modern barns, decaying outbuildings, stables, an orchard, ancient wells and a walled garden. There were piles of tyres and heaps of manure and all the inevitable junk and jetsam that accumulates in barnyards. There was even a cricket pitch indicated on an old map of the land. It was the complete, unabridged, bundled country-life package.

The owner was the first person we'd met on our quest who clearly didn't want to sell his house. He loved the place, but he was getting too old to be running a farm. The cellar was full of his cherished tropical fish, cichlids, and he showed us them first. There were a confusing number of rooms – attics and pantries abounded. There was a welcoming comfy generosity about the place. We walked over the land with the man, Mr Taplin. I'd started to like him the moment we arrived. He was particularly pleased about the drains, and we kept stopping to inspect pipes, soakaways and trenches. In London you flush the loo and that's the business dealt with. Out here it was just the beginning of an epic journey. The foul waste pipe ran under the garden and through the farmyard to a septic tank. The purified effluent from the septic tank discharged into a gully. The gully, sprouting lilies and irises, ran past the Dutch barn and expelled into the primary ditch. The ditch gradually became more of a stream as it converged with the outputs of the rainwater run-off manifold and the field drain matrices. He said he'd show us the field drains if we wanted to inspect them, but that they were quite complex. The main ditch neatly bisected the farm, taking a scenic detour through the lake. On the far side of the lake it resumed its journey, towards the Evenlode and, once in the Evenlode and heading for London, the matter was out of our hands.

Then he showed us where his favourite horse was buried. It was a sunny spring day, and I'd known since before I'd got out of the car that I wanted to live here. It was perfect. Mr Taplin's car, which we'd parked next to, was of a similar vintage and in similar condition to our own.

Claire wanted to see the woods. So did I. We walked over the heath. A large number of big black birds were circling and whirling over one end. 'Wow,' we said, 'look at all those birds!'

'Well, I've not been at 'em for a couple of years,' Mr Taplin said. 'They want taking care of.'

'What do you feed them on?'

'Feed 'em? No, take care of 'em. Let 'em 'ave it!'

I'd been a vegetarian for seventeen years. 'What do you mean, let 'em 'ave it?'

'Well, I come down with the twelve-bore, and let 'em 'ave it.'

Apart from shooting the birds, he seemed like a really nice man. He smoked Embassy Number Six and painted in watercolours. He was unhurried and peaceful, enjoying the moments as they sailed past.

For many years the property had been a notable shorthorn dairy cattle farm, but mad cow disease and foot and mouth had brought it to its knees. It was a wreck, but we loved it.

The house in Mercer Street had a balcony with some window boxes, but no garden. I sold the house and Dave bought the aeroplane and we bought the farm. It was going to be quite a leap up to two hundred acres.

12

beginnings and endings

Geronimo

Claire got pregnant in a castle on our honeymoon, which was the best thing yet. The worst thing about the early stages of pregnancy is that it's practically all you can think about, but you're not supposed to tell anybody. I thought it was obvious anyway. We had to go to Marks & Spencer every week to get bigger bras, and pants. It's best not to tell anyone the news in the first twelve weeks, because a quarter of pregnancies miscarry in the early stages. If all looks good at the twelve-week scan, you're in with a good shot. At that stage you get graphs and comparative statistics on the likelihood of various aspects of the foetus being 'normal'. Normality was a condition I had been shirking all my adult life. I suddenly found myself longing and wishing for something absolutely typical. I wanted everything about the baby and the pregnancy to be as ordinary as possible. The more in the middle of a line something was, the better I felt about it.

I think it is impossible for anybody with a vivid sense of

reason to know how they would feel about continuing a pregnancy with complications until confronted with the situation.

Claire's older brother Robert was physically disabled and he only lived until he was four. She sometimes says she can remember stealing his toys and then she goes quiet. Our consultant wanted to know exactly what was wrong with Robert, but we couldn't trace his medical history and we only had one photograph of him. From what we could piece together, he had a genetic condition. When we spotted an unmistakable little willy on the scan, and it was clear we were having a boy, things went into overdrive. A Harley Street genetic specialist explained there was a fifty-fifty chance that Claire would be able to have healthy male offspring. It took him about an hour and lots of new words to explain why. Claire had to have her DNA flown to Switzerland for testing. At the time when we should have been breaking the happy news, we had even more to think about, but the little racing heartbeat had become the most precious thing in the world.

I liked the doctor. I like experts. I never met a true expert I didn't like. Knowledge is an irresistible, benign enchantment. Genetics wasn't as well understood when Robert was alive, so it was difficult to know what the exact cause of his troubles might have been. It might not have had a name, back then. In Switzerland, they were looking for translocated XX anomalies. That was the main worry.

We went back to see the doctor and he said Claire's XX department was all located fine and dandy. I stood outside of myself for a moment. We'd both become preoccupied with the possibility of having to face a difficult decision. I suddenly found I had a lot to say, more than ever before. I couldn't stop talking. I felt weightless. Claire was cracking a huge smile. The doctor was enjoying the moment and we blethered for ages. He reckoned it was all going to be fine but we still shouldn't tell anyone until all the results were back, but that was really just a formality.

Then there was a phone call saying he wanted to see us again. I went into a bit of a panic. Why did he want to see us again? He said it was all Jim Dandy. There was nothing left to say on the matter, just loose ends to tie up. We didn't have to go and see him about million-to-one-shot loose ends unless there was bad news. I couldn't keep my cool. We got the first appointment we could and sat on the edge of our seats staring at him wide-eyed, the two of us.

'Everything OK?' he said. We both pointed out he was the best one to tell us that. 'Oh, yes. No worries there, nothing to worry about. Just, you know, wanted to see how you were getting on, all part of the service, ahem.'

I felt my bodyweight disappear again, but as I floated down this rendezvous suddenly all seemed a bit pointless. The guy was a gene specialist, not a midwife. Midwives are the people you talk to about sore bosoms, milkshake cravings and all that stuff. My genetic make-up was doing fine thanks, no problems there as far as I could tell at the moment, doctor, cheers. Claire's DNA was evidently scrubbing up OK, too, so really, all fine. All fine in the gene department, thanks very much.

As we were leaving he asked if he could have a couple of tickets for the Blur gig at Brixton Academy!

The Hospital of St John & St Elizabeth in St John's Wood, 'John and Lizzie's' to its guests, often has more paparazzi in attendance outside than patients on the wards within. Among the photographed it's the most fashionable private hospital to launch your latest progeny. The Portland Hospital is still the hip place to get your ears tested, and I wouldn't go anywhere else, but for celebrity childbirth it's got to be John & Lizzie's. They have very big baths on the birthing unit, almost as big as the ones in the Mercer Hotel. They sell the candlelit New Age homoeopathic, yogaromatherapy delivery package. These things are all popular among famous women.

We started going to visualisation classes. The idea of the

'Visualisation for Childbirth' course is to form a clear picture of what the birth is going to be like, so that you know what to expect and you're not wildly dreading a big painful unknown. It definitely helped take some of Claire's fears away. We lay on big cushions in a fug of ylang-ylang and sandalwood, imaginizing calm taxi rides to familiar surroundings, soft music playing at the birth centre, a nice big lovely bath, and then a most wonderful natural, extraordinary thing happening. We went into great detail. I often happily dozed off in the sessions. It harked back to childhood bedtimes. There's a part of the brain that just can't resist stories, the same part that likes experts. We seem to need them and there's something about visualisation that's better than television, or films. It's like a very intimate, tailor-made radio play and it casts the listener in the lead role. I thought the acupuncture business Claire was having was probably bunk and people who talk about 'energy' are, frankly, silly, but there was something fair and simple about this kind of hocus-pocus. Of course it all went out of the window when the contractions kicked in.

I distinctly remember hearing Claire say, 'I don't WANT to go in the bath. I want some DRUGS. I want some drugs right NOW. GIVE ME SOME DRUGS!' She'd been in the 'birthing pool' for hours and hours and nothing was budging. More and more people arrived and the lights got brighter. It was definitely all moving away from the calm candlelit herbal scenario we'd been working on. It was four o'clock in the morning when the obstetrician arrived, big, black, smiling and wearing an Arsenal top.

There is a part of everyone that recoils at the thought of seeing their loved one up on the jacks being poked around by a rubber-gloved gooner. Some fathers choose not to be at the birth of their children; it's quite a trend. Some mothers prefer to have their super best friend as a 'birthing partner'. I couldn't have missed it. I was down at the business end gawping and crying.

The baby was stuck in the birth canal, and a medieval-looking contraption called a ventouse, a kind of plunger like you'd use for sorting out a blocked sink, was squidged on to the little head somewhere on the other side of Claire. She was huffing and puffing, and the gooner was working up quite a sweat, too, as he pulled and heaved on the end of the plunger in the bright lights. It was hard, physical toil, like a strange tug of war. Some of the people were cheering on Claire's team. 'PUSH, CLAIRE, GO ON, GOOD GIRL!' I was with the doctor. 'PULL, PULL, NOW! NOW! COME ON THE ARSENAL!' By the time they'd separated, the baby had a cone-shaped head. He was covered in goo and was the most beautiful thing I've ever seen. No one's ever ready for that feeling.

Building

The new house didn't look in too bad shape. We thought we'd strip the wallpaper, redecorate, live in it for a while and modernise when the right time came. A lot of plaster seemed to be coming off with the wallpaper, so we took off some of the plaster. The walls were damp. With the walls exposed, you could see that some of the beams were rotten. The beams were rotten because the roof was leaking. So the roof had to come off. By this time it was obvious that the plumbing could do with an immediate overhaul and the electrics needed a good looking at. Old houses are like that. I'd dealt with builders and architects before, in London. Architects are a discrete genus of the species of *Homo sapiens*. To be a successful architect requires a similar mesmeric charm that is the bread and butter of the film director, the television evangelist, the hypnotist and the Pied Piper of Hamelin. They arrive with their little satchels and their propelling pencils. Everything about them says calm; from the crisp white sheets of paper they use to cast their spells, to their supernatural patience.

They retreat, taking your dreams with them in that little satchel, and return with goblins, pixies and demigods who turn your house into dust. If all goes well you live happily ever after, but the plot thickens and takes unexpected twists along the way. People who've had babies bang on and on about what hard work it is. Having had a baby and builders at the same time, I'd say that builders are harder work, but I wouldn't bang on and on about it. Other people's builders are even less interesting than other people's babies.

Building wasn't something I'd ever viewed as a particularly creative process, not like art or music. Art and music happen in your mind and live there. Building, when you're able to build anything you like, starts in your mind and then you live there. Artists and musicians enjoy a cachet that eludes the builder, but I'm starting to think that building is the most primal and satisfying of all the creative urges. As a steel beam was being craned into place, I turned to the structural engineer and said, 'I guess it's sculpture really, isn't it?'

'That's not what we facking call it, mate! Hur, hur, hur.'

It's easy for your dreams to run away with you, but, when all is said and done, a house is just a house. A home is something else and I gradually realised I had one. Even when it was mainly a building site it was where I wanted to be. We lived in the chaos with an ancient cooker and an open fire, doing nothing at all whenever we could. I didn't want to go anywhere else. I'd landed.

I bought a digger. There was a huge area of concrete behind the house, about an acre, I think. I'm not sure if anybody actually knows how big an acre is. I've never been able to find out for sure. The area it covered was bigger than a football pitch and smaller than a cricket pitch. It was for making silage on. Silage is what cattle eat in the winter, fermented grass. I couldn't see us needing quite that much silage ever, so I bulldozed the whole lot and a machine as big as a ship came and crunched it all into little pieces. Bulldozing concrete is about the closest feeling you can get to playing the bass in a rock and roll band. They are connected.

Now I was a builder again, like I had been when I failed my 'A' levels. When I worked on building sites, I dreamed about being in a band and the band was playing to huge crowds. I always knew it would happen, I just didn't realise when it did that I'd be onstage dreaming I was on a building site.

There is always someone banging something somewhere on a farm. It's a kind of heartbeat, and it's as natural as the sound of a cock crowing.

There was a point when I realised that 'farm' is just another word for 'building site'. A farm is a process, a continuous cycle. There is no conclusion. There were piles of manure, piles of rubble, a mountain of crunched concrete, heaps of wood, all kinds of stuff in mounds. My first inclination was to get rid of the piles and clear the place up, but piles are a farm's vital organs. Some of the piles grew and some shrunk, but they were all being fed and milked, it seemed. I soon started to collect piles and talk about them and, indeed, to them.

We bought a couple of thousand sheep. Sheep are a good place to start. They are easy to look after and they don't need any expensive equipment, not like babies.

Singing

My granny didn't believe that we'd called our baby Geronimo. She kept asking what his name really was. I said that sometimes we called him Big Ears, and sometimes we called him Skippy, but his name was definitely Geronimo, and he wore it well. His first word was 'digger' which rang nicely with my new sense of purpose.

I saw the advert for the singing group in the doctor's surgery. While being weighed, Geronimo had scored a direct hit on the health visitor's slacks with a vigorous spray of baby wee. They really hate that, health visitors. They say, 'It's all right, happens all the time', but it sours the atmosphere. Then he'd had his latest injections and he'd screamed and screamed at the nurse. Until then, I'd thought trumpets were the loudest thing in the world. It's got something to do with their range. Trumpets play in the same register as shouts and screams. The Red Arrows taking off, or standing onstage at Glastonbury, sandwiched between towers of amplifiers and a hollering multitude, doesn't give you quite the same impression of loudness as being in the same room as one other person who is playing a trumpet. And trumpets don't get near to babies on the perceived loudness scale. It's got nothing to do with decibels. There is something very subjective about the ear's response to babies screaming.

We'd suffered a punctured dummy at Tesco a couple of weeks earlier and he'd gone into paroxysms of anguish. I figured that being deprived of his binky for an hour or two would do him good, toughen him up a bit. If you've ever wondered what it's like to be really, really famous, try pushing a screaming baby around a supermarket for a few minutes. You look up and all eyes are on you. People stop what they're doing and stare at you; they ask you if you're all right, they nudge and point, they interfere. 'No, he's fine, he's absolutely fine,' I'd said. But they weren't buying it. My nonchalance made them more concerned. Some had started to follow us and by the time we'd got to the beans aisle we had to abort the mission.

The surgery was full of screams here and wee there, and I was evacuating as swiftly as possible. I was halfway out of the door when I saw a little card pinned to the wall advertising a singing group for mums and babies. I paused to take down the number, avoiding the collective gaze of the waiting room.

I assumed they meant dads as well as mums. I arrived slightly late at the village hall, but I stood outside suddenly finding the need to pluck up courage. I was never nervous about going onstage or talking to rocket scientists on live television. I wasn't fazed by Hollywood starlets or foozled by bullying billionaires. But I felt nervous now. Even when I picked up my guitar and sang Joe Strummer a melody I'd written for him it hadn't been this bad. I was terrified. I was about to tiptoe into the delicate skein of the real world and I hadn't been there for years.

When I got through the door the mums were singing a song about shaking a parachute, and shaking a parachute. Some babies were crawling around. Some were under the parachute laughing and some were trying to break things and fight each other. It's invigorating to observe babies en masse.

The unaccompanied sound of mothers gently singing to their little children is the sweetest music I've ever heard. I was the only dad there. It was like being back in the French department at college, another matriarchal super-civilisation.

A lot of the well-known nursery rhymes are folk tunes as old as the hills. They're a part of the human condition, and they lift the spirits like love in the morning. We sang 'Giddy-up horsey', did more parachute shaking, then there was one I'd never heard involving lions and rivers. The hits kept coming, though. I think it's the best band I've ever been in.

I became more and more engrossed, messing around in the parish. The more things I did, the more other things suggested themselves. It felt like I was in the right place. My usual response to being told 'There is a TV crew at the door' is to panic. The news media only normally hound you because some heinous escapade has come to light or something nasty is brewing. It's never normally a good sign, even if it does make the cleaner feel glamorous. There were actually two TV crews and a *Sunday Times* journalist in attendance by the time I got to the front door. They were all smiling, though. They took it in turns to explain that our tiny, local rural community had been voted 'England's Finest Village' by *Country Life* magazine.

Not since arriving in Japan for the first time, poor and practically destitute, to be overwhelmed by fanatical fans at the airport, had I felt quite so ridiculous as I did now in this Cotswolds village. Being big in Japan wasn't something I'd ever bargained for. It was just a huge slice of luck that Japan existed at all and that its people wanted to buy our records and give us presents. I had the same feeling of outrageous good fortune now as it became clear that somehow we'd landed on our feet.

Of course the notion of the best village in the country is just a bit of harmless nonsense. In fact, it made our neighbourhood the scourge of the shire. The surrounding villages, some of which have a nicer duck pond and better preserved stocks, a higher-ranking celebrity resident or less low-cost housing, were unified in their disapproval. But I felt vindicated. When we were in the process of buying the farm, almost everybody I knew had sought a quiet word with me. They all expressed their concerns about my buying a random tumbledown ruin in the middle of nowhere. It had bewildered people and now it suddenly looked like a pretty neat trick.

Gardens

I don't know how much sense it would make to live in the country if I wasn't married. Cities are distracting, erotic places, but love flows uninterrupted in the countryside. I suppose that's why we moved here, because we wanted to be together. That's the best thing about living in the country, being in a world of your own with the person you love. I was never happier than when sailing on the random breeze of fortune, but now I was settled. I still wanted to travel, but in order to travel, rather than drift, I need a home. Some people have lots of houses, but you can only really have one home, somewhere that you long to be when you're not there, somewhere in which you can happily do nothing at all, where all your things are.

I had been nocturnal for many years. Cities only really come alive at night; that's when all the good stuff happens. The great outdoors flourishes in the sunshine and the pleasures of the countryside are subtle and lasting, rather than short and sweet. All happy endings imply gardens. That's just the way it is.

I had been a vegetarian for twenty years. I'd fought my way around the restaurants of the world, sending things back that had bacon sprinkled on them or chicken stock in them, enduring many a plate of overboiled vegetables, and the disdain of proud chefs everywhere. Japan was the most difficult place to fulfil the vegetarian dream. I had taken special training to make sure I could order vegetarian food in Japan, but it's complicated. Vegetarianism is just not a notion to the Japanese. You have to explain the whole concept, every time you order a bowl of noodles. Still, more often than not it would be a disaster. 'I'm sure this is fish,' I said to the girl from the record label, holding up a morsel with my chopsticks. 'No, not fish,' she said. 'What is it then?' 'Is *made* from fish. Is not fish.' It was hopeless.

I think my vegetarianism stemmed from a wish to take a benevolent but passive role in nature. That role changed when we moved to the farm. You can't be a passive farmer. I had no idea what was going on. It was two hundred acres of unknowns. I don't know what would have happened if we hadn't found Paddy. Paddy is a kind of farming adviser called a land agent. It's the equivalent of a manager in showbusiness, or, probably more accurately, someone who you pay to be your dad. Paddy walked all over the land with us, inspecting fences, hedges, ditches, weed infestation levels. He appraised the state of the roofs and gutters around the farmyard, he applied for grants, he told me to see so and so about such and such. He took care of the business, and I learned a lot from him very quickly. He said we had to do something about the rooks. They were taking over. Rooks eat all the other birds' eggs, so unless you keep them under control you end up with just rooks. The West End is teeming with rodents. There were heart-stopping rats bigger than cats in Endell Street. Mercer Street was more mouse and pigeon territory. Rentokil would come and put their traps down and that would take care of it, but there's no easy way to deal with rooks. The only way to control them is to shoot them. It was a difficult situation for a vegetarian. In the end I resigned myself to the fact that you're being a lot more benevolent with a twelve-bore than you are when you order the nut roast. It was a short step from whacking rooks to munching on a bacon sandwich.

It was the final step in a complete volte-face. I didn't recognise myself any more. It only seemed like a minute ago that I was the number one slag in the Groucho Club, a boozy lascivious metropolitan vampire pacifist with too many friends. Here I was early in the morning, fresh from kippers with my wife, standing in a field alone with a shotgun. I let 'em 'ave it.

Beagle II

It was our first Christmas on the farm, 2003. Beagle was due to land on Isidis Planitia, a flat and relatively friendly part of Mars, early on Christmas morning. There was a media centre in London that had satellite links with mission control in Darmstadt. I drove up to London with my dad in the dead of night. We got there in an hour. Naturally, Colin Pillinger and his wife and the whole Beagle team were there. There were journalists, TV crews and one or two interested public figures. Everett Gibson, from NASA, was there, still showing everyone his meteorite. There were mince pies and crackers and the atmosphere was more than festive. It was tense, very exciting – the story of Beagle had become a media phenomenon. There was massive popular support for the sideburned swashbuckler and his spaceship.

We knew the lander had separated successfully from Mars Express, the mother ship, and was spinning its way towards the Martian surface. It was hard to believe it was happening. 'Parachutes should have opened,' said Colin. The whole room was silent. The whole city was silent. It was Christmas morning after all. I formed a mental picture of the chutes opening in the thin Martian atmosphere and the tiny machine that was taking us further into the space age. There was a lot riding on it as it hurtled, red-hot, supersonic, towards the virgin landscape. What might happen? What might we know this time tomorrow? Money, reputations, years of hard work were suspended from those remote gossamer parachutes.

Ten seconds to impact. Colin was talking to mission control on a headset. He'd been addressing the room, but now his attention was with them. We were holding our breath, waiting to hear the musical call sign that indicated Beagle had landed and was functioning. But there was no signal. It never came.

I still think Beagle was a success, in many ways. It was a triumph of aspiration, if not a victory for science. The world doesn't leap forward by committee. It needs leaders. It needs leaders with big sideburns.

Queen

I jumped in a taxi on Oxford Street. 'Buckingham Palace!' I said, became aware of what I'd said and laughed out loud. I was often saying, 'Follow that car', and even, 'Lose the car behind us' wasn't unusual, but I'd never said 'Buckingham Palace' to a taxi driver before. I thought he might have had more to say about it. He merely declared solemnly that Marble Arch was completely solid. For a moment I thought he was attempting some spontaneous architectural criticism, but he was referring to the traffic and not to the monolithic, eternal qualities of the structure itself. We picked our way swiftly and silently through the magic maze of Mayfair, eluding the petrified chaos of the main roads.

My experience of taxi drivers, and in fact more or less everybody, is that people naturally tend to underestimate each other. Very successful people are often refreshing because, being used to success, it's what they identify with and what they tend to expect and see more of in people.

I once got in a taxi at Sloane Square. The driver and I were talking and he inevitably asked me what I did all day. I told him I was a musician – I was in a chatty mood. Not as chatty as him, though. He naturally assumed that I was a struggling musician. People usually do. He treated me to a well-prepared 'Don't you give up on it, my son' soliloquy. 'You'll get there in the end,' he said. I wondered where the hell he was talking about. I'd asked him to take me to Claridge's.

I went to a drum shop, once, with Ben Hillier. He was the hot record producer of the moment. He was in between finishing *Think Tank* for Blur and starting a record with Depeche Mode. Ben has a thorough academic grounding in rhythmic principles and occult knowledge of metric pulse systems. He'd played timpani in orchestras when he was twelve; he'd engineered drum sounds on U2 albums; he'd programmed beats for Paul Oakenfold; he'd found the man with the cannons that we used on 'Jerusalem'. I've never met anyone who knew more about drums than Ben. If ever there was a bona fide drum expert, it was him, and he'd just walked into the drum shop. He was looking at a vintage Gretsch kit. It was a beauty, very expensive. He was asking questions about it that I didn't understand. The man said, 'It's a bit unnecessary for a home studio, if that's what you're looking for.' He was quite dismissive. It wasn't what Ben was looking for. He was looking for something that could grace Abbey Road. He was definitely being underestimated.

We were arriving at Buckingham Palace, now.

'Where do you want, mate?'

'I think we need to go in where those policemen are standing, by the photographers, see?'

'*In?!* Yaw goin' *in*? Idunbelieveit! Twenny-farve years I been waitin'! Twenny-farve years!'

'Jesus, I didn't think you were very impressed. How long do you think I've been waiting to say it?' He wanted to know everything then, but there wasn't time.

I noticed Beth Orton going in, giggling, and I relaxed a little bit. It was a reception for the music industry, but I hadn't known exactly what to expect.

It was the best party I've ever been to. I've tried to work out why. There was no sex or drugs or rock and roll. It was purely about music, in all its shapes and forms. I was talking to a tin-whistle player for a while. Then I spotted my manager. He was hosting a little huddle that included Status Quo, Peter Gabriel and Phil Collins. He was doing his Basil Brush laugh and telling stories. I had no idea that he knew all these people. I went to say hello, but got talking to a lady from the Nordoff-Robbins Music Therapy Foundation. She introduced me to an academic from the Guildhall School of Music. Like myself, most people had arrived without their wives, partners or friends. There were no plus ones, which meant that everyone had to talk to each other, rather than huddling around in their customary cliques. Everybody who turned up was quite excited about being at the palace, apart from Brian May, who was leaning unceremoniously against a fireplace, with his mad Louis Quatorze hair and aristocratic features, giving the impression that he was often there.

I caught up with my manager and he said, 'Come on, you've got to meet the Queen.' 'Where is she?' I spotted her; she was with Beth Orton and they were both giggling. The Queen seemed to be really enjoying herself, and why not? It was a great party. Mastering the two-minute encounter is part and parcel of being in a famous band. Music has a supernatural effect on people; I know, because I feel it myself. Meeting the people we have stirred is a delicate business. It's not big-headed to suggest that sometimes members of the band spent the merest of moments with people who would really cherish the encounter and take the memory to the grave. The Queen, who does that kind of thing more than anybody, is really, really good at it, the uncontested world champion of the brief encounter. She made her way around the whole room and made everyone feel special. It's tiring being anti-royal. I've felt much better about everything since I had a chat with the boss.

I think all rock stars start by wanting to destroy the world. Then their dreams come true and they end up trying to keep it like it was before they started.

It's Twins!

It was Boxing Day 2005. We'd had dinner with the Duke and Duchess of Somerset. We kind of gatecrashed. We'd just confirmed that Claire was pregnant, days pregnant. It was really icy on the roads and really late. I'd done most rock star things, but I'd never driven a car into a tree until that night. We were almost home. I put the brakes on to slow down for the hairpin bend at the top of our valley. Nothing happened. We just kept going. We were heading for a Cotswold stone wall at deadly speed. I mounted the verge to lose some pace but lost control and we glanced off a mature oak, *Quercus robur*. It was a hell of a wallop. Six inches further to the left and we'd have hit it smack on. Claire might have lost her legs. As it was, she lost the baby a few days afterwards and I just don't know how closely linked the two events were.

We were on holiday in the Maldives six months later and Claire just couldn't get out of bed. She wanted taramasalata for breakfast, but it wasn't that kind of hotel. I think men can tell when their wives are pregnant. I always knew before we did the test. It's the rising shape of the breast that gives it away, more than the *à la carte* thing. I said we weren't having ice cream this time. No way. It's hard to watch your wife eat ice cream, especially when you're really happy. I put on four stone when Geronimo was born, slightly more than Claire did. I'd worn out a pair of running shoes getting that stuff off. We both thought it might be twins. Claire was just so tired and hungry. We told the doctor and the doctor said, 'Don't be ridiculous, you don't want twins. It's complicated.' And sent us for a scan.

As soon as the ultrasound image came up on the computer screen, it was blindingly obvious what was happening. For the untrained eye, it's hard to tell exactly what's what on an early scan. It's all a bit abstract. I was definitely looking at a diptych, though, two of everything. Yep, there were two tadpoles, two doughnuts, two wiggly bits, two croissant things; twoness abounded and multiplied and filled the screen. It was doubled up. It was dual-aspect. It was a completely two-nique situation. The mirror symmetry spoke a primitive language that a monkey would have understood. I looked up at the consultant and raised my eyebrows. He just nodded.

'Yep,' he said. 'Not much doubt about that.'

Claire had her head in her hands and her mouth was open; she was speechless. I realised that was what I was doing too, holding my head and gaping. I don't know if it's a learnt or primal reflex that causes that reaction – hands on ears, eyes and mouth wide – but it seems to be the universal mechanism for expressing sudden, unexpected, uncontainable elation. We told the grannies on Christmas Day. I thought about it and decided that the exact point when Christmas peaks is halfway through lunch, after the goose and before the cheese. So that was when we told them. I filmed their reaction and they both do that exact same thing. They put their hands on their heads, curl forwards and open their mouths. It's a super-smile, reserved for just a handful of occasions in a lifetime when it is suddenly clear out of the blue that something wonderful has happened and things are going to get immeasurably better from now on.

I was sidelined by the news. We were at the neighbours' house on Boxing Day and I was talking to an eminent elderly lady. Old ladies are a vital part of life in the country. The Cotswolds does a very good line in golden grannies. They seem to know more about gardening and pianos and local history and who's who and what's what than anybody. I was telling her my plans to bulldoze all the building rubble into one large heap in the distance, making a satisfying megapile. I explained how I was going to put a shed on the top and apply for planning permission to be buried underneath it with my guitars. At the mention of guitars, she said, 'Oh, are you the one who . . .' I thought she was going to say, 'is in that band?' I prepared myself to be bashful, but she said, '. . . whose wife is having twins?' And that was me all of a sudden, Claire's husband, the twins' dad. I had a new identity. Bands and families aren't that dissimilar. I had a new band now, or rather Claire did.

Claire got really big. We had fat rapper tracksuits on standby. I thought they were the only things that would fit. One of her friends told her that she wasn't going to be able to pull her own pants up when it got to the end. Another one said she'd need a wheelchair, for sure. I'm not sure how badly Claire needed to hear those kinds of things, or how badly the people who said them wished it was them having twins instead.

It didn't get that far, though. I was in London when Claire phoned and said she thought her waters had broken. It was three months early. She was rushed to the regional maternity unit and told to lie very still. They said it would be great if she could just stay as still as she could for about the next three months or so. She'd been there for a week when I got the call, the call I had been getting every day, 'Get down here, I think they're coming', followed by a mad dash and panic and then, nothing doing.

It was the morning of Easter Monday, about two-thirty, when the phone rang. This time it wasn't Claire who called. It was a midwife. She said, 'I think it's worth your while coming down.'

It was a familiar run, by now, but it was an eerie sprint to the hospital that time. The roads were immaculate. It was dream-like. I didn't see another person or vehicle as I gunned the big old Merc through the ghostly empty night the twenty-odd miles to Oxford.

Hospitals are buzzing the whole twenty-four hours, especially maternity wards. There were always a couple of people smoking outside the entrance to the women's centre and there were people around the drinks machine, waiting and wondering.

Claire was crying when I got to the ward. 'I'm sorry,' she said. It wasn't her fault. I held her hand. We'd been briefed on what to expect if she gave birth this early when she was first admitted. It wasn't exactly what you want to hear. Serious risk of brain damage, almost certain to be breathing difficulties, possibility of blindness, and that was just the 'B's.

The babies were definitely on their way and they were both breech and they were weak, especially the one whose waters had broken. The safest option, said the consultant, was an immediate emergency Caesarean. I didn't have any better ideas.

The operating theatre was as white as an art gallery and as bright and busy as a TV studio. There was the surgeon and her assistant, the anaesthetist, a nurse for each baby, a specialist for each baby and doctors and people with clipboards. All you could see was eyes. Everyone had masks on.

I was sitting by Claire's head behind a curtain that ran along the top of her chest. I'd been talking to my friend Robert about Caesareans. His wife had one. He said it was absolutely fine as long as you don't look over the curtain. The only trouble is that all you want to do is look over the curtain.

It was true. I was leaning over. Claire wanted to know what was going on. I didn't want to tell her. They'd painted her tummy with gloop, sliced it open and the surgeon was in there up to her elbow, rummaging.

When she pulled twin one out by his feet, like a rabbit coming out of a hat, he didn't make a sound. I was sure he hadn't made it. He was limp and silent. Claire was saying, 'Is it OK? Is it OK?' I said of course it was. It was a lie as far as I was concerned, but a good one. They were still fishing around for twin two. He was squeaking a bit when he got out, so that was all right.

I felt so confused. Claire was in a daze. The babies were whisked straight from the theatre into intensive care, where all the life-support apparatus was situated. No one can tell you what's happening at this stage, no one can say, 'It's fine, don't worry', because no one knows. It's best just to let them deal with it. It was my job to look after Claire. I couldn't do anything else.

We got back to the ward and I asked the nurse as discreetly as I could when we'd know if there were any problems. I was really worried about the one who hadn't made any noise or movements. She said brightly, 'No news is good news, so try and get some rest.' I called Mrs Swann, the piano teacher, to say we couldn't make it today, because the babies had arrived. She said, 'Congratulations!', and I hadn't realised until she said that magic word what had actually just happened. It was all so touch and go, I hadn't even called the grandparents.

As the days in intensive care went by, I wondered when I'd be able to stop worrying. Blind panic had mellowed to acute anxiety, which in turn had settled right down into chronic mild apprehension with occasional spasms of intense anguish, all mixed with the chest-beating rapture of fatherhood. It was weird, like moose cheese: too much flavour to deal with.

The special care birth unit was as hot as hell, and the torment was as exquisite. This is where the sick babies from all points west were brought to fight for their tiny lives. It was always hard to walk through that door. Sometimes we'd visit and there'd be a new arrival, parents sobbing in the wake of some terrible complication. It was most heart-rending when the parents were young. We never knew if it was going to be us next up for some bad news.

But the little boys, who to start with would fit in the palm of my hand, fingers like matchsticks and faces like tiny old men, grew stronger. It's the first twenty-four hours that are the toughest. Then if they can make the first week they're in with a good chance. But it's always day-by-day, hour-by-hour, minute-by-minute, in neonatal intensive care. After eight weeks in Oxford and a fortnight in Banbury, we brought them home. It was a close squeak. Twenty years ago they wouldn't have made it.

Toys are better now, as well. They don't know they're born, kids today.

Today and Tomorrow

It's half my life ago, nineteen years, since the first rehearsal when we wrote 'She's So High' and it's nearly four years since *Think Tank*. It was a mad steeplechase on a mad horse, but writing about it all at last has made me realise just how much I loved every single minute of it, while it was happening. No one can be wise until they have been properly foolish, or feel well at home until they've spent time wandering in the wilderness. Having spent so much time together, all four of us in the band have grown up in our own quite different ways since that last record, we've all learned to stand on our own two feet as individuals. Damon's sold millions more records, Graham has found peace and filled it with his own noise, Dave's gone into politics and I'm a Renaissance man. I think we all needed to do that before we could face each other again.

On my last birthday, Graham came out to the farm. I had seen him for a couple of years, but we were both wearing tweedy suits and thinking about the same new things. He wants to move out to the country, too. He brought his new guitar with him, a customised Martin acoustic, built especially for him. He played it while I cooked lunch. It was just like at college only it was a better lunch, and a nicer guitar. 'I'm up for having a jam with the others,' he said, rather surprisingly.

I was just happy to see him again. It's companionship that makes any journey worthwhile. I'd taken a running jump at everything and somehow, instead of falling, I'd risen, weightlessly and effortlessly, lifted higher and higher by the arms of the people who surrounded me.

Flying Tony brought the Bonanza over today. I'd sold it to Dave for a generous price and he still lets me use it occasionally. I drove cross-country to Enstone aerodrome with Claire and Geronimo. The flying club usually only does Pot Noodles and crisps but there was a barbecue going on this morning and burger smoke wafted amid the avgas fumes. There were planes coming in from all directions and the usual murmur of covert excitement that is the happy atmosphere of all small airfields.

'Where do you want to go?' said Tony.

'Shall we just go and look around?'

The earth fell away once more. My wife, my child, my friend and I were airborne, a racing bullet at the exact centre of a perfect three hundred and sixty degree horizon, the whole world below us, and God knows, the boundless open universe above. It was a late September day. The haze of high summer had dissolved and the air beneath our wings was a sea of perfect clarity, England in its green glory, below.

England is beyond all doubt the prettiest country from the air. It is more intricately fascinating than the yawning stitched quilts of continental Europe, more vivid than any other landscape.

Those small meadows are impractical for farming but unrivalled in their brilliant perfection. And right in the middle of the prettiest part of England's green and pleasant land was the farm. I hadn't seen it from the air since I'd bulldozed the concrete or planted the vegetable garden, dug the lake or knocked down the asbestos carbuncles. It was a miraculously transformed ruin; it was a phoenix from the flames; it was a very big house . . .